Publishing Director: Alison Goff
Creative Director: Keith Martin
Executive Editor: Julian Brown
Executive Art Editor: Geoff Fennell
Editor: Karen O'Grady
Design: Louise Griffiths
Production Controller: Sarah Scanlon
Picture Research: Zoe Holtermann, Rosie Garai

First published in Great Britain in 2000 by Hamlyn,
a division of Octopus Publishing Group Limited
2-4 Heron Quays, London E14 4JB

Distributed in the United States and Canada by
Sterling Publishing Co., Inc
387 Park Avenue South
New York, NY 100016 - 8810

Copyright © Octopus Publishing
Group Limited 2000
ISBN 0 600 59837 3

A catalogue record for this book is
available from the British Library

Produced by Toppan
Printed in Hong Kong

hamlyn

Chronicle of
Celtic Folk
Customs

A Day-to-Day Guide to Folk Traditions

Brian Day

Contents

How to use this book

Each chapter in which customs are listed refers to either a calendrical, agricultural or ecclesiastical period.

The chapter starts with general notes on the types of custom peculiar to that period.

Events of variable date are listed seperately from those of fixed date – it is advisable to check with local tourist offices when these events will be happening before travelling.

March customs

M arch with its lengthening days was a hard-working month for the Celts, and relatively little time was spent festively. Cold dry March winds were feared for their effect on shoots, as Isle of Man weatherlore tells us. The people there, and other Celts, started ploughing and sowing. Brittany had abundant weatherlore this month. The tides brought seaweed for food and fertilizer, and was much used by the Scots, Irish and Welsh. Apart from collecting seaweed for fertilizer, the type of seaweed called laver (*Porphyra umbilicalis*) was eaten. In Wales it was collected mainly on the south coast, and washed and boiled (for about five hours) to form a gelatinous purée called laverbread. **Laverbread with Oatmeal and Bacon** *(see p.197 for recipe)* was served for breakfast.

Variable Dates

Edinburgh Folk Festival, Edinburgh   Lothian
EDINBURGH IS THE PRINCIPAL CITY OF SCOTLAND.

Fixed Dates

1st March St David's Day
CELTIC St David is the patron saint of Wales who died this day in AD 589. He founded St David's Abbey in Pembrokeshire, known for its strict regime and life of austerity. He was said to have saved the monastery at Glyn Rhosyn from destruction by Irish invaders by converting them to Christianity. A daffodil is worn, and leeks are eaten. St David is known to have been a vegetarian, modelling his spartan existence on that of the desert monks of Egypt. Leeks are said to drive evil spirits away and to purge the blood, especially if eaten in March. This may explain their adoption as an emblem of Wales and by Welsh troops, the latter practice first recorded at the Battle of Meigen in the 7th century. It is said that St David gave the idea to the Welsh leader Cadwallader for his battles against the Saxons. King Arthur, whom the Welsh claim to be one of their own, was said to have insisted his troops wear a leek in their caps to be distinguished from their Saxon foe. St David was also the patron of flocks and ships. David's mother St Non adopted the daffodil as a symbol because it grew in the Vale of Aeron where her son was born. It became the Welsh national emblem in 1907, being championed by LloyGeorge.

58 March customs

For quick and easy reference the following symbols accompany every folk event:

✳ Mixed Celebration, Feast, Sing-Song, Commemoration, Opening of Season, Mock-Mayor Election

☗ Pagan Custom, Wassailing , Fertility Rite, Sacrificial Rite, Harvest Custom

♚ State Event, Crown Event, Civic Custom, Curfew, Courts

✚ Religious Custom, Wake, Rushbearing, Clipping, Beating Bounds, Walking Day, Blessing, Pilgrimage

✋ Music, Dance, Drama, Arts

♟ Parade, Trade Procession, Trade Ceremony

✿ Fair, Carnival

▦ Land Rights, Quit Rent, Auction, Civic Dole

☻ Charity, Dole

◉ Game, Contest, Competition, Sport

Each event is accompanied by a symbol denoting the type of custom (see key on opposite page).

SCOTLAND

☗ Whuppity Stourie (or, wrongly, Scourie), St Nicholas' Church, Lanark   Strathclyde
This is a centuries-old tradition after the resumption of bell-ringing after the layoff from October until February. There is a peal of bells at 6 pm, when boys run three times round the church, then fight each other with paper balls suspended on string while the bells sound. Until the 18th century the fight was with caps against rival youths from New Lanark, at a site at Wellgate Head. The victors paraded back singing a traditional victory song. Today, at the conclusion of the paper mace fight the Provost throws pennies at Hyndford Place for children to scramble for.

The bell-ringing and fighting may be a vestige of an ancient ceremony to drive out the dark forces of winter, or, more likely etymologically, to drive away the spirits travelling in clouds of dust (stour) that settle on crops in spring. The sound of the bells achieves the same effect as banging on pans and trays or whirling caps or paper balls. Going three times round a sacred object was a Druidic practice. However, there are other suggested derivations, none of which can be regarded as certain.

LANARK IS ON THE A73 SOUTH OF CARLUKE.

WALES There is a custom on this day called Cymhortha, the visiting of anyone in the village too ill to plough their fields. Neighbours took an ox, plough and a special stew made from leeks, of which Wales has several types, including **Leek and Ham Soup** *(see p.197 for recipe)*, **Leek and Potato Soup** *(see p.197 for recipe)* and **Cawl** *(see p.198 for recipe)*. Cawl is a stew/soup and was once a staple diet of rural Welsh families.

In soute-east Dyfed people rose early to sweep the fleas from their doorsteps.

3rd March St Winnol's Day
CELTIC St Winnol (or Winwaloe) was a Breton who became an abbot in Cornwall. The churches at Landewednack and Gunwalloe, both at Lizard Point, Cornwall, are dedicated to him, and he was also venerated in Norfolk.

The regions where each event takes place are listed.

Directions to the event are provided.

Captions relate to listed events, where more information is given.

Gathering wrack for manure

1st – 3rd March **58**

Illustrations have been chosen to show scenes characteristic of the custom.

Introduction

This book describes the Celtic Folk Calendar, a term which implies a common cultural origin for those customs of the Irish, Manx, Scottish, Welsh, Cornish and Breton Celts which are associated with specific dates, seasons or other calendrical periods. The customs of the more distantly related Celts of Asturia and Galicia in north-west Spain are not considered in this book. Calendrical customs may be communal or family-oriented, involving historical, religious or folk activities such as devotions, re-enactments, preparation of foods or natural medicines, performing arts, games and crafts. Their origins may be clearly known to the people concerned, such as local historical or religious commemorations, but may also be of unknown provenance, surviving only as habit, divination, legend or superstition. By presenting for each day or period the features of the relevant custom as practised in the individual Celtic nations, the common cultural core becomes abundantly clear as you follow them day by day in this book.

The headings **CELTIC, IRELAND, ISLE OF MAN, SCOTLAND, WALES, CORNWALL** and **BRITTANY** will be seen throughout. Customs found in all Celtic areas, and descriptions of common historical, cultural and religious heritage, are included under the heading Celtic. Customs now extinct in the mother lands may be found in emigrant communities, such as the USA, Canada, Australia and New Zealand.

Those specific to individual Celtic nations are under the appropriate national heading. In some cases there is a lack of corroborative evidence in the form of written or pictorial records from certain Celtic areas in certain periods, and it is not always possible to substantiate the belief that a particular custom was once widespread over the whole of Celtic Europe. In such cases the tradition alone will have to suffice. So successful has been the suppression of Breton culture by the French in the past that we must draw heavily on the tradition that the Bretons kept their Cornish customs for some time after travelling to Brittany in the 5th and 6th centuries AD to escape the Anglo-Saxon invasion of southern England, at least as far as local circumstances would permit. The sections on Brittany in this book lack some of the local historical detail of the other sections, therefore, but there is a comprehensive selection of current Breton folk events. Short biographies are given only of Celtic saints, and only non-Celtic saints venerated in the Celtic lands are mentioned. For more details of non-Celtic saints, the Julian and Gregorian Calendars, the Ecclesiastical Calendar and the Easter Cycle, see the author's *A Chronicle of Folk Customs*, which also describes the English Folk Calendar and gives details of customs introduced into the Celtic lands by the English.

Celtic folk customs have a complex history. They are part of the common tradition of Western Europe but have distinctive local variations. The latter are bound up with many associated factors such as climate, geographical characteristics, soil and geology, local flora and fauna, and, of course, social structure and organisation. Each custom is normally complex in that it has several interwoven ingredients, and examples of these are history, myths and legends, devotional practices past and present, divination, natural medicine, music, dance and drama, culinary traditions and recreational habits. Even if we accept that in Druidic times the folk culture was reasonably uniform throughout Celtic Britain and Ireland, which is by no means certain, we have then to disentangle the effects of profound changes brought about by contact with the Christian Church and Anglo-Saxon and Scandinavian settlers and the consequences and subsequent history of those changes to calendar, agriculture, religious belief and practice, financial obligations, pattern of settlement, social organisation and general way of life. Driven as they have been to the western edge of Europe, after suffering many assaults on themselves and their culture, it is not surprising that such a beleaguered people has lost some of its once distinctive character. Many customs referred to here are, therefore, no longer practised, but it is to be hoped that Celtic readers, on learning about their folk heritage, may be moved to revive what has been lost.

Such customs as have survived are clearly stated as current, and are described in the present tense, with date, location, travel directions by road, and starting and finishing times where customary. Events which are of local preserve are not necessarily open to the general public, and where this is known appropriate advice is given. Any important information about the origins of these customs, including the underlying beliefs and traditions associated with them, is attached to the description. From this information you will see how many currently held customs reflect the complex social, philosophical and religious history of the Celts. It is not uncommon to find a mixture of Druidic, Catholic and Protestant elements in a religious ceremony, and that same mixture may be present in Catholic Ireland, Brittany and the Western Isles, and in Protestant Scotland, Isle of Man, Wales and Cornwall. Similarly, elements introduced by the English have fused with local Celtic features to create a secular mixture every bit as interwoven as the religious one, particularly in the Lowlands of Scotland, the eastern part of Ireland, the Isle of Man, the Marches of Wales, and Cornwall.

Plougastel Daoulas, Calvaire

The Celts traditionally used whatever food resources were available, even to the extent of seaweeds requiring five hours or more to cook, so close were they to that precarious boundary between subsistence and starvation. Much food was seasonal, and they tried to vary the taste of staple foods by adding seasonal extras, such as the way the Irish added onion, leeks, peas, parsley or nettles to champ. The single meal dish, such as a stew or broth, was an everyday dish, but on special occasions separate dishes were the norm. For feasts an ordinary item such as an oatcake would be made with spices and dried fruit, and would contain charms on divination days. These variations, along with riotous games and rumbustious music were an expression of joy for a temporary relief from subsistence drudgery. Traditional recipes quoted have full instructions, with measures and temperatures in both imperial and metric units. Games and other activities are generally described sufficiently for people to understand or actually take part themselves, and it is to be hoped that all the entries in the book will encourage parents to recognise the value of passing on these aspects of common culture to their children so that they grow strong and tall from their own roots rather than from a graft on another rootstock.

In an essentially rural society like that which once existed all over the Celtic lands changes sanctioned by civic or Church authorities took some time to reach remote parts, and sometimes never did. Rural folk took rather more notice of changing patterns of weather and temperature, growth and activity among plants and animals, the changing positions of stars, planets and the moon, and other natural phenomena, than they did of the calendar. Solstices and equinoxes may change through the course of astronomical events whereas dates like Midsummer Day were traditionally fixed. The original Druidic lunar calendar found itself in competition with the Roman (Julian) solar calendar, introduced in 46 BC, adopted by the Anglo-Saxons and Anglo-Normans. The agricultural seasons tended to reflect better the former and this led to parallel rural and urban reckonings.

When the Gregorian calendar was introduced in 1582 it was not adopted at the same time throughout Europe, with Catholic countries doing so immediately and Protestant countries doing so in their own time. Among the Celts the Scots were the first to adopt it, in 1599, with England, Wales, Ireland, the Isle of Man and Cornwall doing so in 1751. But in rural areas, in Scotland and the Isle of Man particularly, the Old Calendar, as the Julian calendar was called, persisted, making the task of ordering folk customs calendrically a difficult one. Not all sources say which calendar, Old or New, is referred to when a date for a custom is quoted. There is also the inescapable problem posed by the fact that the ecclesiastical origins of both calendars mean the retention of variable dates for the Easter Cycle. Customs may, therefore, be on a fixed date, a variable date, at a fixed interval from a fixed or variable date, periodic, irregularly seasonal or dependent on natural phenomena like the tides, or when the local community chooses. Some events held at weekends or on public holidays may have been moved from weekdays for commercial or logistical reasons, or from days no longer public holidays. In all cases, entries in this book are placed as near as possible to the time when they normally fall.

The fact that folk customs are followed long after they have ceased to be of direct practical consequence shows that they also have a social function that is not related to their age or frequency but to their value as a binding force within the community. This fact is often misunderstood by those seeking to replace folk customs by activities seen as more socially or spiritually desirable. Certainly in the 19th century English philanthropists and evangelists tended to regard old Celtic ways as a hindrance in Victorian progressive society and a legacy of a pagan, uncultured past. They failed to appreciate the practical origins and usefulness of much folklore, and the fact that an attack on folk customs, and the traditions and beliefs attached to them, is an attack on folk culture itself, with all that means in terms of ethnic pride and identity.

A typical rural Celtic community in times before the advent of mass communication and travel was self-sufficient and isolated both geographically and socially. Most of what was eaten was locally grown, and utensils, tools and other essential items made by local craftsmen. Such interdependence gave rise to a strong community spirit, where conformity and convention were the norm and individualism looked upon with disdain or suspicion. The villagers knew one another intimately, as they did their environment upon which they depended so critically and which they collectively sought to understand and control. In such communities people took on many roles, but the people they met while doing so were always the same. They shared, they belonged, and they handed down their skills and ways. This produced a common outlook on life, and estranged them from the landed gentry whose attitudes, social conventions, language and religion may well all have been alien.

Folk customs helped cement such communities together, as they require communal effort and involvement. They were regarded as a solid foundation on which to build the future, and gave people a measure of stability and confidence to face that future. Even activities which evolved for purely practical reasons, such as harvesting or sheep-shearing, become events that everyone joined in, even neighbouring villages in a mutually co-operative arrangement, to share the banter, discussion, jokes, story-telling, work-songs, refreshments and feasting to mark their successful conclusion. Even when the working practice ceased the tradition was often maintained because of its social value. Maintaining community spirit was felt to be particularly important through the days of winter, and this led to many winter customs outliving others and outliving the original functions of them.

It has been something of a rearguard action by the Celts to save the remnants of their folk culture that have survived the changing times, the Anglification of the Celtic lands, and the active determination of various Church denominations to rid the Celts of what was seen as pagan heritage. There is much in these pages for those who wish to reverse this trend and revive old customs, despite the fact that the circumstances which gave rise to them have long since disappeared. Even in a modern setting they would be an expression of Celtic identity unsurpassed in its ability to generate cultural pride and that sense of uniqueness which all communities like to feel and to be able to justify. It would also help to re-create the community spirit which was such an impregnable feature of Celtic rural communities long ago, which only the harshest of measures by the English and French authorities could fracture. There are many cases of customs being preserved by the personal interest of one individual or family, or by the great sense of history and togetherness to be found in isolated communities.

It was in the 19th century that these independent rural communities gradually and irreversibly changed. Influences from urban areas increased, as trading for consumables and more advanced equipment, implementation of new laws and administrative arrangements, the spread of alien religions and moral codes by evangelists and philanthropists all had their effect on the highly customised lives of the rural Celts. Ancient traditions were abandoned, remoulded, or forced out, surviving only if they conformed to a new scale of social values. There was a sustained attack by Christians on pagan ceremonies such as the worship of the sun, water spirits and the various natural forces that controlled the Celts' vulnerable lives, with attempts to replace them with ceremonies of Christian import, even if their provenance was totally invented for the purpose. Some saints were invented solely to divert worship of pagan beings towards a Christian 'commemoration'. This was done extensively to give a new meaning to practices at sacred wells and pagan religious sites which proved impossible to eradicate. The vibrant merry-making which accompanied many pagan celebrations, much of it outpourings of relief at a successful harvest or other critical activity, were suppressed or banned by law.

Once the train and car had broken for ever the isolation of the rural Celts relationships developed with outsiders which were to loosen local ties and see the importing of commercial goods, new ways, new attitudes, and values which only had substance if the society whence they came was also embraced. It was not only this process that threatened folk customs but also the growing feeling among the villagers themselves that they were unsophisticated and primitive. People feeling ashamed of their culture are the easiest of prey for the zealous, articulate evangelist, adept at persuading their new converts that folk customs were an intolerable, sinful distraction from the objective of spiritual salvation. In Wales and the Isle of Man, for example, travelling Methodist preachers condemned folk customs as pagan and popish, and vigorously diverted the people towards dependence on the chapel for their spiritual needs and leisure pursuits. Thus, the chapel replaced the village community spirit as the focus of their lives, and folk customs, traditional music, dancing, sports and games all lost ground as the pattern of life changed and new social structures emerged. As if in a final effort to complete the destruction of Celtic calendrical customs, gradually, modern hybrid customs, such as those at Christmas, New Year and Easter, to name but three examples, replaced the distinctive local celebrations in the Celtic communities, leaving but few traces of them today.

In remote areas where there was no tradition of writing down aspects of folk culture, only oral communication, we have to rely on the written notes and diaries of travellers, though it must be said that not all recorded customs faithfully, some colouring their descriptions by interpretations influenced by their own culture or simply by prejudice. Sources written in Celtic languages are therefore more reliable than those written by visitors, particularly from England, who tended to use deprecating descriptions and to write from first impressions instead of from any understanding of Celtic folk life.

The decline of the Celtic languages has been another factor in the general decline of Celtic folk ways. Within a native tongue are special vocabulary, modes of expression, descriptive terms, references and general style of communication which cannot be replaced by an alien language like English. Oral tradition cannot succeed if children no longer speak the language of their parents and grandparents, because gradually the vast repository of tradition is emptied by not being used, replenished or handed down. When education in Celtic languages was stopped by the English and French authorities, and children punished and shamed when they spoke them, generational ties were weakened and respect for the role of the elderly as the bridge with the past lessened. Even those children who could understand their grandparents became less and less interested in what came to be seen by them, under alien influence, as an outmoded way of life with nothing left of value, and, therefore, nothing worth preserving.

The author, who regards everything in this book as worth preserving, invites readers to contact him through the publisher with details of current or recently discontinued customs which have not been included in this edition. Please supply notes on the custom, its origins and precise location, and, if possible, photographs. Village or town names alone are not sufficient as there is often more than one place with a particular name in a county.

Whoever you are this book is for you. If you are Celtic, or of Celtic descent, and were brought up in, or in the ways of, one of the Celtic nations, this book will explain many of the things you and your ancestors were brought up to do but never really knew why or how they arose. If you are not Celtic, or have not been brought up in a Celtic nation or in the Celtic way, the book will go a long way to explaining why those distinctive people you know, live among, or have heard about, behave the way they do throughout the year.

The Folk Regions of the Celtic Lands

CELTIC These regions are not simply Ireland, Isle of Man, Scotland, Wales, Cornwall and Brittany. The customs of some parts of the Celtic nations in the British Isles are much influenced by neighbouring English customs or by the customs of immigrants from other parts of the British Isles. The former applies to parts of east Wales, east Cornwall and lowland Scotland, and the latter, through English and Scottish settlement, to the Isle of Man and Northern Ireland, and through English settlement in Cornwall, south west Dyfed in Wales, the south Wales valleys, parts of the north Wales coast, and eastern areas of the Irish Republic. Both consequences have occurred in Brittany through French influence and immigration. For this reason, folk regions do not necessarily correspond with administrative regions. Boundary changes for the latter in Wales and Scotland must be taken into account when comparing accounts of customs in books published before 1972 with those described afterwards.

Variations in folk customs have also been brought about by religious differences, such as the contrasts between Protestant Northern Ireland, Catholic Northern Ireland and the Catholic Irish Republic, and also between the larger proportion of Catholics in the Hebrides compared with elsewhere in Scotland. Areas settled by the Norsemen still show differences in custom to a degree depending on how long the settlement lasted. There are relatively few vestiges now in eastern Ireland and the Isle of Man, rather more in the Hebrides and north-east Scotland, and many more in Orkney and Shetland. This is particularly evident for Midsummer Day, and Midwinter Day and Yule celebrations, which had no counterparts in the old Celtic year. Other differences have come about through normal geographical separation and lack of travel and interaction, such as between north and south Wales, and between the Highlands and Lowlands of Scotland.

Much folk 'tradition' surrounds the megalithic monuments in the British Isles and Brittany, but as far as is known the Celts were not the builders of these.

Three groups of Celtic languages evolved, the Goidelic (Irish, Manx and Scots Gaelic), the Brythonic (Welsh, Cornish and Breton), and Gaulish. The Irish language gave rise to both Manx and Scots Gaelic through Irish colonisations, and Cornish gave rise similarly to Breton.

IRELAND The four historic provinces of Ireland, and the counties they consist of, are Leinster (Dublin, Meath, Louth, Westmeath, Longford, Kildare, Offaly, Leix or Laois, Wicklow, Carlow, Kilkenny and Wexford), Munster (Waterford, Cork, Kerry, Limerick, Tipperary and Clare) and Connaught or Connacht (Galway, Mayo, Sligo, Leitrim and Roscommon), all in the Irish Republic, and Ulster, which has three counties remaining in the Irish Republic (Donegal, Cavan and Monaghan) and six in the United Kingdom (Down, Antrim, Derry or Londonderry, Tyrone, Fermanagh and Armagh).

In the 17th century Ulster saw an influx of English and Scots Presbyterians who settled in large numbers, introducing many customs and aspects of social and agricultural organisation not seen before in Ireland. The native agricultural system was tribal, based on the clachan, a family commune, whereas in the English Pale a feudal system operated. Large families were common and blood ties strong, there being strong social pressures on young people to marry, have children and perpetuate tradition. Communities were often isolated by lack of roads, bogs, mountains and other types of terrain which restricted travel. This led to self-sufficiency, preservation of old, labour-intensive ways and tools, and a uniquely varied and ancient folk tradition. Nowhere in the British Isles had so much survived for so long.

The Great Famine of 1845–47, coming as it did after a period of unprecedented social and economic change, heralded the decline of the Irish folk society and the Irish language. The loss of oral culture, the handing down of traditions within the family and community, led to the loss of the lore and legend in which these traditions were enshrined, from which this westernmost outpost of Indo-European folk culture never recovered.

In Ireland the areas where Irish is still spoken are collectively called the Gaeltacht, which embraces Counties Donegal, Mayo, Galway and Kerry, with pockets in the south near Cork, in Co. Waterford and Co. Meath.

ISLE OF MAN The ancient division of the island, with its traditional occupations of crofter, farmer and fisherman, was into six sheadings. Each one had the duty to provide a manned and armed warship for the King of Man. The island had 16 parishes. Sheadings have been discontinued for formal administration, and the island is now a single administrative unit.

There were two dialects of Manx, North and South, separated by the central hills of the island, but by the 1920s English was the principal means of communication. The last native speaker, Ned Maddrell, died in 1962.

SCOTLAND Under The Local Government Act 1972 Scottish counties were absorbed into Regions, and three Islands Areas were created. The Islands Areas are Shetland, Orkney and Western Isles. The Regions, and the former counties they include, are Highland (Caithness, Sutherland, and Ross & Cromarty except north Lewis, Inverness except the southern Hebrides, and Nairn); Grampian (Moray, Banff, Aberdeen and Aberdeen City, and Kincardine); Tayside (Perth except south-west Perth, Angus, Dundee City, and Kinross); Central (south-west Perth, Stirling, and Clackmannan); Fife (Fife); Strathclyde (Dumbarton, Renfrew, Argyll, Bute, Ayrshire, Lanark, and Glasgow City); Lothian (East Lothian, northern Midlothian, West Lothian, and Edinburgh City); Dumfries and Galloway (Wigtown, Kirkcudbright, Dumfries); and Border (Peebles, Selkirk, southern Midlothian, Berwick, and Roxburgh).

In the 6th century the area between the Pentland Hills and the Pentland Firth was inhabited by Picts, as was most of Galloway. Brythons were in Strathclyde, while Gaels were in Argyll and the southern Hebrides having crossed from Ireland in the previous century. The Brythonic language called Cumbric lingered on in the border area of south-west Scotland and north-west England until the 10th century. The south-east, Lothians and the Merse were occupied by English. Later a few Flemish settlements sprang up on the east coast, and Norsemen colonised Caithness, parts of the west coast and the Hebrides, and Orkney and Shetland. By the 17th century English had penetrated far into southern Scotland, first into the eastern lowlands up to and around Edinburgh, then into the western lowlands. By the early 20th century the Gaelic language was more or less confined to the north-west coast and the Hebrides.

WALES The Local Government Act of 1972 created eight Welsh counties from the 13 originally created in 1930. This meant that Flintshire and Denbighshire became Clwyd; Cardiganshire, Carmarthenshire and Pembrokeshire became Dyfed; Newport and Monmouthshire (which was removed from the jurisdiction of the Lords Marchers in 1535 – which made it part of England) became Gwent; Anglesey, Caernavon and Merioneth became Gwynedd; Montgomery, Radnor and Brecknock became Powys; the municipalities between Aberdare, Pontypridd and Bridgend became Mid Glamorgan; Cardiff, Barry, Cowbridge and neighbouring areas became South Glamorgan; and Swansea, Neath and Port Talbot became West Glamorgan.

The Goidel Celts were in Wales before the Brythons, possibly coming from Ireland, but then the Brythons moved in from the east to occupy an area from south-west England to the River Clyde. Later there were migrations into Wales from south-west Scotland and north-west England. The Romans occupied parts of Wales for mining and for military reasons, and when the Roman Empire declined Christianity was introduced into Wales. Then came Anglo-Saxon, Norse and Norman settlements, and in south-west Dyfed Flemish and Huguenot immigrants. Gypsies came to Wales in the 17th century. In the 19th century English and Scottish farmers settled in north Wales, while in the south demand for labour in mining and industry brought Cornish miners, and Irish, Scottish, English and Jewish workers. In the 20th century north Wales attracted more English settlers to work in industry and tourism.

In the 16th century Welsh was still spoken in parts of Chester, Shropshire, Herefordshire and Gloucestershire. In Shropshire it survived into the 19th century, and around Oswestry into the 20th century. Most Welsh speakers now reside in the north of the principality.

CORNWALL Cornwall once consisted of two regions, West Penwith and East Penwith, the former where Cornish culture was strongest and the latter more influenced by English customs. Administratively it has remained a single county.

Although the ancestors of the Bretons left Cornwall in the 6th century to escape the Saxon invasions, Cornish and Breton remained mutually intelligible up to the 14th century. Breton continued in use despite the imposition of French, only slowly losing ground, whereas Cornish was rapidly replaced by English and ceased to be a vernacular language by the end of the 18th century. There is evidence that Cornish was regularly used in the 19th century by Cornish miners who went to work in South Wales coal mines after the closure of their Cornish tin mines. However, in Cornwall itself anglisisation had led to the loss of much Celtic folk culture, many customs having been acquired from elsewhere in south-west England.

BRITTANY La Basse Bretagne, the western Breton-speaking part, consists of Morbihan, Finistère and Côtes-d'Armor. La Haute Bretagne, the eastern French-speaking part, was Loire-Atlantique and Ille-et-Vilaine, but in 1972 the département of Loire-Atlantique was removed from Brittany. Bretons talk of the two faces of Brittany, Armor (the sea) and Argoat (the woods). They identified first with their pays, then with the commune (village), not with a region or province.

Celts from Central Europe reached Gaul in the 6th century BC, and called it Armor, the land of the sea. They were joined by the Cornish who took refuge in Brittany in the 5th century AD after the Anglo-Saxon invasions of Cornwall and Wales. Cornish prevailed and became Breton, only slightly influenced by Gaulish. French influence came much later.

There are four main dialects of Breton, Cornouailles in Cornouaille (south Finistère), Léonard in Léon (north Finistère), Trégorrois in Tréguier and the Bay of St Brieuc, and Vannetais in Vannes and the Morbihan Gulf. Vannetais, which has the most French influence, is more distinct than the other three, which are closely related. Currently the language is spoken to the west of a line drawn to the east of Guingamp, Pontivy and Vannes and to the west of St Brieuc and Loudéac. At its maximum extent in the 9th century it was spoken almost to the outskirts of Rennes. In the 19th century the French government started its unsuccessful campaign to eradicate Breton.

Types of Folk Tradition in the Celtic Nations

CELTIC Most surviving traditional Celtic customs arising from the Druidic era have changed considerably through the agencies of the Church, civil authorities, changing local circumstances, and influence from English settlers with different traditions. The Church used various means to eliminate, suppress or absorb pagan customs, such as threats of damnation and excommunication, shaming, assimilation into a religious custom or one invented for the purpose, or reinterpretation on a religious theme. As many celebrations got out of control, with danger to life and property, civil authorities were forced to restrict, curtail or even ban them, and the Church often worked hand in glove with the civil authorities to achieve these ends, notably in the days of the Puritans and heyday of the Methodists.

Many customs have been introduced from England, replacing local Celtic customs. This is particularly true of modern accoutrements associated with the celebration of Easter and Christmas, of Guy Fawkes' Night, and of certain aspects of the celebration of May Day. These customs are described in detail in the companion volume *A Chronicle of Folk Customs*. The areas most affected are those where English settlement and influence were greatest in the past; the areas preserving their Celtic language and culture were least affected by these offshoots of English rule.

Saint days were holidays and days of feasting for the parish, centred on the church dedicated to the saint. Churches were often built on the sites sacred to pagan belief, by sacred wells or sites which were thought to be inhabited by supernatural beings or animals, all to which homage was paid or sacrifices

Breton game of Broken Pots, Brittany

made. The saint was often chosen as a near replacement of the deity in terms of their patronage or relevant aspect of their life, even inventing a saint if one was not readily to hand.

Many types of custom are found in all or several Celtic areas, but some are characteristic of one. There are surviving examples of traditional dance festivals; folk dramas; folk and carol singing; parades and trade processions; a variety of pagan rites, including fire festivals, saining (ritual purification), divination, wassailing, fertility rites, sacrificial rites, barring-out, animal cults and harvest customs; pagan customs given a Christian context, such as blessings, well-dressings, boy-bishop elections, boundary walking, wakes and fairs; purely religious customs, including pilgrimages; civic ceremonies, including the Scottish Ridings; manorial customs, introduced by the English, such as courts leet and baron; charities and bequests; sports, games and contests; and numerous others, for example, historical commemorations, culinary festivals and mock-mayor elections. This book does not deal with wholly private customs, such as those of schools, colleges, universities, clubs and regiments, that have no folk elements, nor with wholly commercial events.

Classification symbols have been used for the current folk events described under each relevant date *(see p.7 for symbols listing)*. These will help those planning to visit the places where the events are held to see under what type of custom the event can broadly be classified. Many customs have a mixture of elements, so any attempt at classification is necessarily imprecise and can only refer to what is now the dominant element. For example, most current religious customs have surviving pagan elements, just as most current pagan customs have intruding religious elements, so it is the currently dominant element that has been used for the classification. The 'General' category is a miscellaneous grouping of celebrations not falling comfortably under any of the other headings and which are principally commemorative or festive.

Traditional dance festivals are found mostly in Scotland (Highland Gatherings) and Brittany, but include the International Eisteddfod in Wales. Morris dancing crept into Cornwall and Welsh border areas but is exclusively English in origin.

Folk dramas like mumming plays have a number of elements, both pagan and religious. Disguise, hence the word guisers, may have been used when civil or church authorities were trying to eliminate the custom by recognising and apprehending participants, but is likely to be much older, perhaps guarding against being seen and abducted by witches, faeries or evil spirits. The hero-combat play is common, in which a self-proclaimed warrior or saint kills an adversary, who is then revived by a comic doctor. Decapitation of a leading player and resurrection may be linked to the death of the old year or season and the birth of the new, the changing calendars explaining why mumming is at various times of the year. There are also fertility elements. Mumming developed a religious context when the Church used it to act out biblical stories for the illiterate (miracle or mystery plays). This goes back to the 9th century, but later Merchant Guilds took over the performances on their guild days. Mumming also has characters whose function is solely to entertain and collect money, and others dressed as animals, possibly survivals of pagan animal cults with human as well as animal sacrifice. It was regarded as a great honour to wear the head and skin of a ritually slaughtered animal. Remnants of animal cults are commonest in Scotland. Animal characters also appear in many dances and parades.

Folk carol singing is alive in Wales and Brittany. Traditional times for carol singing were Eastertide, May Day, Whitsuntide and Christmas, although there are carols for other times of the year as well, such as Corpus Christi. Carols exist for many festive occasions during the year, as they were originally songs with refrains to accompany round dances. Many folk carols were the victims of the attention of the Puritans, although some have survived.

Parades are held for a variety of purposes, religious, civic and trade, the former surviving best in Brittany and the latter two in Scotland.

Fire ceremonies have complex associations, as they are influenced by Norse fire-worship and midsummer and midwinter solstice vigils, hence those on St John's Eve, St Peter's Eve and at Yule, the latter mostly in the north of Scotland. The traditional Celtic bonfires at Beltane and Samhuin had a saining purpose, to purify the people, animals, air and fields, and prepare for the new season, so that all will be fertile and bathed in sunlight and the powers of darkness overcome.

Saining involved cleansing rituals such as sealing house and byre and burning juniper inside, and sprinkling with sacred or first-drawn water. Protective plants such as rowan were hung up, and the air purified by the smoke and heat from bonfires and torches.

Divinations were practised at strategically important foci of the calendar, such as on the eves of Beltane (1st May), the start of summer, and of Samhuinn (1st November), the start of winter, on the old Celtic calendar, and also to a lesser extent of the other quarter days of Imbolc (1st February) and Lughnasadh (1st August). On the solar calendar, particularly in areas of Norse settlement, divination would be done on Midsummer Day and Midwinter Day, and at the vernal and autumnal equinoxes, corresponding to the quarter days on 24th June, 21st December (sometimes 24th or 25th December), Lady Day on 25th March, and Michaelmas on 29th September. When New Year's Day was moved to 1st January, divinations were moved to 31st December, although in all cases there were areas where people kept to the Old Calendar dates. The convergence of the pagan and ecclesiastical calendars caused some to be moved, for example, St Bride's Day divinations to Fastern's E'en in Scotland. The making of oatcakes was often part of the divination.

The most common themes for divination ceremonies were marriage prospects, future occupations or circumstances, and who would die and when and how. Many divination rites involve sunwise per-ambulation, doing this or other action three or nine times, placing secretly or illicitly acquired objects, often nine, under the pillow to induce dreams of future spouses, or looking over the left shoulder to see a future partner observing the rite. Walking nine times around an object was a common prelude to invoking the appearance of an apparition of one's future partner, or a vision of one's fate. Nine seems to have a mystic significance in divination. Outdoor divinations were done between sunset and dawn. Other divinations used harvest items and tools, and relied on the behaviour of leaves, nuts, apple pips, beans and wheat grains in the fire; dropping egg, molten wax and molten lead into water to observe the shapes; making a traditional divination dish, sometimes with charms inside; spreading ash to read the prints or patterns; observing snail trails or the shape of cut and tossed apple peel; and many more. The hazel tree was thought to be the source of wisdom, hence the popularity of its nuts in divinations.

Being the end of the Celtic year, Hallowe'en was a natural time for divination to look into the next, and babies born on this day had 'second sight' and could see what others could not. The Celts believed that the souls of the deceased had to pass through water to get to the underworld, and this is the origin of Apple-Ducking, for apples were talismans with the power to see into the future. This became a game of ducking into a bucket of water with apples floating in it, to bite one or stab it with a fork held between the teeth. A related game is Snap-Apple, in which crossed sticks are suspended from the ceiling, an apple on one arm and a lighted candle on the other. It is spun, and those present try to bite the apple without getting singed.

Barring-out customs occurred at times of change in calendrical, seasonal or religious observance, such as on a Quarter Day, on Shrove Tuesday before Lent, and on St Nicholas's Day. The customs include the Welsh Mari Lwyd midwinter custom, the shutting out of teachers on Shrove Tuesday for an extra day's holiday, and the exclusion of reapers from the farmhouse at the end of the harvest.

When Christian missionaries sought to replace pagan seasonal fertility rites in fields and fisheries, designed to ensure good yields and catches, they substituted blessings and thanksgivings as the reason for the activity. The beating of the earth to awaken sleeping spirits became Beating of the Bounds, or Perambulation, often done in Ascension week. This is a walk around the parish boundaries by the vicar, churchwardens and parishioners to mark and aid recollection of the parish boundaries in the absence of mass literacy and maps. Boundary walks or rides became social as well as religious events, and some arose by civic charter rather than out of religious observance.

Wells and springs have long been sites of water worship and of water sprites. The Church built chapels on these sites to try to Christianise rites held there, rededicating them to saints, and introducing well-dressing as an expression of thanks for the water supply. The relative freedom of villagers with wells from water-borne diseases helped to encourage acceptance of the rededication. They were visited on Sundays and saint days, but on certain other days, such as New Year's Day, Palm Sunday, Ascension Day, May Day and Whitsun, the water was thought to be more potent, particularly that of healing wells. The pre-Christian custom of leaving offerings to water spirits in return for the granting of a wish, or making an offering in order to leave an ailment behind with it, persisted into the Christian era. Well customs thus acquired a mixture of Christian and pagan elements. Some wells foretold the future by the water level rising or falling to presage disasters, or by reacting when an object was thrown in. Other wells could grant wishes when a pin, coin, bead or button was thrown in. The honouring of wells by dressing with flowers or greenery was done on their saint days, or at Whitsun or Ascension Day. Rag or Clout

(Scottish Cloutie) Wells are dressed with rags after a visit, particularly if curative as the illness is left on the rag, disappearing as the rag decays. To steal the rag is to acquire the illness.

An elected boy-bishop serves from St Nicholas's Day (6th December) to Holy Innocents' Day (28th December), and like schoolboys barring-out teachers this is an example of children taking an adult role as well as commemoration of St Nicholas's avuncular reputation.

Wakes were annual festivals held to commemorate the completion and dedication of the parish church to a saint; the devotions themselves to the saint were called patterns (pardons in Brittany). The word pattern (pardon) came to be used in Catholic areas, and wake in Protestant. Booths would be set up to provide refreshments, and gradually some of the occasions developed into what were called holy fairs. The following day became a holiday, indeed, the word 'fair' comes from the Latin 'feria', a holiday. Sometimes whole Wakes Weeks would be given over to the festivities. Gradually some fairs took on a more practical purpose, enjoyment becoming secondary, and some were established purely for trade, both wholesale and retail, in animals and merchandise. Peripheral activities such as match-making, games of chance, sporting and other contests, and entertainment grew. The Normans granted royal charters to trading fairs. Fairs, then, came to be either Trading or Charter Fairs, established by royal charter or Wakes (or Revels) to mark a church's patronal festival. Church-ale was often brewed on a church's holy day and sold to parishioners to raise money for church repairs and charitable causes. Hiring or Mop Fairs were trading fairs established for the hire of seasonal or permanent workers. At Hiring Fairs labourers would show a token of their trade, such as a mop for maids, a whip for a carter, a straw for a cowman, a crook for a shepherd. Hiring Fairs were instituted by King Edward III after the Black Death. There was such a shortage of able-bodied labourers, particularly on the farms, that all healthy men were required to offer themselves for hire at the nearest fair or market. After the Reformation the fairs outlived most patterns.

The display of a glove or hand outside a fair is a sign that visiting merchants may enter and trade without fear of arrest as long as the charter is obeyed. Delicacies specially sold at fairs are called fairings. The common feature of roasting oxen, rams, boar, deer, etc., to sell the meat to visitors may have its origins in animal sacrifice.

A wake was also a vigil and feast for the just departed on the evening before burial. It was traditional to serve guests burying cakes or biscuits so that they can digest the sins of the deceased. Professional mourners may be paid to attend the funeral and relatives would also hire sin-eaters, often poor women in need of food, who would take on all the sins of the dead person as s/he was brought out of the house. The soul, thus unburdened, would ascend freely to heaven. Bees have a strong connection with death, and if the deceased kept bees the hives would be turned round when the corpse was brought out of the house. People also kept vigil on the eve of the saint day of their parish church.

A number of pilgrimages are still made, particularly in Catholic Ireland and Brittany.

Many civic customs are the preserve of trade guilds, as they strive to advertise and maintain their privilege, authority and exclusiveness. Unlike English boundary customs which are pagan customs put in a religious context, Scottish Ridings are civic occasions.

Manorial Courts are feudal in origin, as shown by the ancient names of officials, and were normally for the administration of common land and other property. They are of two types, Courts Leet, that may also enquire into felonies, but cannot administer punishment, and Courts Baron, that are purely manorial. Other types of ancient Court include Hocktide Courts; courts for grants of rights; Verderer's Courts for the administration of forests; Admiralty Courts for regulating fisheries and waterways; industrial courts, for example, to regulate local mining or quarrying; courts maintaining quality and standards in retailing; and Pie Powder Courts at fairgrounds, so called because they dealt instant justice to offenders, who were often itinerants, as shown by the dust on their feet (French 'pied-poudre' meaning 'dusty feet'. Although surviving courts still have certain powers to supervise and regulate practices, their powers to prosecute and fine are now severely restricted. Most have now gone from the Celtic areas, being originally introduced by the English, but a few survive in Wales and Cornwall. Probably the oldest court in the land is the Coroner's Court.

Doles and charities tend to be feudal, Christian or philanthropic in origin. These days some are distributed by the church, some by private benefactors, and some by executors or trustees of wills in which the donations were provided for – sometimes with eccentric conditions attached.

Traditional sports and games were played at Wakes (days of dedication of the local church), fairs and public holidays. Games played include horse-racing; foot races, particularly in Scotland; Cornish and Breton wrestling; hurling in Cornwall and Ireland; Highland Games in Scotland and similar gatherings for traditional Breton sports; and mass football in many areas of Scotland (Ba' Games) and Wales. Happily some games have disappeared, such as bear-baiting, bull-baiting, cock-fighting (almost), biting the head off a sparrow and pulling the head off a suspended goose, with a greased neck, by riding past.

Electing Mock Mayors was once common in poor towns with more wealthy neighbouring towns. It was a way of poking fun at what they regarded as the pompous ceremonial of the election of the real Mayor. For example, Halgaver Moor in Cornwall elected a Mock Mayor on the same day as its large, important neighbour Bodmin. Some elections were held on Feast Days. The office of Mayor was instituted by the Normans, replacing the Saxon Portreeve, and it has been said that the election of Mock Mayors was a deliberate act of defiance towards the Norman imposition, done with much satire.

In addition to those mentioned there are many customs which are highly individual to a locality and which do not fit into any of these categories. One thing is undeniable; many customs have echoes of more profound pagan rituals, however harmless they may seem now.

IRELAND Feast days in a parish would be holidays for parishioners, but not to forget devotions at the saint's local shrine. These devotions, when organised, were called patterns (pardons), and were held at parish churches before the Reformation. Many were on traditional sacred sites dating from before the arrival of Christianity in Ireland. During the period from the late 16th century into the 17th century, when many Catholic buildings and much property was confiscated or destroyed, patterns were held outside by the ruins or round dedicated wells. With no strict control possible over what transpired, more and more secular elements crept in, and some degenerated into general merry-making. In Presbyterian Ulster there were similar gatherings called 'sacrament Sabbaths', and these too attracted itinerant traders. Fairs, called 'holy fairs', grew up around the patterns and sacrament Sabbaths, at which there were sales of goods and livestock, games and sports, horse-racing, and much drinking and brawling. The most notorious of these fairs was Donnybrook Fair in Dublin. Under the Penal Laws of the 18th century patterns were banned as 'popery', but the restrictions were widely flouted. When the Catholic Church again exerted influence over such events their character had irreversibly changed, partly due to the desperate economic circumstances of rural folk in the mid-19th century, and partly due to the zealous attitudes of upper-class clergy with no roots in the countryside. Generally, between May and November, gatherings were large, but in the winter months they were small and local because of the weather.

Among surviving gatherings and pilgrimages we have the midsummer gathering at St Ronogue's Well, near Cork, and another at Gouganebarra Well at the source of the River Lee. Pilgrimages to St Patrick's Purgatory on an island in Lough Derg, Co. Donegal, have been made since medieval times, once featuring the carrying of penal crosses or portable wooden crucifixes.

May and November, the start of summer and winter respectively, were the months considered most important for fairs, particularly for cattle sales and hiring workers. The Spring fairs (February and March) and Lammas fairs (July and August) were principally for horses, sheep and wool. Other fairs were held at Easter and Whitsun, and on saint days where the festival associated with a local patron saint attracted a fair. It was the custom on closing a deal for the seller to hand back a sum called the 'luck penny' as a goodwill gesture, and on hiring someone that person was given 'earles', or 'earnest money', but had to hand over their bundle of belongings as security against failure to turn up. Matchmakers were to be found at fairs, who would arrange trial marriages for a year. Other visitors included peddlers, musicians, ballad singers, gamesters and beggars, as well as those seeking rivals to settle old scores.

ISLE OF MAN Manx customs have inevitably been influenced by the mixed population on the island, from Pre-Celtic, through Irish Gaelic, Scandinavian, immigrants from Lancashire and Derbyshire (followers of the Stanleys), and Scots smugglers from Galloway. May Day customs, for example are Celtic, whereas the All Hallow E'en and the battle between summer and winter are largely Scandinavian. The fact that a first-footer on New Year's Day is lucky if dark shows the Celtic preference then. After this dilution by immigration came the suppression by the Methodists, leaving the Celtic culture of the island in a much reduced and fragmented state.

The ancient Manx Celts venerated natural objects such as water, trees and hills, and also the elemental forces of nature, the seasons, the sun and moon, light and darkness, as these ruled their lives. Typical of a farming and fishing community, there was a preoccupation with weather and weatherlore, but it was faeries, bugganes, spirits and witchcraft that were held responsible for mishaps, diseases afflicting family and livestock, and crop failures. These supernatural forces were felt to be strongest at the onset of winter at Savin, the start of the Celtic New Year on 12th November (Old Calendar) or 1st November (New Calendar). Wheat has been grown for at least 4000 years on the island, but oats and barley grow better in most places and came to be used more often for bread. It is interesting to note the hierarchical language used to refer to produce. Hay was 'saved' in a wet midsummer and potatoes were 'dug' or 'picked', but corn was 'harvested' with much ritual.

It is customary in the Isle of Man to refer to all saint days as feast days.

The island had 750 fairs up to the 18th century, but by 1940 only three remained, Hollantide Fair, Michaelmas Fair and St John's Fair on 5th July. By law, fairs were never held on a Sunday, so when a calendar date for a fair fell on a Sunday the fair was moved to the following Monday.

Visiting wells was a strong custom but this too has sharply declined. Sunday was a favoured day, but the busiest days at wells, particularly at curing wells, were Ascension Day and the first Sunday in August. Before they acquired associations with saints, at the behest of the Church, wells were thought to be the habitation of water spirits, some malevolent, who were venerated, feared and placated by offerings. A variety of other creatures and beings was also thought to live in them. Rag and Pin Wells represent a dual Christian/pagan tradition. The usual custom was to throw in coins, pins, beads or buttons, then drink the water, then say a prayer (a Christian invocation), then add to its decoration or place a votive offering such as a flower or rag on a nearby bush or tree. The supplicant's ailments will be left behind with the offering, and disappear as it decays (a pagan belief). There are no wishing wells on the island. Wells near summits were particularly sacred.

SCOTLAND In medieval times plays were held on festival days (play-days), under the auspices of a mock 'Abbott' (essentially a Lord of Misrule). The play was often the centrepiece of general entertainment involving minstrels, musicians, jugglers and tumblers, and also pageants and ridings. The principal play-days were associated with Candlemas, Corpus Christi, St John's Day and St Nicholas' Day, but there were also plays about other biblical episodes. They were held on playfields, and all large burghs had one. They were banned in 1555 during the Reformation as both pagan and popish, and so vigorously were they suppressed that only the Goloshan, performed by guisers at Hogmanay, remains. The Calvinist Kirk abolished feast days in 1560, and thereafter religious ceremonial diverged in character from the still Catholic-influenced western isles.

Early June in towns in southern Scotland sees the start of the Riding of the Marches (boundaries), the riding round the often extensive tracts of common land belonging to burghs (chartered towns) and traditionally used for gathering stones and wood, grazing stock and cutting peat. Some of the customs embrace older elements such as from Beltane rituals (particularly those taking place at or near Whitsuntide), the medieval May Game, and religious perambulations on saint days. The burgesses of a burgh are responsible for checking the marches of the common land, indicated by natural features or planted markers. The Ridings came about in the 16th century through the need to protect land from incursions and to assert ownership because of raiding by the English, land-grabbing and rivalry between burghs. Before that there was much land theft, raiding, rustling and general lawlessness, and it was the job of sheriffs to ride regularly round keeping order, enforcing boundary rights and also wood-, peat- and bracken-cutting rights. The Ridings became a tradition in the 19th century and today these Ridings, which are mainly in the border region, are re-enacted each Summer, despite the fact that many boundaries have long since changed. They are civic and secular, as opposed to the religious perambulations of bounds in England.

A typical pattern for a Riding is for an elected Cornet or Standard Bearer and their Lass to be kirked, then given charge of the Burgh Flag by the Provost and invested with the sash of office. The flag is 'bussed', that is, bedecked with ribbons. There may be a ride-out of the cavalcade before the main ride. There is a Cornet's Ball in the evening. Early next day, carrying the Burgh Flag, the Cornet leads a cavalcade round the marches, usually starting at the Mercat Cross or Town Hall, and the boundary markers are ceremonially checked. The procession returns, the flag is handed back to the Provost and the burgh map signed. Often the ride ends with the Cornet's Gallop. The event also usually incorporates the crowning of a Festival or Summer Queen. Often a whole week of festivities is organised, ending with a banquet for the leading players. The titles given to key participants vary from burgh to burgh. The crowning of a local girl as the Queen, with a Court of attendants, has in many places become a children's festival, with a procession through the town and sports and games to follow.

Highland Gatherings serve the same purpose in the Highlands as the Burgh Festivals in the Lowlands, there being few burghs in the Highlands. The first recorded gathering was in 1819 at St Fillans, Tayside. Normally, they are held in summer or autumn, and consist mainly of sports events, dance competitions and piping competitions for the war pipes. A typical opening would be with a procession of clansmen in kilts, bonnets and with claymores, led by pipers. Foot races arose out of the tradition of runners used to communicate with, summon or warn clansmen, in the latter case by carrying a fiery cross (crann-tara). The races were either on the flat, but including a hurdle, or up to a hilltop. Tossing the caber grew out of the customary way to get a felled trunk over a gully or burn. The aim is to toss it so that it makes a vertical semi-circle and lands in line with the thrower. The Braemar caber is 19 ft long and weighs 120 lb. Other traditional events are putting the stone, throwing the weight (56 lb), throwing the hammer (an iron ball on a chain), jumping and wrestling. In the solo bagpipe competitions the pibroch (piobaireachd) is played, the two most prestigious competitions being at Inverness and Oban. The three main dance competitions held are for the Sword Dance (Gille Callum), the Old Trews (Seann Triuthas), and the Highland Fling. There may also be judging of reels and strathspeys.

Gatherings of note are at Aboyne, Braemar (the largest), Cowal Gathering (Dunoon), Inverness (now only a piping competition), Lonach (Strathdon), and Oban. However, there are many smaller ones worth visiting, for example that on South Uist where the piping competition attracts fine players. The Gatherings usually end with a ceilidh.

WALES Saint days were celebrated with a variety of customs. They were usually held on Sundays, but sometimes began on Saturday and lasted until Tuesday. Relics of saints were carried in procession. There were several in honour of the Virgin Mary, and at Gwyl Fair y Gwirodau there was carol singing, the songs being about the life of the Virgin, walking round a fire, and much drinking. Gwylmabsant was observed in every parish with games (such as foot races, leaping, hurling, wrestling and football) and other entertainments, as well as cock-fighting, bull-baiting and bear-baiting, visitors often being put up overnight by making beds on the floor. Football matches were held between parishes, the losing team providing beer for the winning team. In the 18th century some clerics tried to stop or limit these celebrations, one reason being the brawling and drunkenness that accompanied them. Furthermore, the gentry became used to using Sunday as a day for taking an outing or calling on friends, and so the character of Sunday in Wales changed for all sections of the community.

CORNWALL Cornwall has a large number of saints, one for every parish, and therefore many feast days. These were celebrated on the nearest Sunday and Monday to the dedication day, which were called Feasten Sunday and Feasten Monday. A typical Sunday meal was a joint of meat and figgy-pudden (baked or boiled suet pudding with raisins). On the preceding Saturday baking would be done, for example, of plum cake, 'light' currant cakes raised with barm (yeast) and made yellow with saffron, and 'heavy cake' – a rich currant paste (pastry) made with clotted cream and eaten hot.

On Feasten Days standings (stalls) in the streets traditionally sold gingerbread nuts and sweet-meats. There were fairground amusements such as swings and merry-go-rounds, and eventually fairs. Gloves displayed on poles indicated the local ownership of the fair as well as access being allowed to visiting traders.

Many villages elected Mock Mayors in their feast week, and at the end of a day in which he was thoroughly spoiled he was thrown in a stream or rubbish tip. Pelynt's Mock Mayor, for example, was royally treated, wined and dined at each public house then dumped in Old Shute Pond.

Cornish miners were always very superstitious and particular about their rituals, perhaps a reflection of the dangers of their job, and there was a great deal of folklore and custom associated with tin mining. A Stannary Parliament once represented tin miners in Cornwall and Devon, but now there is no industry to represent as the last working tin mine, a 2600 ft deep, 300 year old mine near Redruth, was closed on 6th March 1998.

BRITTANY Brittany has many springs and wells, which were a feminine symbol and part of an ancient cult of water. The early Christians built chapels on the sites and rededicated them to saints. Many were thought to have healing properties. The sun was a masculine symbol, and likewise Beltane sites of sun and fire rites had chapels dedicated to St Michael built on them.

The most distinctive feature of Breton churches is the parish close, consisting of a triumphal arch, a Calvary, and an ossuary or charnel house. A Calvary is a large sculpture group of episodes from the Nativity and the Passion of Christ, displayed around a crucifixion scene. When the churchyard was full, graves were opened and the bones taken to the ossuary. The skull (chef) was sometimes put in a marked box for the relatives to honour. The parish close was often used as an open-air pulpit. It included shrines to local saints.

The chapels, calvaries and pardons are testimony to the strong Catholic faith of the Bretons. Formerly, almost every village and every shrine had its pardon, and it served also as a family reunion. On the last Sunday in August is the pardon of Châteauneuf-de-Faou, an example of an old-style pardon closely linked to the lives of the people. The pardon came out of the Catholic Church's tradition of granting indulgences to parishioners on saint days in order that their sins might be pardoned. The ceremonies often include the taking of vows, blessings of people, animals or venerated objects, and the seeking of cures. Generally they commence with Mass, proceeding to open-air services, a pious procession in which banners, statues and relics are carried, and in the evening confession and vespers. Sometimes pardons end with secular functions and events such as fairs and festivals of Breton arts and sports. Pardoners took a gift back home for those who could not attend. This was called 'their share of the pardon', and might have been a Pardon Ball, a big shiny ball (in red, green, yellow or blue) to hang on the rafters, a religious object or toy. On the evening of a pardon a rice pudding would be made, cooked at the baker's.

Breton folk-tales are particularly well preserved. Like their wisdom and history, they were handed down orally in the family or propagated by minstrels, and these tales, steeped as they are in Celtic mythology, are still known today. Many refer to the coming and going between this world and the beyond, a passage more frequent at certain times of the year like Beltane and Samhain. They also tell of fantastic creatures, faeries and enchanters, giants and korrigans, mermaids, talking animals, and kings and princesses who can change shape.

Folk and Ecclesiastical Traditions

CELTIC From early Irish and Welsh literature we learn that the pre-Christian religion of the Celts was Druidism, which centred around the sun and nature, but included the belief that the living and the dead occupied different, but inter-connected, worlds. They believed in life after death and buried food, ornaments and weapons with the dead. The Druids taught that transmigration of souls occurred to other worlds, to one where there was no sickness, no unhappiness, no old age or death, and where time passed very slowly, or to one where suffering and sorrow reigned. Growth and fertility, and the powers determining them, were essential aspects of many rites, focusing principally on the sun and the phallus. The latter's power was more evident to the ordinary Celt than the distant might of the former, and fertility rites had an orgiastic side. Astronomy and herbalism were well-developed and important practices. Druidism also had much local character in the form of cults and deities, which persisted in that, after Christianisation, locally made saints were very common. There are compelling similarities between Druidism and Indian religions.

It is difficult to construct the Celtic pantheon as more than 400 gods and goddesses are known. Two gods connected with important festivals were Belenus, God of the Sun, venerated at Beltane (1st May) and Lug, the Great God of the Celts, at Lugnasadh (1st August). Lug was preceded by Nuadu as king of the gods and succeeded by Dagda, the good god. There is no evidence of actual sun *worship* at Beltane, but its crucial importance was clearly recognised. Wells, rivers and sacred trees were venerated and had patron gods and goddesses. The oak was the most sacred tree to the Druids, with yew and beech among others.

The entrance to the Celtic world of the gods was through water, which is why offerings were made in peat bogs, lakes and other watery places. The Celts placated, invoked and venerated rather than loved or worshipped their gods. Many gods appeared in triple form, and had three associations. The number three was sacred, signifying completion, so human sacrifices were killed three times, for example, by garrotting, stabbing and impaling. The number nine, being three times three, was also sacred. On sacrificial days, when an animal was offered to a god for his/her consideration or protection, or on feast days, no work was done and there was general celebration and feasting, the sacrificed animal being divided up among the tribe or clan. While conquerors of Celtic tribes, and imposers of new religions like Christianity, were able to suppress the day-to-day power of the Druids, their culture and influence proved enduring. Celtic social organisation was tribal, each tribe having a chief, with a regional group of chiefs under a king, but the Druidic priesthood structure went across this organisation, even though each tribe had its own deities. This pan-Druidic authority partly explains the

Helston Floral Dance, Cornwall, c.1910

survival of Druidic customs and beliefs long after the Druids themselves were replaced. Examples are midwinter evergreen decorations, plum puddings, and kissing under the mistletoe; apple-ducking at Hallowe'en; and placing earth and salt on the breast of a deceased person before burial. There are still remnants of their four great quarter day festivals, Samhain, the great feast at the end of summer; Imbolc, the feast of purification for farmers and the start of lambing; Beltane or Beltine, the great feast at the end of einter, when cattle were purified; and Lugnasadh, the harvest and first fruits festival.

There were three orders in the Druidic hierarchy, the Bards, who were singers and poets, the Seers (or Vates), diviners and natural philosophers, and the Priests or Druids proper, who, in addition to their religious function, looked after moral standards and administered justice. There were no temples, icons or other images, rites being held outside, usually on high places to be closer to the sun or in a grove of their sacred tree the oak. The many stone circles in the British Isles were not built by Druids. Shrines were erected only under Roman influence. The Druids predicted the future by divination, often from observation of natural phenomena or the behaviour of slain animals or human victims. They were recruited from the warrior class, but ranked higher. They educated the class as well as performed their religious and ritual duties. In resisting the Romanisation of Britain they made themselves targets for suppression, but as the Romans did not subjugate Ireland Druidism survived longer there than in Britain.

The early Christian Church focused its attention particularly on Celtic fertility rites and the demonisation of Celtic gods, replacing them with Christianised versions, often of distorted or invented provenance. Many aspects of the Druidic cult of nature were not wholly incompatible with a Christian stance, and the replacement was not a violent affair. For example, as the Druids believed in the immortality of the soul they were able to accept this aspect of Christianity, and also the correspondence alleged by the early Christians of Christian saints with Celtic deities. Even the symbol of the sun endured as the circular motif in the Celtic cross.

Christian missionaries were in Britain in the 4th century, and by the close of this century St Hilary, St Martin and St Ninian were working among the Picts of Strathclyde. The first Celtic Christian Church was monastic, not diocesan. St Patrick in AD 431 established the Church in Ireland, and one of its missionaries, Colum or Columba, founded a monastery on Iona in AD 563 which was his base for the conversion of Scots from the Firth of Forth to Shetland. St Mungo carried on the work in southern Scotland. Columba died in AD 597, the year that Augustine arrived in Kent. At that time Ireland, Scotland, Wales and south-west England were largely Christian, but the Lothians, The Merse and the rest of England were pagan. The remainder of southern Scotland was Christianised by St Cuthbert from Lindisfarne, and missionaries from both Lindisfarne and Canterbury dispersed throughout England. The Norse colony of Orkney and Shetland was not fully converted until the first Christian King of Norway, Olaf Tryggvason, imposed Christianity on the islands in AD 995.

The Celtic Church was increasingly Romanised, but after the Reformation only in Ireland did the Catholic Church remain the state religion. Records of church festivals in early times are scant, but we know that in the 1st century Sundays, Easter and Pentecost were celebrated, and in the 2nd Lent and the birth of Christ were added. In the 4th century, in an effort to replace Celtic gods and heroes in people's affections by Christian martyrs, and so transfer their homage, the Church instituted saint days, as well the process of Christianising those festivals and associations which the Celts would not abandon. The *son* of God, not the *Sun,* was worshipped at Yule, and Bride, the Celtic Goddess of Spring, was replaced by St Bride of Kildare, her festival day becoming Candlemas Eve. Beltane was associated with the Holy Cross, but this was relatively unsuccessful. Midsummer Day, dedicated to the Norse god Baldur, was rededicated to St John the Baptist. Lammas was Christianised by presenting a loaf in church, and Samhuinn, the festival of the dead, became Hallowmas. These changes, however, did not eradicate the old ways and beliefs completely, as the product of generations of observance becomes deeply ingrained in people's consciousness. What happened was that religious and folk customs became hybrid celebrations, with elements of Druidism, magic, the supernatural and Christianity in evidence, a cultural hot-pot which remains with us today.

The overlaying of pagan customs by Christian ones has hybridised the Calendar too, with the variable dates being largely descended from ecclesiastical tradition, notably for Shrovetide, Lent, Easter, Hocktide, Rogationtide, Whitsuntide, Trinity and Corpus Christi, collectively called the Easter Cycle, with Harvest dates being largely determined by the weather.

One of the legacies of the Church's attempt to eradicate devotions to, and the memory of, pagan gods is the zealous way in which early Christian clerics moulded the lives of saints, even inventing episodes, to fit them for the purpose of replacing those gods in the spiritual affection of the people. Some saints appear to have been wholly invented, for example St Catherine of Alexandria, and these were indeed removed from the Roman calendar when it was overhauled in 1969. Some that remain, such as St Anne, still defy historians looking for evidence of their existence. It appears that devotions to the Earth Goddess Anu were redirected to St Anne, alleged to be the Virgin Mary's mother, but almost certainly invented.

Many saint days were common throughout the Celtic region, and there were a large number of them, but others were local, often confined to a single village as is commonly the case in Cornwall and Brittany. Many saint days were abolished first in Protestant parts of the British Isles, being retained for a time in Catholic Ireland, but even there the English authorities finally rationalised the situation by establishing, in 1871, national Bank Holidays. The first such holidays were Good Friday, Easter Monday, Whit Monday, the first Monday in August, Christmas Day and the first weekday after Christmas Day, although some local feast days persisted for a time. In compensation for the loss of saint day holidays weekly annual leave was granted by employers.

A Druid revival began in the 18th century, inspired by classical and medieval literature, and there are people today who call themselves Druids and perform what they claim are Druidic ceremonies. They and their activities are not considered in this book, as there is no evidence that any of the rituals that they perform are in fact authentic, nor that the practitioners have any cultural descendency from the real Druids.

IRELAND The feasts and fasts of the Catholic Church were much more numerous in the past than they are now. Fasting meant a restriction to one meal a day, while abstinence meant refraining from certain foods. Ordinary abstinence referred to meat, but Lenten fasting obliged the faithful to have only one meal a day, containing no animal products at all, including milk, butter, cheese, fats and eggs. In addition to Lent, including Sundays in Lent, the Lenten fast was expected on the Advent fast days. The situation with regard to other days of fast or abstinence was not uniform in Ireland because of the power of bishops to change the days of obligation in their dioceses, thus causing local variations in folk traditions. The Advent fast was abolished in 1917, and milk products and eggs removed from the obligation of abstinence. Later, the obligation of abstinence on ordinary Fridays was abolished, although many continued it voluntarily.

During the time of the Penal Laws, under English rule, many Catholic ceremonies lapsed, but they resumed when the Catholic Church was allowed to reinstitute its religious calendar.

Generally, the traditions of Protestants in Ireland, largely descendants of English and Scottish immigrants, have remained quite separate from those of the majority Catholics.

ISLE OF MAN The island was Catholic before the Reformation, but became Protestant after it. From the 18th century, Methodists opposed Celtic customs strongly, and the early Wesleyans took particular exception to Celtic music and dancing, and the use of the Manx language. Churchgoers using Manx were regarded suspiciously, Manx hymns were discouraged or scrutinised carefully in translation, and traditional Manx services, like the Christmas Eve Oie'l Voirrey, were replaced or subjected to considerable modification.

SCOTLAND The Celtic Christianity brought to Scotland by Columba in the 6th century was largely displaced by Romanised Christianity from Northumbria up to the 8th century when Roman Catholicism took over. Scotland remained Catholic until the Reformation. Reforming Protestants challenged Catholicism in the 16th and 17th centuries, and after the 1688 Revolution Covenanting Presbyterians and Episcopalians vied for power, the former becoming dominant and establishing the Church of Scotland in 1689. An Act of 1712 protected the Episcopal Communion. After the Reformation, Catholicism was mainly to be found in the Highlands and Hebrides, and the Roman Catholic Church was formalised again in 1878. However, most Catholic elements in folk traditions had by then disappeared, feast days as early as 1560 by order of the Calvinist Kirk.

WALES The arrival of Christianity saw the beginning of a sustained attack on Welsh folk culture, resulting in massive loss of folk-tales, songs and other musical and oral heritage. Initially the ruling classes embraced Catholicism, and Christianisation of pagan associations began, such as the linking of wells with saints. After the Reformation landowners took up the new religion, while the rural folk clung to their mixture of pagan and Christian beliefs and ways. After the suppression of Catholicism in Elizabethan times, Methodists and Non-Conformists increased their influence in Wales. Calvinism and Arminianism spread in north Wales, while Baptists and Congregationalists were more successful in the south. There were pockets of Quakerism among old families, and Unitarianism on the borders of the old counties of Cardiganshire and Carmarthenshire and in parts of Glamorgan. It was the Methodist Revival of the 18th century by stern puritans which saw the banishment of many ancient Celtic traditions.

Surviving churchyards which are oval or round in shape denote a previous grove of trees sacred to the ancient Celts, such as those at Llanfechain, Powys; Cilcenin, Dyfed; and Derwen, Clwyd.

CORNWALL John Wesley and Methodism came to Cornwall in the 18th century. The tinners (tin miners) were converted and their customs began to wane under attack from the Methodists. Throughout Cornwall old Celtic religious practices were replaced and Methodist hymns replaced folk songs. To preserve Cornish culture, the first Old Cornwall Society was set up in St Ives in 1920, to be followed by others, eventually leading to the creation of the Federation of Old Cornwall Societies.

BRITTANY During Roman times Armorican Gaul was a land where the Druids wielded considerable authority, but once the Catholic Church was established the Bretons remained loyal to it, as they do to this day.

Brittany claims 7847 saints, many of local adoption, and few actually canonised by the Vatican. Tro-Breiz is the tour of Brittany visiting the cathedrals of all seven founding saints Samson, Malo (the Welsh monk Maclow who set up home near the rock here in the 6th century), Brioch, Tugdual, Paul the Aurelian, Corentine and Patern who came with the Cornish in the 5th century. These were linked with the seven original bishoprics at Dol, St Malo, St Brieuc, Tréguier, St Pol-de-Léon, Quimper and Vannes. Until the 16th century every Breton was expected to make the Tro-Breiz to all seven shrines. There is an Islamic-Christian pilgrimage, called Le Vieux Marché, to the chapel of the Seven Saints on the fourth weekend in July. In the Breton flag, the Gwenn ha Du (White and Black), the five black stripes represent the original bishoprics of Upper Brittany (Rennes, Nantes, Dol, St Malo and St Brieuc) while the four white stripes represent those of Lower Brittany (Léon, Cornouaille, Vannes and Tréguier). The field of ermine in the flag evokes the Duchy of Brittany.

The Celtic Year and Quarter Days

Folk custom is heavily pre-occupied with two fundamental needs, to feed and to reproduce. Fertility was essential to both, and to ensure it the forces of nature had to be honoured and sacrifices made. It was clear that there was a relationship between the cycles of day and night, and of the seasons, on the one hand, and the movements of sun, moon and stars on the other. Activities and festivities were synchronised with the life cycles of important plants and animals, key events being the death of vegetation at the start of winter and its renewal in spring.

For rural folk the notion of a calendar was principally agricultural, but time also came to be reckoned in lunar phases in the pre-Christian era. The Celts had two seasons, summer starting at Beltane (1st May eve), when cattle were put out to pasture, and winter starting at Samhain (1st November eve), when cattle were brought in from the fields. The oldest Celtic calendar was lunar, with 12 lunar months and an intercalary period of 12 days, each of which had the name of one of the months. This may be the root of the view that the weather on each day of the last six days of December and first six days of January, or on the first 12 days of January, typified the weather to be expected in each of the 12 months to follow. In Brittany these days are still called *gourdeziou*, or 'over-days', and it may also explain the Welsh terms *dyddiau dyddon*, and *coelddyddiau* or 'omen days'. In Irish and Welsh folk-tales a limit for an undertaking of 'a year and a day' is common, and may have the same origin.

Ancient myths show that the Celts personified the months and credited them with attributes. In surviving Breton folk-tales January is portrayed by snow and cold, February by icicles, March by hail, April by buds, May by green grass, June by hay-making, July by hatching eggs, August by the harvest, September by cold north winds, October by mist, November by big drips and streams, and December by shivers and chills. In other tales they have occupations: January is often a ploughman, but has a warm house; February a tailor, but his house is cold and short of food; and March a barber, but penniless, for example.

The Ancient Celtic Year began with Samhain (what is now the eve of 1st November) and continued through three other quarter days, Imbolc (the eve of 1st February), Beltane (the eve of 1st May) and Lughnasadh (the eve of 1st August). A festival marked each one, and such was the enduring nature of these celebrations that elements of them survive today.

The old Manx seasons were summer (starting on May Day) and winter (starting on Old Hollantide Day, 12th November). Later spring came to mean February to April, summer May to July, autumn August to October, and winter November to January. Each of the three months in each season is known as the first, middle and last month of the season.

The non-Celtic people of Britain used the solstices and equinoxes to divide the year, with Midsummer Day and Midwinter Day (or Yule) the most important festival days, particularly for people of Norse descent.

On account of the mixed traditions in the British Isles two other sets of quarter days arose, one based on the astronomical cycle and the other based on the agricultural seasons. These are known from at least medieval times. The former set had quarter days at Christmas (25th December, near the winter solstice), Lady Day (25th March, near the vernal equinox), Midsummer Day (24th June, near the summer solstice) and Michaelmas (29th September, near the autumnal equinox). These were used for legal purposes such as for hirings and rents in England and Celtic areas under direct English administration. The latter set was very close to the old Celtic Year and had quarter days at Candlemas (2nd February, the start of spring), May Day (1st May, the start of summer), Lammas (1st August, the start of autumn) and All Saints' Day (1st November, the start of winter). These were called cross-quarter days, and they were considered unlucky by the Church because they were old pagan festival days.

The Scottish quarter days were Candlemas on 2nd February, Whitsun or Old Beltane on 15th May, Lammas on 1st August, and Martinmas or Old Hallowmas on 11th November.

There are few vestiges of the old Celtic calendar remaining in Brittany. The public holidays in Brittany are 1st January (New Year's Day), Easter Monday, 1st May (Labour Day), 8th May (VE Day 1945), Ascension Day, Whit Monday, 14th July (Bastille Day), 15th August (Feast of the Assumption), 1st November (All Saints' Day), 11th November (Armistice Day 1918) and 25th December (Christmas Day).

Apple Bobbing at Hallowe'en, Scotland

January
customs

The Bretons, who personified all months, and lived in the southernmost Celtic land, called it January the Chilly, and icicles were 'January's Teeth'. The dark lifeless days inspired visiting and mutual support to maintain community ties. The calendrical significance of January varied according to whether Celtic, Anglo-Saxon or Norse tradition was followed, with Yule continuing all month in the north of Scotland, but Christmas elsewhere originally on 5th January (or 6th January according to which tradition you follow) but today effectively ending on New Year's Eve.

January was a time of hope for good weather and crops, and thoughts of spring. Forces both good and evil vied for control of people's lives, and these had to be appeased or combated by the appropriate rituals. Having enough food and keeping warm, and maintaining the health of livestock, were constant preoccupations in rural Celtic society, as was the interpretation of portents all around. When you live on the edge of subsistence, the temptation to try to predict the future is well-nigh irresistible.

Variable Dates

CORNWALL In January the relief from flooding from Loe Pool is commemorated. It is Cornwall's largest lake, separated from the sea by a sandbank called Loe Bar, and it often flooded. In order to relieve the flooding local people cut a channel in the sandbank, and bought permission to do this from the Lord of Penrose Manor by presenting him with a purse containing three halfpence.

Fixed Dates

1st January New Year's Day, Circumcision
CELTIC New Year's Day is awash with superstitions and practices whose function is to ensure that the family has good fortune in the coming year and starts as it means to go on with family, household and finances intact. People rose early, all possessions were brought into the house, nothing was lent, no debts were paid, leftover food was used up and the house ritually cleaned. Omens abounded, particularly in the behaviour of fires and weather. Freshly drawn well water was especially potent in its cleansing and healing properties. Gifts, called Handsel, were given to children, friends and callers, in the latter case when they called as first-footers bearing symbolic items

signifying a wish that the household would have good luck, warmth, prosperity and nourishment. To forget meant bad luck, and not to give them refreshments was bad manners. The appearance of the first person to cross the threshold is highly significant.

The familiar theme of death and rebirth is a feature of mummers' plays traditionally performed on this day.

ISLE OF MAN This day was often called Little Christmas. Fiddlers would go from house to house to rouse the occupants with music, and their wives would follow the next day for payment, usually food or drink. The English tune 'The Hunt is Up' was a favourite.

SCOTLAND This is called Ne'er Day, and when in 1600 it became 1st January it brought it into the 12 days of Yule, and those celebrations done on Twelfth Night were done instead on New Year's Eve. Also moved were rites formerly done on old quarter days, such as first-footing, saining and divination. At the end of the Celtic Year people gathered at stone circles or mercat crosses to see in the new year, and the Church encouraged them to gather in churches instead. The burning of the old year out survives as an element of several Scottish Yule/Hogmanay customs.

The first to get out of bed took sowans or the pint to the rest of the family, and then fresh food to the animals. Sowans was an oat gruel made by fermenting the inner husks of oats after winnowing and threshing, filtering and boiling the liquid until it thickens. Leftovers were used up, in dishes like **Potted Stilton** *(see p.193 for recipe)*, and potting was a favourite way of preserving foods like game and meat to be eaten at Winter celebrations like Hogmanay.

This morning, men can traditionally demand a kiss from any woman they know.

A traditional drink on this day is the **The Pint** *(see p.193 for recipe)*, made from beer, whisky, sugar, eggs and nutmeg, and drunk with shortbread.

In the Highlands they have **Athol Brose** *(see p.193 for recipe)* made from whisky, honey, oatmeal and cream.

Sowans sweetened with honey or treacle, with whisky added, and hogmanay bannock (for breakfast, it being bad luck to break it earlier) were eaten. **Black Bun** *(see p.193 for recipe)* – originally Twelfth Cake, a rich fruit cake – and cake and kebbuck (oatcake and cheese) were also eaten at this time.

First footing in Edinburgh

A popular main course for dinner was goose or beef, followed by plum pudding . In north-east Scotland and Aberdeenshire boys would go begging for food and money to give to local poor or elderly people. This was called 'thigging'. In Aberdeen on this day there was once a large trade procession.

In the Highlands, today was a saining day and before the purification began, water delivered from 'dead and living fords' – streams that were crossed by funeral processions – was drunk and sprinkled everywhere.

Children once went holming today, which involved whipping each other's legs with holly until blood was drawn. Each drop represented a year of healthy life.

New Year visitors in disguise are called guisers. Children with blackened faces and in disguise go around (as at Hallowe'en) singing or reciting begging rhymes for food (such as slices of Black Bun) or money. Typical food offered is sweet cakes or sugared bread. The tradition of begging rhymes existed from Sutherland to Fife, and also in Orkney and Shetland. Going from house to house giving New Year blessings and receiving gifts was characteristic of the Lowlands. A traditional first-footer refreshment was whisky and warm **Petticoat Tails** *(see p.193 for recipe)*.

New Year's Day sport was played, Shinty (or Camanachd) in the Highlands and Handball or Football in the Lowlands. In Kirkwall a New Year Ba' game was played.

Shinty *This game, as played long ago, with its aerial as well as ground-level combat, was like clan warfare with a few rules. No-one called 'Time!'; one team called 'Enough!!'. As now codified it is played by teams of 12, 45 minutes each way, on a field 200 to 145 yards long by 100 to 70 yards wide. There is a hail (goal) at each end. The ball (formerly called the shintie and made from knotty wood) is made of leather-covered cork and struck with a caman (a wooden stick shorter than a hockey stick, and formerly made from a sheep's backbone) on either side. Its rules are too complex to record here, but it has elements of hockey and lacrosse.*

Handball *This is similar in objectives to soccer except that the ball can be caught, thrown, bounced or struck with the palm, but not kicked except by the goalkeepers in their goal-circles. Players must not enter the goal-circle.*

Today in East Wemyss, formerly on Auld Handsel Monday (the first Monday of the new year on the Old Calendar), the game of Yetlins was played, and may have been more widespread as it derives from an imitation of the passage of the sun at the winter solstice.

Yetlins *Such games involved either rolling wheels down hills or hurling iron balls from the hip along a level track. The game died out during World War I, and was played along the rocky shore called The Skelleys, between two large boulders. A game was called a 'hail', and was won by throwing an iron ball, in the smallest number of throws, from one boulder to the other. The balls were 3 in in diameter and weighed 3 lb. Long ago wave-rounded stones were used, and most recently a leather strap was employed to project the balls.*

Another game played today, and again formerly on Old Handsel Monday, was 'A Bawbee She Kyles' in Kirkcaldy until the 1950s.

A Bawbee She Kyles *Three rows of three holes, each with a diameter of 6 in, were cut in the turf. The rows were 1 yard apart, and a Mark was made on the ground 10 yards from the nearest row. A 5 in cannon ball was cast from the Mark to try to 'kyle' (drop or roll) it into the hole. Each player threw a ha'penny (bawbee) down before his throw. When a ball was kyled the player took the kitty. There was betting on the outcome.*

In Shetland this was the second day of Yule, called Helya's Night. Milk-an-mel was eaten. After Christianisation children were blessed today and committed to the care of the Virgin Mary. Five Grülacks (The Gentleman, a 'carrying horse' and three others) went from house to house in the morning with a greeting song, getting food in return, which the 'horse' took back for the New'r Night Feast. The day in Shetland was a working day for everyone, to establish the pattern for the rest of the year.

🌑 The Pint Ceremony, Lanark Strathclyde

Local pensioners assemble at the District Council Offices in the morning to receive a pint and one pound. The money comes from the interest on three debts dating from 1662 – called a Mortification – which was originally used for a number of causes such as sending five poor boys to the local Grammar School and providing a large glass of mulled ale for retired burgesses.

LANARK IS ON THE A73 SOUTH OF CARLUKE.

🌑 Ne'er Day Ba' Game, Kirkwall, Mainland Orkney

After a preliminary game on Christmas Day, the main events of this street football tradition, played with a cork-filled leather ball, take place today. At 10 am the Boys' Game starts in front of the Cathedral at Mercat Cross. The Men's Game gets underway at 1 pm, between the Uppies and Downies (representing the two parts of the town).

KIRKWALL IS THE PRINCIPAL TOWN OF ORKNEY.

🌑 The Boys' Walk, Dufftown Grampian

This was originally a reunion of distillery apprentices belonging to the Juvenile Society, a mutual benefit society. Today, boy and girl members parade through the town collecting money for local worthy causes, with evening entertainments to conclude.

DUFFTOWN IS ON THE A941 SOUTH FROM ELGIN.

WALES Young people in South Wales villages would rise early and conduct saining rituals with freshly drawn spring water. In south-west Dyfed towns like Tenby this custom survived until as late as the 1950s.

The collecting of calennig (New Year's gifts) by children from door to door was a characteristically Welsh way of giving gifts today in Gwent, Glamorgan and south-east Dyfed. Between early morning and noon children went round with an apple or orange skewered with corn and evergreen sprigs. Three skewers were added to provide a tripod-like support and a larger one by which to hold it. It was sometimes covered with flour and studded with nuts and raisins. Householders would give food or new pennies. The custom has survived, but not the carrying of the apples or oranges. It is reminiscent of the English gift of an orange stuck with cloves given in Gloucestershire and Hereford and Worcester, especially to godparents. The giving of Christmas boxes is a 20th-century introduction from England. Calennig may have its origins in the Roman custom of strena, a pagan symbol of fruitfulness in the year to come.

Fruit was taken out to hens so that they would lay well all year.

Right: Collecting Calennig on New Year's Day, South Wales
Left: Calennig Apple, Wales

Mari Lwyd did the rounds today. Mari Lwyd (The Grey Mare) is a horse character in a midwinter barring-out custom, surviving today in Glamorgan and south-east Dyfed. In Glamorgan and Gwent it was associated with Christmas Night, but elsewhere in Wales it was abroad in the New Year and Twelfth Night. It is often done in conjunction with wassail singing. A horse's skull (or a wooden skull) is fixed on a pole and carried by a bearer entirely covered by a white sheet. Ribbons and other decorations are sown on the sheet area covering the skull, including black cloth ears. The eyes are usually of glass and the lower jaw is sprung so it can be snapped. Sometimes it is buried after use and dug up next year, to be whitened with lime ready for use again.

A 'leader', using reins with bells on, takes it from house to house accompanied by 'Sergeant', 'Merryman' playing the fiddle, men in beribboned clothes singing a song, sometimes also by Punch and Judy, and asks for admittance. Usually this is refused with a good excuse. If one cannot be thought of then the party is admitted and given free beer. They make a fuss of the women. Punch and Judy may have blackened faces, and Punch carries a poker that he uses to beat the ground. Sometimes the men wear suits decorated with ribbons, and Judy may carry a broom, like Bessy, to sweep around the house like New Year sweepers. This is a similar job to Mollie who accompanies the Hooden Horse in Kent, and to Our Lass who accompanies Old Tup in Derbyshire, although she did not normally carry her own broom. Records of Mari Lwyd start at the end of the 18th century, and the custom seems to be composite with elements of pre-Christian wassailing at the approach of spring, a pagan horse-cult, mumming and medieval miracle plays. Lwyd can mean holy or grey, and Mari could be Mary or Mare, but which is not certain.

Mari Lwyd, Welsh Folk Museum, St Fagan's, Cardiff — South Glamorgan

Their primitive horse-character leaves in the early hours, and until mid-January it visits a number of places, such as Llantrisant and Pontypridd in Mid Glamorgan, Ystradgynlais on the West Glamorgan/Powys border, and Ammanford in Dyfed.

CARDIFF IS THE PRINCIPAL CITY OF WALES.

Mari Lwyd, Llangynwyd, near Bridgend — Mid Glamorgan

At midnight from the 12th-century thatched public house Yr Hen Dy (The Old House) Mari Lwyd begins her rounds.

TAKE THE A4063 NORTH FROM BRIDGEND, THEN LEFT ON AN UNCLASSIFIED ROAD AFTER COYTRAHEN.

CORNWALL Some swept dust inwards, some outwards. Doorsteps were sanded for good luck, so that visitors brought some in on their soles.

BRITTANY This is a public holiday, and not a religious feast day, although it was customary to have a big family meal at noon.

It was customary to go visiting and extend New Year greetings and good wishes, including the hope for healthy bowels. This might last all day. Children also did the rounds, asking, in rhyme, for money.

2nd January

SCOTLAND This was the third day of Yule in Shetland, called Tammasmas E'en (or Tunderman's Night, or Thor's Night). No work was carried out nor games played after sunset. The Church rededicated it to St Thomas. Byaena Sunday Brose was eaten, prepared from smoked cow's or sheep's head.

First Monday in January

IRELAND This was Handsel Monday, when children visited relatives, neighbours and friends for handsel – usually small gifts of money or cakes, which it was unlucky to refuse to give.

SCOTLAND This was called Auld Handsel Monday, and until the end of the 19th century was a holiday for labourers and servants. There was a tradition of giving gratuities to employees and the needy in the area, often a hearty breakfast, and to make sure the recipients were awake horns were blown outside their houses or musicians played and sang. Typical foods provided were Yule Brose, haggis, black and white puddings, beef, ale and whisky.

Families went visiting or out for walks, and there were fairs held. Street musicians would strike up and stalls selling **Kelso Gingerbread** *(see p.193 for recipe)*, sweets, fruit and treacle ale appeared.

Visitors to houses would be offered porter with shortbread, currant loaf and pies. A typical dinner would have been powsowdie (sheep's head broth), goose, beef-steak pie, and plum pudding or currant dumpling. Barn dances were held in the evening.

In some places this was considered the end of the Daft Days, so it was Uphalieday. The next day was called Roking Day (a rok is a spinning wheel) because spinners started work again.

Mari Lwyd, Cardiff, Wales

4th January
ISLE OF MAN On Old Christmas Eve Spinners stopped work until 6th January.

5th January Twelfth Night, Epiphany Eve, Old Christmas Eve, Wassail Eve
CELTIC Various remnants of the old Twelfth Night celebrations survived for a time in the Celtic areas after the change to the Julian Calendar, until gradually they were moved to Christmas Eve and Christmas Day. A special cake was baked, with tokens inside; the lucky finders being made King and Queen of the revelries. All would drink from a communal bowl called the Wassail Bowl, containing a mixture of fruit and spiced ale. Poor people in fancy dress (Guisers) would take the bowl from door to door, singing carols and offering good wishes with the drink, in the hope that they received gifts. They might also dance or perform a mumming play. Celebrations in the parts of Scotland originally settled by Norsemen were distinctive today and tomorrow.
ISLE OF MAN This was Old Christmas Eve in times past, and many people stuck to it long after the calendar change. It was customary to grow Sweet Cicely in Manx gardens, an aromatic plant called 'Myrrh', which tastes and smells of aniseed. At midnight people went outside with lanterns to see if shoots had appeared and if any had bloomed. The flowers open for an hour only.
SCOTLAND Twelfth Night is called Auld Yule, and celebrations centred round a wassail bowl.

There is a Christmas flowering thorn at Queen Mary's College, St Andrews, Fife, which blooms traditionally on this day.

This was Yule E'en in Shetland. The whole house was cleaned and everyone put on fresh clothes. Sowans was eaten. Yule cakes were baked between sunset and sunrise, one for each member of the family. Yule **Brunies** *(see p.193 for recipe)* were cakes shaped like the sun with a hole in the centre.

A light was left burning all night, and outside was left a basket (kishie) of peat and, to keep trolls away, an iron blade.
WALES In the evening a large loaf, like **Bara Brith** *(see p.194 for recipe)*, or pile of cakes or a single large cake – such as **Teisen Lap** *(see p.194 for recipe)* or **Twelfth Night Cake** *(see p.194 for recipe)* – was made and divided between Christ, Mary, the Magi and those present. A ring was hidden, and whoever got it was elected King (or Queen) of Misrule, or a dried bean and pea were hidden and the finders elected King Bean and Queen Marrowfat. Only one person must put bread in the oven, as more than one are sure to quarrel.

Three customs also done on this day were Mari Lwyd, wassailing and hunting the wren. Hunting the wren, which was thought to embody the evils of winter, and parading it round in a wren-house (or Cutty Wren) decorated with ribbons was last done in Pembrokeshire in the 19th century. Young men mainly carried out the custom, singing wren songs, at night, making sure to visit newly married couples, who always welcomed them. Sprinkling the couple with water while in bed adds a fertility element. The hunters offered the wren for sale for beer money.

Wassail in South Wales today involved carrying a cake, baked apples, sugar, and warm beer and spices in a 12-handled vessel to a house where lived a newly married couple, or one recently moved to a new house. They sang, and those inside answered with alternate stanzas. After admission they shared the drink first, then the food. This has the appearance of a consecration ceremony, similar to marriage customs.

In south-west Dyfed poor females went sowling, which was begging for any food eaten with bread, such as cheese, meat or fish.

CORNWALL All Christmas cakes must be eaten by Twelfth Night, and all decorations taken down.

Guising, or geese dancing, with blackened faces and some in animal skins, was done on or around Twelfth Night until recently. A death-and-resurrection drama about St George was the usual play performed. The last recorded group were the St Ives guizers with their processional dance.

6th January Twelfth Day, Epiphany, Old Christmas Day, Uphalieday

CELTIC As with Twelfth Night, different Celtic areas preserved the Old Christmas Day celebrations to a different extent, with Catholic Ireland having the most subdued day and Scotland the most festive. As the last day of Yule in many northern areas, rituals associated with a threshold occasion such as divination, particularly for marriage prospects, were done, as well as feasting, games and general merry-making.

IRELAND This day was also known as Little Christmas.

A recent custom is Nollaig na mBhan, or Women's Christmas, when husbands, sons and boyfriends treat their wives, mothers and girlfriends respectively in appreciation of what they have done for them.

ISLE OF MAN This was the last day of Yule. Fire was never borrowed today, but purchased instead. The herring fishermen's Boat Supper was sometimes held on this day. Wells were often visited, possibly encouraged by the Church to distract people from pagan practices associated with the last day of Saturnalia.

The ceremony of Cutting Off the Fiddler's Head was a Twelfth Day tradition carried out at dances at which the fiddler played. His other function was as a matchmaker. He would lay his head in a girl's lap and someone would ask him who such-and-such a girl shall marry – giving the name of a local girl present. The fiddler's answer was greeted accordingly by those in the know, with mirth, tears, anger or happiness.

A game similar to pairing valentines was played. A master of ceremonies (mainshter) was elected and he appointed a girl (legad) for every boy as their partner. The boy bought food and drink for the legad. Then the White Mare (laare vane) came in (with its wooden horse-head, snapping mouth and covered in a sheet; cf. the Welsh Mari Lwyd) and much merriment ensued.

Another game was Goggins or Noggins.

Goggins *Symbols of various trades, such as water for a sailor, grain for a farmer, etc. are put into mugs, and these are put on the hearth. Girls are blindfolded and must choose a mug. The symbol in it is that of the profession of their future husband.*

SCOTLAND This was also considered the last of the hallow days of Yule, and all evergreen decorations were burned.

This was Yule Day in Shetland, and on the island of Foula, 30 miles west of Lerwick, Shetland, this is still Christmas Day, and called Yule. Christmas trees are now flown to the island, but there are still many Norse elements in their celebration. Their Christmas meal, prepared beforehand on Yule E'en, consists of reetsit (salted smoked mutton), potato soup (tattie soup) and bread made with caraway seeds. People visit each other on round trips, meeting up at 9 pm in one house for feasting, drinking and dancing. In former times, when the whole of Shetland celebrated this day, there was abundant custom. The first to rise brought a peat in for every member of the family and put it on the fire. The person who's peat lasted longest would have the longest life. Yule Brose was eaten at a candlelit breakfast, to wait for the rising of the Yule sun. Wandering musicians played and greeted householders, as the women cooked for the feast and the men and boys played Ba'. After eating there was story-telling in the old Norse tradition, and the creation of Norn rhymes called Veesicks. Then the gue (a two-stringed fiddle) would strike up for singing and dancing. A feature of Shetland Yule until Four-and-Twenty Day on 30th January was the bands of guisers (Grülacks) dressed in straw with conical, beribboned straw hats. They announced their arrival with a gunshot, and the gudeman of a house would greet them similarly. After doing a sword dance and reel for the household they were then given refreshments and money. As the Norn language and customs faded Scottish traditions replaced them. Veesicks were only made in Norn and have now disappeared.

WALES This day came to mark the end of the Christmas period, which previously ran on to Candlemas. The Yule Log was taken out and decorations taken down.

Some villages clung to Christmas Day celebrations today, for example, Llansanffraid, Gwynedd.

CORNWALL Cornish guisers are called Goose Dancers, and wear Twelfth Day fancy dress.

Some kept Christmas Day here up to the 19th century, but feasting and merriment happened in other households too. A Twelfth Day cake was made and in it were hidden career divination tokens. After the candles were lit games were played, such as Robin's Alight (Jack's Alive in East Cornwall).

Robin's Alight *A stick is set alight and whirled rapidly in the hands of the first player, who repeated: 'Robin's alight, and if he goes out I'll saddle your back.' The stick was passed on. Whoever let the spark die had to pay a forfeit (or pawn): 'Here's a pawn and a very pretty pawn! And what shall the owner of this pawn do?'*

After midnight supper, for which there is a record of a 'pie of four-and-twenty-blackbirds' being served, divination was done.

BRITTANY This is called the Day of Kings. In Dinan there was a custom among young people to go around the town reciting the Life of Herod in verse. One child, an innocent or simpleton, was dressed as a Jewish child and had his neck ceremonially cut with a wooden sword. Plays on this theme exist, dating from the 18th century.

On this day suitors used to visit girls they were seriously interested in courting. Popular girls had their house full, each trying to be the twelfth visitor, as this would ensure that they would be chosen to marry her.

7th January St Brannoc's Day, Old St Stephen's Day

CELTIC The 6th-century Welsh saint St Brannoc, who is buried at Braunton, Devon, sailed to south-west England from Wales in a coffin made from stone. It was said that he could tame or cure any animal.

IRELAND Christmas decorations came down, all evergreens being burned, not put on compost heaps, or kept to add to the fire under the pancake griddle on Shrove Tuesday.

ISLE OF MAN Some herring fishermen held their Boat Supper today.

CORNWALL The inhabitants of St Agnes in Scilly held a feast today in honour of their patron saint St Warna. Her well was cleaned and guns fired over it.

First Monday after Twelfth Day

CORNWALL On Scilly young men and women celebrated by exchanging clothes and dancing.

9th January St Fillan's Day

St Fillan was an 8th-century Scottish pioneer of a cold-water immersion therapy for lunatics, who were taken to St Fillan's Pool in the Strathfillan Valley, near Tyndrum, Central Region. One of his caves is at Pittenweem, near Anstruther, Fife.

11th January Old New Year's Eve

ISLE OF MAN Some herring fishermen held their Boat Supper today.

Burning the Clavie, Burghead, near Elgin Grampian

This fire festival seems to have Druidic and Norse elements, and may be as much as 1500 years old. Burghead is known to be a Pictish site. The word 'clavie' comes from the Gaelic 'cliabh' meaning 'a basket'. A whisky cask is sawn into two unequal parts, the smaller bottom part being nailed to a 'spoke' (an 8-foot salmon fisherman's pole). The nail used is iron-free, giving rise to the theory that it is a pre-Iron Age custom, and is driven in with a stone not an iron implement. Herring cask staves reinforce the structure to make a cage, into which the clavie carrier puts his head. The clavie is filled with wood and tar, and torched with burning peat. All items used for this ceremony are given or borrowed, not bought. The Clavie King has a crew of five. Only local families take part.

At 6 pm the Clavie King leads the procession up Doorie Hill. It is bad luck to stumble. Faggots from the clavies were traditionally thrown through any open door, where they were received gratefully as protectors from the evil eye. Once at the top the clavies are rested in stone holders after circling the knoll sunwise, then they are smashed and their contents tipped out down the hill. Villagers make great efforts to retrieve a piece of tar, as a good-luck charm and protector from evil.

In the past boats in the harbour were circuited with torches as a protection and a libation made to the sea-god.

TAKE THE A96 WEST FROM ELGIN, THEN RIGHT ON THE B9013.

12th January Old New Year's Day

ISLE OF MAN Some herring fishermen held their Boat Suppers today.

WALES When the calendar changed in 1752 some New Year's Day customs were transferred to this day (yr Hen Galan). An example is the farmers' feasts for those who helped with the harvest. Also, agricultural lettings and other agreements were reckoned from this day. In parts of Dyfed Hen Galan is still celebrated.

Hen Galan Festival, near Fishguard, Cwn Gwaun region Dyfed

In the morning children march and sing through the streets, begging for gifts (calennig). In the evening, in farmhouses, feasting (noson lawen), story-telling and singing are enjoyed.

THIS REGION IS TO THE SOUTH-EAST OF FISHGUARD.

Burning the Clavie, Burghead

✦ Hen Galan Service, Llandysul Church, near Cardigan   Dyfed

This is a public service, featuring the local style of singing known as pwnc. The service consists of the catechising of 13 Sunday Schools, each of which recites portions of the Scriptures, followed by each of the 13 choirs singing an anthem.

A Church Sunday School Festival was founded here in 1833 by the Reverend Enoch James to counter the custom of holding a mass football match with the village of Llanwenog, in which the 8-mile pitch between the villages had the two churches as goals. It became so violent that a fatality occurred, and it was abandoned.

TAKE THE A484 EAST FROM CARDIGAN, THEN LEFT ON THE A486.

Monday after 12th January   Handsel Monday

SCOTLAND This was Old New Year's Day in some areas, and called Handsel Monday until 100 years ago. Rich people gave gifts to the poor, and pupils gave gifts to their teachers. The pupil giving the most generous gift was made King, or Queen, for the day, and had the power to grant a day's holiday. Handsel money was spat on for luck and put into an empty pocket. Street markets sprang up to sell treats such as treacle sandwiches, plum pudding, steak pie, goose, pig's head and powsowdie (sheep's head broth). Sports and dancing were also popular today, as well as visiting or first-footing.

Landowners on Islay, Strathclyde, served Buntat' Breac (mutton stew), whisky and porter to the local people.

Tuesday after 12th January   Roking Day

SCOTLAND Roking Day saw a continuation of Handsel Monday activities in many parts, but for spinners it was time to resume work on their rokes or spinning wheels. This is the equivalent of St Distaff's Day (7th January) in England.

13th January   St Mungo's Day

CELTIC Born Kentigern in the 7th century at Culross, Fife, St Mungo is known to have founded a church on the site where Glasgow Cathedral was later built, and in which his burial place is. Mungo means 'good friend', a name suggested by one of his mentors St Serf of Culross. Also buried on this site is Fergus of Kernach, another of St Mungo's mentors.

SCOTLAND This was once celebrated as Ne'er Day (New Year's Day) in Foula, Shetland.

16th January   St Fursey's Day

CELTIC St Fursey was a 7th-century Irish mystic.

🎧 **Up Helly A', Scalloway**
TAKE THE A970 WEST FROM LERWICK.

17th January St Anthony's Day, Old Epiphany Day
BRITTANY St Antoine was the patron saint of pigs, and a chapel to him in Musillac was a place of pilgrimage, presumably for pig farmers rather than pigs. In Saint-Melaine, Ille-et-Vilaine, there was a fair dedicated to him.

20th January St Agne's Eve, St Vigean's Day
CELTIC St Vigean was a 7th-century abbot, originally from Ireland, but who founded a church at St Vigean, near Arbroath, Tayside.

Traditionally this was a time for divination to reveal a future spouse, which in Scotland meant throwing grain in a field then returning home to look in a mirror.
SCOTLAND St Vigean's Fair was held today at the town of this name near Arbroath, Tayside.

21st January St Agne's Day
CELTIC St Agnes became the patroness of maidens and was revered by the Cornish for the way she resisted surrendering her virginity to the Cornish giant Bolster.

24th January St Paul's Eve
CORNWALL Miners had a holiday today, called Paul Pitcher Day. They set up a pitcher of water and threw stones at it until it shattered. Then they would buy a new one and fill it with beer to drink. In the villages, during the evening, it was Paul Pitcher Night, when groups of youths threw broken pitchers or other vessels at doors, saying, 'St Paul's Eve and here's a heave!' The first heave could not be objected to, but if a second was thrown then summary justice could be meted out. In East Cornwall the pitchers were filled with sherds, earth, or worse.

St Paul's Eve fair, Newlyn, Cornwall 1880s

25th January St Paul's Day, Conversion of St Paul, St Dwynwen's Day, Burns' Night

CELTIC St Dwynwen (or St Dwyn) is the Welsh patron saint of lovers. Her shrine at Llandwyn Island, Anglesey, was visited by courting couples and by farmers with ailing livestock.

SCOTLAND This is Burns' Night, first held by a group of friends of the poet Robert Burns (1759–1796) in 1801, and nationally since 1859. He was born into a farming family on this day in 1759 in Alloway, Strathclyde, and died on 21st July 1796. The first Burns' Club was founded in Greenock in 1801. His songs and poems drew heavily on folklore, custom, divination, superstitions, witches, ghosts and the local scenery and way of life, and they feature in gatherings on this night. The normal pattern for the evening is supper, speeches and songs, as much as possible using his Lallans (Lowlands) dialect. After grace the **Haggis** *(see p.194 for recipe)* – minced mutton, offal, oatmeal and spices boiled in a sheep's stomach – is piped in, in sunwise procession, and cut with a St Andrew's Saltire. Whisky is poured and the supper, often including **Scotch Broth** *(see p.194 for recipe)*, sheep's head broth (powsowdie), wind-dried cod with horseradish and egg sauce (Cabbie Claw), and smoked haddock (Finnan Toasties), eaten.

After the speeches and toasts, Burns' recitals are given and his songs are sung, finishing with Auld Lang Syne, all joining hands crosswise. This is not a folk custom, but tends to be treated as though it is.

30th January

SCOTLAND In Shetland this was Up-Helly-Aa, or Four-and Twenty Day, or Twenty-Fourth Night, the last day of Yule. Trolls were abroad and were at their most mischievous. Nobody went out unaccompanied and without protective charms, and babies were sained and guarded. Dances were held in the evening, and just before midnight the trolls were driven back to the underworld by loud noises. Lerwick used to have a custom of dragging blazing tar barrels on a sledge from the docks through the town. This was replaced in the 20th century by a revival of the Norse tradition of Burning the Galley, on the last Tuesday in the month. There may have been two boat-burning traditions in Shetland, one when the bodies of kings and chiefs were sent to Valhalla, and the other when Vikings burnt their longships after settling, as a means of expressing their determination not to return to Norway.

🎧 Up-Helly-A', Lerwick Mainland Shetland

Shetland was Danish until 1469, and the Scandinavian influence in this fire ceremony is plain for all to see. The name of this spectacular ceremony means the End of the Holy Days, that is, the end of Yule, traditionally on the 24th day of Yule on the Old Calendar, that is, the 30th January. The dragging of blazing tar barrels on sledges was banned in 1874 on account of the rowdy behaviour of the horn-blowing guisers accompanying it, and was replaced by a torchlit procession and the burning of a 31-foot Viking longship, complete with 11 heraldic shields and oars on each side.

Other longship burnings in the period from January to March are at Girlsta; Northmavine; Cullivoe on Yell; and Brae.

LERWICK IS THE PRINCIPAL TOWN OF SHETLAND.

31st January St Bride's (Bridget's, Brigid's) Eve

CELTIC It was an ancient belief that the Celtic Goddess Bride visited the poor and hungry tonight and blessed and provided for those who made her welcome. Preparations for her visit were accompanied by much ritual, both within the house and about the village. The Church transferred this belief to St Brigid of Kildare, an Irish abbess.

IRELAND A typical supper would have been sowans, **Colcannon** *(see p.194 for recipe)* or **Champ** *(see p.195 for recipe),* **Dumplings** *(see p.195 for recipe),* apple cake and fruit cakes. **Boxty Bread and Pancakes** *(see p.195 for recipes)* were also popular. Pancakes were eaten from plates on rush crosses.

It was believed that St Brigid visited households to bless them, and in order to make her welcome a rush mat was left outside for her to kneel on, and bread for her and a sheaf of corn for her white cow left on the step. A bed made from rushes or birch twigs was put in front of the fire. Further protection was obtained by making, out of straw or rushes, St Brigid's Crosses. After sprink-ling them with holy water they were hung up over the door in house and byre to keep fire and evil away. There were regional designs, but most featured lozenge or diamond shapes, originally symbols of the sun or eyes. The rushes were pulled, not cut, and were overlapped sunwise (left to right). Another shape made was the swastika, a three-legged one being put up in the byre.

Groups of young people went from door to door offering blessings in return for food or money. They displayed a straw effigy of St Brigid or a decorated doll dressed in white. An image of the saint was called a Brídeóg or Biddy. Biddy Boys would go in fancy dress or in girls' clothes, wearing straw masks. Many counties held St Brigid Processions, with a girl dressed in white carrying a St Brigid's Cross.

Another custom was to place on an outside windowsill a silk ribbon, called St Brigid's Ribbon (Ribín Bríghid, Brat Bríde, Bratóg Bríde, St Brigid's Mantle), or other item that goes round the body such as a scarf, sash or belt.

In western parts of Co. Galway visitors to a house brought a St Brigid's Girdle (Crios Bríde), which was a large looped plaited straw rope, with plaited straw crosses attached. Householders would cross themselves, say an invocation to St Brigid, and go through the girdle three times. Still larger ones were made for passing cattle through. This custom is still observed in Co. Galway west of Loch Corrib and in the Aran Islands.

ISLE OF MAN This evening is called Laa'l Breeshey. Householders stood outside their doors with armfuls of rushes and chanted an invitation to Bride to come in and bless the household, to bring luck and fertility. The rushes were strewn on the floor to make a bed for her, and a candle would be kept lit by food and drink left for her.

SCOTLAND A corn figure representing Bride was formerly made tonight. It was decorated with flowers, greenery and shells, with a bright shell ('the guiding star') placed over her heart. Maidens dressed in white carried the effigy in procession, receiving gifts or food from householders. There was a feast in the evening. A similar effigy was also put by women into a decorated woven corn cradle, which is put alongside a peeled wand of birch, broom or willow outside the door. The women called out to Bride and bade her enter. Ashes spread on the step would be checked next morning for footprints or wand marks, which would signify Bride's blessing on the house and farm.

February customs

By the end of February people hoped that winter's worst was over. Spring preparations could now be made, lend rented, workers and equipment hired, unwanted animals sold at new stock purchased; many of the transactions were done at stock and hiring fairs. Salmon and eel fishermen prepared for their catching season, but took the precaution of having their nets blessed first. Indeed all ensured that whatever their livelihoods depended upon was blessed. Keen eyes continued to look for omens in the natural world.

Variable Dates

Septuagesima Sunday **Lost Sunday, Third Sunday before the beginning of Lent**
This can also fall in January, depending on the date of Easter.

Sexagesima Sunday **Second Sunday before the beginning of Lent**
This can also fall in January, depending on the date of Easter.

Early February
SCOTLAND

Up Helly A', Nesting Shetland
NESTING IS A BAY ON THE B9075, NORTH OF LERWICK.

Up Helly A', Girlsta Mainland Shetland
GIRLSTA IS NORTH OF LERWICK ON THE A970.

CORNWALL

Hurling the Silver Ball, St Columb Major & St Columb Minor Cornwall
See Shrove Tuesday for details.
TAKE THE A3059 EAST FROM NEWQUAY; ST COLUMB MINOR IS REACHED FIRST, THEN ST COLUMB MAJOR.

1st February St Bride's Day

CELTIC This was the Celtic quarter day of Imbolc, and the Festival of Lambing, which may explain the abundance of weatherlore for this day. The Celts used to sacrifice a cockerel to the sun, choosing places of known malevolence such as crossroads or confluences of rivers. To the Celts the cock's crow served the purpose of warning the sun of rising malevolence. The day marked the end of winter, and the sacrifice ensured a productive spring. As on other quarter days people seeking to retain their youthful looks bathed their faces in the morning dew.

The veneration of Bride, (or Brigid, Bridget), a 6th-century (AD 452–525) Irish cowherd from Kildare who became an Abbess, was a deliberate Christian substitute for the cult of the Celtic goddess Bride, daughter of Dagda, whose cauldrons were never empty. St Bride's life was embroidered by the Church in medieval Ireland to give her the revered attributes of the goddess. In this way St Bride became a model of generosity and provider of food to the hungry. She became goddess of the hearth, smithying, poetry, healing and marriage. Wells dedicated to her had water with fecund properties, and she would be invoked to induce pregnancy and ease labour pains. As if this amount of virtue in one person was not enough, the Church even made St Bride the midwife of Mary.

As the first day of spring, many Celts prepared for sowing and other food production activities, although some did this on the 2nd, such as in parishes dedicated to St Bride where no work was done today, only invocations to her. Omens giving clues about the forthcoming spring were looked for in the weather, tides, and movements and behaviour of wildlife.

IRELAND The turning of wheels was avoided on this day, so spinners, seamstresses, millers, carters, and similar tradespeople would stop work. Even cycling was frowned upon. There would be no work done in parishes dedicated to this saint, such as in Dabhach Bhríde, in Liscannor, Co. Clare, and in St Brigid's Stream, Faughart, Co. Louth.

The water from wells dedicated to St Brigid was sprinkled in house, stable and field, while invoking the saint's blessing.

SCOTLAND On Barra and other islands of the Outer Hebrides people made Bride's Beds out of straw or rushes and implored Bride to come to the house and sleep there a night, to bring luck and fertility to the household. Local fishermen cast lots for fishing banks today.

St Bride of the Isles was a mythical figure among communities in the Highlands and Islands.

In the Highlands, this afternoon was a traditional time for cock-fighting, whereas in the Lowlands this activity was done on Fastern's E'en.

2nd February Candlemas Day, The Presentation of Christ, Feast of the Purification

CELTIC At the Roman festival of *Februa* (mother of Mars), candles were carried through the streets and women observed purification rites. This may be the origin of the candlelit processions on this day of mothers who had borne children the previous year, which the Church embraced in celebration of the purification of Mary. Candles were blessed and distributed to the congregation. The Catholic Church chose this day for Candlemas in the 5th century to try to replace the ancient Celtic feast of Imbolc, which heralded the start of the lambing season, and was dedicated to the Celtic Goddess of Youth and Fertility, Bride.

IRELAND This festival lapsed during the time of the Penal Laws, but was revived afterwards.

People donated candles to their local church, or took their own to be blessed and then kept them alight in their homes.

ISLE OF MAN The Church tried to transfer festivities from the 1st to the 2nd to eliminate the memory of Bride. Hence many customs are the same on the two days.

By Candlemas, which was regarded as the middle of winter, half the stores of fodder and fuel laid down should remain.

SCOTLAND Today marked the end of the 40 days of Yule. It was a quarter day, and divination was done in Shetland.

The first Monday of Candlemas Term in Scottish Universities was a holiday called Mealie Monday, as it used to be the day when poor students returned home to replenish their meal-sacks with oatmeal.

This was a traditional day for the Jethart Ba' at Jedburgh, Roxburghshire.

WALES A blessed candle was placed in a window as a sign that this was the last day when it would be needed to work by. Divination customs were practised.

The 'Churching of Women' or 'Thanksgiving after Childbirth' was quite common in Wales. In times past the Church in Wales used the Mari Lwyd custom to commemorate the Purification of the Virgin.

A Candlemas Fair was held at Rador Forest, Powys.

CORNWALL A Candlemas Fair was once held at Looe.

BRITTANY Blessed candles were kept in the house, and lit for protection whenever there was a thunderstorm or illness.

3rd February St Blaise's Day, St Ia's (Ives's) Day

CELTIC St Ia was an Irish virgin who fled to Cornwall.

CORNWALL Candles are still lit to honour St Blaise, the patron saint of sufferers from a sore throat and of woolcombers, in the church at St Blazey.

First Sunday in February

CORNWALL St Blazey in East Cornwall was named after St Blaize, said to have landed at Par nearby. He was invoked by sufferers of toothache. Applying a candle from a church dedicated to him was said to cure it, as it did sore throats and cattle diseases.

Day before Feasten Day
CORNWALL

✪ St Ives Procession, St Ives   Cornwall
The Mayor of St Ives leads a procession through the town as a prelude to the Feasten Day celebrations.
TAKE THE A30 EAST FROM PENZANCE, THEN LEFT ON THE A3074.

First Monday after 3rd February Feast Monday, Feasten Day
At wakes and other celebratory occasions in Cornwall **Feasten Cakes** *(see p.195 for recipe)* were eaten.

⊕ Hurling the Silver Ball, St Ives and Lelant   Cornwall
The day's events celebrate the dedication of the local church to St Ives (Ia). This is a local type of handball game, less violent than that at the St Columbs, and traditionally between Toms, Wills and Johns against the rest. A silver-coated cork or wooden ball is annointed at 9.30 am at the Venton Ia Well and then thrown ('dealt') by the Mayor at 10.30 am from the churchyard wall to a gathering of children, who proceed to pass it among themselves in a scrum. The game moves along street and beach between the two goals, which are two basketball nets. If there is no score, the child holding the ball at noon is awarded a crown piece (25p).

Formerly there was a hurling match with the neighbouring village of Lelant.

At 11.30 am the Mayor throws pennies for other children to scramble for. At 7.30 pm the final event is started by the Mayor, a game of rugby.
FROM THE A30 SOUTH OF HAYLE TAKE THE A3074 NORTH THROUGH LELANT FIRST AND THEN TO ST IVES.

9th February St Teilo's Day
CELTIC St Teilo is connected with churches at Penally, Dyfed, where he was born, Llandaff Cathedral, Cardiff, where he was bishop, and Llandeilo Fawr, Dyfed, where he died.

12th February Old St Bride's Day
ISLE OF MAN Kirk Bride Fair was held, formerly on 1st February.

13th February Old Candlemas, St Valentine's Eve
CELTIC Not only on St Valentine's Day itself, but also on St Valentine's Eve, unmarried young men would put the names of female acquaintances into a vessel and draw them in lots to determine

whom they might marry or seek a relationship with. Later, eligible girls adopted the same practice. Boys would sometimes wear Valentine slips on their sleeves and court and treat the girls whose names were written on them. This custom has been superseded by the sending of Valentine cards.

SCOTLAND This was calving time, when milk supplies traditionally first became available after Winter.

School rooms were lit by candles bought from gifts of money from pupils to their master. Later this became just a donation. The pupil(s) who gave the most were afforded special privileges for six weeks and made Candlemas King and/or Queen. The other pupils paraded them on crossed hands (the King's/Queen's Chair), and were given the afternoon off for ball games. At Kelso a pole with a gold ball atop was carried at the head of the procession. The Jethart Callants' (lads') Ba' was played at Jedburgh today, the Men's Ba', and the older custom, on Fastern's E'en.

Gyro Night was held in Papa Westray, Orkney, on the Tuesday after the first full moon in Spring (Old Candlemas Day). A Gyro was a female monster with a reputation rather like that of a bogey man, and its effigy was at one time burned on bonfires. Two boys dressed in old women's clothes, under which was hidden a rope, and they would knock on doors and assail the person who answered. Bonfires were also lit and straw-rope torches lit.

✠ **Blessing of the opening of the salmon net-fishing season, Pedwell Beach, near Norham on the River Tweed, then at Berwick-on-Tweed**   Northumberland

Fishermen from both the English and Scottish sides of the river assemble just before midnight with their nets for the blessing and offerings of prayers for safe-keeping.

NORHAM IS BETWEEN COLDSTREAM AND BERWICK-ON-TWEED. FROM THE A698 TAKE THE B6470 NORTH, TAKING A RIGHT TURN TO THE RIVER AT NORHAM.

14th February St Valentine's Day, Feast of St Cyril and St Methodius

CELTIC St Valentine, who was renowned for his chastity, has, curiously, become the patron saint of lovers, and in Celtic areas the now universal custom of sending anonymous cards and gifts to those admired is followed.

SCOTLAND The St Valentine's Day ballot was popular in Scotland, as was the sending of a home-made card and a gift to the girl whose name was drawn. There was a belief that the first person of the opposite sex, outside the family, met today would be your spouse. In the border region ballot slips were drawn three times, and if the same name was chosen then this person would be your future spouse.

17th February St Finan's Day

CELTIC St Finan was a 7th-century Bishop of Lindisfarne who wanted to preserve the distinctiveness of the early Celtic Christian Church, and challenged Catholic attempts to dominate it.

Third Thursday in February

SCOTLAND This was a day when the Old Deer Fair was held in Grampian. There is still one in July.

Right and Left: Hurling the Silver Ball, St. Ives, Cornwall

Shrovetide customs

Although Shrovetide fell when daylight hours were few and the weather often poor, nothing could dampen the carnival, pranks and feasting that characterised the four days before Lent, a feature of this time of year since the Roman feast in honour of Bacchus, God of Wine.

CELTIC When Lenten fasting was introduced by the Christian Church, starting on Ash Wednesday, Shrovetide became not only the period when Christians sought forgiveness for their sins but also the last chance for a while of enjoyment and a hearty meal. 'Shriving' is the cleansing of all sins, and a bell was sounded to summon villagers to church on Shrove Tuesday, the day before Lent. As butter, cream, eggs and fat had to be used up, pancakes were a popular Shrove Tuesday lunch, and the shriving bell became known as the Pancake Bell. Meat was either eaten up too or preserved by salting. The word Carnival, associated with Shrovetide merry-making, actually means 'goodbye to meat'! A feature of church, civic and Guild Carnival parades was a number of giant figures. Another sign of the sweeping away of the immediate past was the ritual smashing of crockery.

IRELAND In rural Ireland Shrovetide was a popular time to marry, before the Church's Lenten ban on marriages. Matchmaking started at Little Christmas (Epiphany).

SCOTLAND Many records exist of Shrovetide football from Scotland. Whole communities would take part, using natural or village features as goals and streams as obstacles. The goals might be up to 3 miles apart. Brute force was as important as skill in forcing the ball through the goal. There are records of games between bachelors and married men (such as at Scone, Tayside), and a few of games between spinsters and married women (such as at Musselburgh).

WALES Shrovetide football was played in Wales.

CORNWALL Hurling the silver ball is a street ball game formerly played all over west Cornwall at Shrovetide. The small, silvered ball was passed or scrummed, not kicked, and the game was so vigorous that it drew fierce opposition from Methodists and Victorian prudes.

Hurling *This furious Celtic game has superficial similarity to hockey, but players can catch the ball in the air and carry it for three paces, kick it, and hit it with hands or hurley – which is like a broad-ended hockey stick. The goal is like rugby goalposts. If the ball goes under the crossbar and between the uprights three points are scored. If the ball goes over the crossbar and between the uprights one point is scored.*

BRITTANY The days of Shrovetide were the Fat Days, and cakes were usually made.

Thursday before Lent

BRITTANY Schoolchildren held cock-fights today at school at Nantes, St Malo and other places. See Shrove Tuesday for details.

Shrove Saturday

BRITTANY Shrovetide food was prepared. Rice was cooked for a pudding and sausages were put to soak in water.

Quinquagesima Sunday Shrove Sunday, Sunday before the beginning of Lent

CORNWALL This is the Feast of St Ives.

BRITTANY This was called Fat Sunday, and farmers used to walk round their fields to see if any shoots were showing. Another name for today was Pancake Sunday, as it was the custom to make crêpes, and to take some to the landlord and his family.

Shrove Monday Collop Monday, Peasen Monday

CELTIC On this day remaining fresh meat was cut up into slices called collops. Some of the collops were eaten the rest were salted or hung up until Lent was over.

The Monday of Shrovetide was often used for mischief, and this extended to the 'Barring-out the Master' when children shut out their teachers from school and refused to admit them unless they were given an extra day's holiday.

SCOTLAND Scotch Collops *(see p.195 for recipe)* were eaten.

CORNWALL Only **Pea Soup** *(see p.196 for recipe)* was eaten instead of collops or any other meat, and this day is called Peasen (or Paisen) Monday.

In East Cornwall it was also called Hall Monday. Throughout Cornwall the evening is a night of mischief called Nicky Nan Night, including knocking on doors, unhinging gates, putting rubbish into gardens or even unguarded houses, and spraying water or soot at passers-by. Stolen property was piled up in a public place. On the other hand if a door-knocker was given a pancake the house would be spared any trouble, at least by that youngster!

During the day hurling matches were played. The silver-coated ball was of cork or light wood. It was hurled into the air at halfway to start the game. At St Ives the teams were Toms, Wills and Johns against the rest; At St Columb the teams were townsmen against countrymen; and at Truro married men against unmarried men. The hurlers' motto is 'Fair play is good play.'

BRITTANY Today was a mischief night in Brittany, called 'Ninc-kyn-nan-neuf' (nicky-nan night).

Shrove Tuesday Pancake Tuesday, Last day before Lent, Bannock Night, Brose Tuesday

CELTIC When the Pancake Bell rang, parishioners went to church to be shriven, and after this divestiture pancakes were served at home, leaving the rest of the day for enjoyment before the days of abstinence ahead. The bell was also a signal to shopkeepers to close their premises, and for school pupils to lock out (bar-out) their teachers until granted an extra day's holiday. Those who did not release their energy by hunting or playing sports did so by Lent Crocking or committing other acts of mischief. Children and apprentices who were given a holiday used to roam the streets (going a-shroving) singing Shrovetide songs and asking for pancakes or other little treats. Some fairs were held.

Shrove Tuesday was popular for playing sports, many of which were vigorous, even violent. People who led hard lives, and who had just come through a harsh winter, tended to unwind in ways that today we would find insupportable. Hunting, dog- and bear-baiting, dog-tossing, cock-fighting, and throwing at cocks with sticks, were all practised. The latter practice allegedly arose as a punishment for all cocks because of the part played by one in Peter's denial of Christ. Another tradition says that it started among the Saxons at the time of the Danish invasions. A plan to attack the Danes on a Shrove Tuesday morning was thwarted when a cock-crow alerted them. The white ball in bowls came to be called the cock. No less vigorous than the above was Shrovetide Football (not to be confused with soccer), a traditional Shrovetide game (originally called camping), dating from the 12th century, for which each village had a local variant.

As with many days that were on the eve of an important change, whether it be to lifestyle or of the calendar, Shrove Tuesday was popular for divination and saining.

IRELAND There were no carnivals as in Catholic European countries, Shrove Tuesday being largely a family festival. The fire for making pancakes, to use up eggs, milk and butter, was traditionally fuelled from saved Christmas holly. Different varieties of pancakes were made, including **Irish Pancakes** *(see p.196 for recipe)* and **Boxty Pancakes or Stamp** *(see p.196 for recipe)*.

Meat was the main course, a small piece of which was hung up in the kitchen until Easter Sunday to ensure no shortage in the future.

This was a mischief night in some parts, popular victims being unmarried men, and those who had married again. There was strong public disapproval of bachelorhood and spinsterhood, and of disrupting the normal rules of succession and inheritance when there were children from the first marriage. Typical pranks were blowing horns outside the house, throwing cabbage heads at the door, tying up doors and equipment, blocking chimneys, and sending on fools' errands.

In Skibbereen, Co. Cork, firecrackers were made and let off. Hare-hunting was done, and a portion of its meat hung in the rafters.

There were many marriages today, and much marriage divination.

It was held on the mainland that Easter came a week later on Sceilg Mhichíl, an island off the Kerry coast, and anyone still single by today was urged to 'Go to the Skelligs' by walking to the island at low tide this evening. As a penance, a load of bog-oak or bog-deal was carried back, further evidence of the general disapproval of people remaining single. The names of the unmarried would even be published in taunting doggerel, or on posters advertising 'Grand Excursions to the Skelligs'. In many villages there was public chiding of the unmarried by blowing horns outside their doors, tying animals to their doors, and even rolling cartwheels downhill at their houses.

ISLE OF MAN Crowdy *(see p.196 for recipe)* was eaten for dinner, instead of at breakfast, and meat for supper followed by a large pudding, and pancakes containing divination tokens.

School children barred-out their teachers today, crying 'Bear, bear (bar), give us holly (holiday)!'

Periwinkle Fair was held today until 1834, at Pool Vash, near Balladoole estate, an area with a long tradition of catching and eating shellfish, but it does, of course, fit in with Lenten practice.

SCOTLAND This is Fastern's E'en, Bannock Night or Brose Tuesday. A bannock is an oatmeal cake, and Brose is thick savoury broth. Brose is milk-gruel, and in Orkney it is called Milk-Gruel Night. Scots used to eat meat today lest their livestock took sick. Also, they ate **Fastyn Cock** *(see p.196 for recipe)*, also known as fitless cock, which was a boiled suet and oat dumpling shaped like a chicken.

After the main meal **Sauty Bannocks** *(see p.196 for recipe)* were eaten. The same recipe was used to make 'dreaming bannocks' (bannock brauder) for divination, with the addition of a little soot.

A similar dish in the south of Scotland was called Dry Goose. Other foods included nettle broth, black March cockerel, beef brose, **Cock-a-leekie Soup** *(see p.196 for recipe)* and cream crowdie (see Harvest Customs for recipe). The eating of pancakes was adopted in Scotland. **Pancakes with Beef** *(see p.196 for recipe)* were served.

As a final fling before Lent Ba' games were popular, the whole village (or married men/women against single men/women) taking part, with goals at either end. The ball might be plain, silvered, gilded or beribboned, and struck with hands or clubs. The tradition survived longest in Border, notably Jedburgh, and this was the traditional date of the Men's Ba', reckoned as the Tuesday after the new moon after Candlemas. Originally this was a Shrovetide Football game, but the kicking of footballs was banned in 1704, so a handball or 'hurling' game was substituted. An attempt to ban this in 1848 was overruled by a traditionalist High Court Judge.

Horse-racing was held at Kilmarnock until 1842.

WALES There was a carnival atmosphere in old Wales today, with feasting, merry-making and sport. **Welsh Pancakes** *(see p.196 for recipe)* and **Welsh Oatmeal Pancakes** *(see p.197 for recipe)* were popular, as was their tossing, and this is the only widespread Shrovetide custom surviving. Poor children used to go from house to house begging for pancakes or the ingredients to make them. A pancake bell would be tolled at 11 am for shriving.

Shrovetide (or Mass) Football was played in South Wales, using the whole town as a pitch with goals at each end. Windows would be boarded up as all the local men and boys took part, and sometimes the women too.

Mass Football *Although the rules (or, to an onlooker, the lack of them) differed from place to place, mass football was played in many parts of England, Wales and Scotland until it became formalised as football or rugby in the mid-19th century. Teams were made up of the whole adult and teenage populations of two villages, or of two halves of a town, or of different sections of a community such as married men against bachelors. Sometimes both men and women took part, and a few games recorded have been women-only, such as spinsters against married women.*

Generally the goals are at opposite ends of the parish or town, or are familiar landmarks. Householders boarded up their windows and doors. The ball, a leather-covered bladder, is thrown up at the mid-point of the pitch, and could be kicked, thrown, carried or passed, the passing often being done in a scrum to keep possession. Injuries were many and goals rare, a match often having a time limit, when the side in possession won, or being declared won on the first goal scored.

As if cock-fighting and shying at cocks were not enough, hens that did not lay before noon were thrashed.

Two Kidwelly customs are of interest. Crochon Crewys (Lenten Crock) was an egg-shell or scooped-out turnip with scraps of food in, and it was secretly placed by youths on the window sills of houses. If the householder could rush out and grab them before they ran away they had to shine all the boots in the house. Traditionally they were given pancakes as a reward. This custom may have arisen as a rebuke to families who were known not to fast in Lent, as a rhyme chanted by the youths hints at this. A similar objective, this time a reminder of the observance, was served by the second custom, that of kicking pans and utensils down the streets.

CORNWALL Dinner today was fried eggs and bacon, or salt pork, followed by pancake with currants. In the afternoon, in Penzance, poor people gathered limpets and periwinkles ('going a-trigging') and made **Periwinkle or Limpet Soup** *(see p.197 for recipe)* for supper. Shellfish was called trig-meat.

Also in Penzance, women and boys would stand on street corners, with greased, sooty hands, and rub them on people's faces while pretending to be affectionate. In the afternoon, when the butchers' market was hosed down by firemen, passers-by got drenched. This was an expression of a general custom of throwing water, handfuls of shells, bottles of filth, etc., over people or through doorways. Also, the Nicky-nan boys were out again, and mischief was done such as taking signs down, wrenching off knockers, and removing gates. They would try to enter houses undetected, with blackened faces, and throw broken crocks on the floor. If discovered they would demand money or pancakes to desist. At Mousehole boats were hauled off the shore and put in millponds. In St Ives and Scilly children would knock on doors with stones on strings, and beg for pancakes, whereas in Landewednack they begged for 'Col-perra' – food and money. In Polperro the threat was of throwing a huge stone to break down the door if a pancake was not given.

On the mainland and in the Scilly Isles Lensharding was done by throwing old crockery at people's doors. Sometimes wood or stones were thrown at the doors instead, with demands for money or pancakes. Other mischief also occurred. Shroving songs were sung, asking for money or food, with the threat of damage if nothing was given.

Egg Shackling, St Columb Major Cornwall

The object of most egg shackling games is to try to crack an egg, held by someone else, with one's own egg, without one's own egg also cracking. This game can only be described as conkers with eggs, but at least over a bowl. Two children face each other, eggs in hands, and strike them lengthwise. Those with unbroken eggs play others until only one player is left with an unbroken egg. Traditionally, pancakes were made from the remains, after the shell had been picked out! Another version of this game was called shackle-eggs.

Shackle-eggs *Each child wrote their name on an egg, and the eggs were put into a sieve. The sieve was gently shaken until one egg cracked. This was removed and the shaking continued, until only one whole egg remained. The winner was given a special cap.*

TAKE THE A3059 EAST FROM NEWQUAY TO ST COLUMB MAJOR.

Hurling the Silver Ball, St Columb Major and St Columb Minor Cornwall

The match at St Columb Major lasts from 4.15 pm until 8 pm, with a rematch 11 days later. The contest is at least 400 years old. The shallow trough goals are 2 miles apart, and the large number of participants charge through the boarded-up streets trying to score with the silver-coated apple-wood ball. The ball is 'dealt' (thrown up) from a ladder in the Market Square. Previously an all male match, it is now for anyone on the sides of Town and Country, although both men's and women's matches have been held. In former times the ball was gilded.

Generally in Cornwall hurling matches were decided either on goals or when the ball was carried over the parish boundary, or in more recent times by either. Wesleyan Methodists opposed this boisterous game and caused its decline.

TAKE THE A3059 EAST FROM NEWQUAY; ST COLUMB MINOR IS REACHED FIRST, THEN ST COLUMB MAJOR.

BRITTANY There was a number of songs associated with the making and eating of pancakes, sung by children.

A number of activities were enjoyed today, one such being a game called Écaisser La Grenouille (Dismember the Frog).

Écaisser La Grenouille *The frog is a piece of round polished wood. Two youths stand opposite one another, strike each other's hands three times, then grasp the frog. Their teams then grasp them from behind until they form a sort of rugby scrum, but which is less wide and more like a caterpillar. The two teams, often from neighbouring parishes, try to pull and twist to force the lead youth from the opposing team to release the frog.*

Marbles was popular, and tops were made from spools or were hand-carved. They had to be perfectly pear-shaped and smooth to look static when spun. A nail was driven into the stalk end, and strong, supple string used to spin them. Galoche was Breton quoits.

Galoche *The galoche was a peg of carved wood, stuck into flat ground. Three quoits of iron, 8–10 cm in diameter were used. The players stood 10 metres from the galoche and tossed the quoits to try and knock the galoche over.*

Ninepins was also a favourite, the pins, of three sizes, being carved from wood and hewn to a point at the top.

Ninepins *The pins were arranged on level ground in a 3x3 square. The largest pin (Old Nine) was put in the centre and was worth nine points. The four middle-sized pins, worth five points, were put in the corners, and the four smallest pins, worth one point each, were put between the middle-sized pins. Either wooden balls or round stones were thrown by players in turn to knock the pins over;, highest score wins.*

Schoolchildren held cock-fights in their school playgrounds, parents forming the arena, and the victor was paraded round the town in a wheelbarrow as a makeshift throne, and then they all feasted on the food, such as pork, poultry, bacon, eggs, cider and coffee, they had collectively provided. The girls had a different contest, Egg Breaking.

Egg Breaking *All brought eggs to school and they were pooled and divided up equally between them. Each girl held an egg and tried to break their opponent's egg without breaking their own. The girl who had the champion egg, which might do for as many as a dozen others, was proclaimed Queen.*

Both these activities were recorded from Saint-Lunaire and elsewhere. Another sport was La Courrerie de Coqs (Running the Cocks) or Faucherie de Coqs (Reaping the Cocks).

La Courrerie de Coqs *A stake is driven into the ground (the 'cock') and players arm themselves with a scythe. They are blindfolded and taken some distance away. They reap with the scythe, moving to where they think the stake is, and the one who strikes the stake gets a prize of a cock or rabbit.*

Another activity recorded at St Malo was Tire-Jars (Pulling the Gander's Head Off).

Tire-Jars *A gander is suspended by the feet from a tree, and an avenue of spectators made leading up to the tree. Participants draw lots then in turn ride up to and past the tree, attempting to pull off the gander's head without leaving the saddle. The victor is proclaimed King, and chooses a Queen from among the female onlookers. Each horseman also then takes up a woman behind in the saddle and they ride in cavalcade to a feast.*

The game of soule disappeared in the mid-19th century because it was stopped on account of brawling, but had been played since the 13th century. The ball was thrown and kicked, and its last stronghold was in and around Saint-Glen in the district of Moncontour. A custom last recorded in 1680 at Saint-Perrieux was that the last bridegroom of the year, or if none, of the preceding year, had to supply a soule (or boule) of wood for a Christmas contest.

The children would be taken out to see the Carnival procession. In some areas Carnival, or Mardi-Gras, is a big, riderless horse carrying pancakes on its back for distribution. The children go to great lengths to convince it that they have been well behaved and deserve a pancake. Elsewhere another tradition exists, for the children wait at crossroads, where crosses are found, and strike the horse with cudgels as it passes. A further custom is to put a bone, with some meat still on it, on the ground for the children to dance over, after which they throw it in a corner and say they have buried it. This harks back to the meaning of the word Carnival, 'goodbye to meat'. Sometimes the burial of Mardi-Gras is more realistic, in that a straw figure of an old man, or a boy dressed as a strawman, is accompanied in procession by mourners, laid down in a mock grave, and then wept and grieved over with much pretend emotion. The boy who plays Mardi-Gras keeps this name as a nickname all year.

Traditionally this evening all the cats in a village would congregate and serenade the residents.

Second Saturday after Shrove Tuesday
CORNWALL

🌑 **Hurling the Silver Ball** St Columb Major

TAKE THE A3059 EAST FROM NEWQUAY TO ST COLUMB MAJOR.

Hurling the Silver Ball at St. Columb Major, Cornwall

Lenten customs

Lenten customs were formerly principally of religious origin or of a nature that reflected the togetherness of a family as its members adapted to fasting and other forms of abstinence and the change of routine that necessarily accompanied them. The unmarried and others who failed to observe the expected formalities were frowned upon, and even ostracised, before relaxation of the rules at the end of Lent returned ordinary folk to the normal austerities of late winter, which in themselves were quite enough to bear.

CELTIC Long before the Church's inauguration of fasting for 40 weekdays (the six Sundays in Lent are not fast days) people were forced to eat sparingly because either stores would by now be running low. Strict fasting permitted one meal per day, not containing meat, eggs, dairy produce or wine, but fish and shellfish were allowed. As sex was forbidden Lenten marriages were rare and more or less ceased by common consent.

IRELAND Lent was faithfully observed in the past, and eggs, milk and milk products were not even eaten on a Sunday. Most fat used in cooking was animal fat, so the ban on animal products was highly restricting. A typical breakfast would have been porridge, black tea and bread, the latter being leavened with yeast rather than the usual soda and sour milk. Oatcakes would be made unleavened. At midday the meal would be potatoes, with fish (particularly herring), shellfish, seaweed (the edible kind is called dulse) or onions, and again black tea, which was often drunk on its own in the evening. A sour drink was made by fermenting crushed oats in water.

There would have been no visiting or merry-making, and many even stopped smoking and drinking alcohol. By the mid-19th century, however, the strict fast (black fast) was only a feature of Ash Wednesday and Good Friday.

ISLE OF MAN Normal fasting rules were observed.

SCOTLAND Lent fasting ceased in Calvinist Lowland Scotland after the Reformation, condemned as popish superstition.

A typical dish eaten in Lent was **Lenten Kail** *(see p.197 for recipe)*, a spring greens soup.

WALES Fasting and other abstinence lapsed in Protestant/non-conformist Wales after the Reformation, as did most aspects of Catholic self-denial. A few customs survived for a time, such as the wearing of black, and, until quite recently, waiting until after Lent before marrying.

CORNWALL In East Cornwall, at the beginning of Lent, a straw figure dressed in cast-off clothes, called Jack-o'-Lent, was dragged through the streets, burnt, hanged, shot at and otherwise abused. He represented Judas Iscariot.

BRITTANY In Catholic Brittany Lent was solemnly adhered to. As on Fridays through the year fish was eaten. Fasts and vigils were twice a week. No marriages happened in Lent, or, if possible, before Palm Sunday. Weddings normally took place on a Tuesday, with the celebration going from tavern to tavern until the end of Thursday.

Variable Dates

Ash Wednesday First day of Lent

CELTIC Traditionally this is one of the two days when Christians endured fast and abstinence, the penitent wearing sackcloth and sprinkling ashes on their heads during the penitential service. The connection between penitence and ashes is an ancient one, the ashes being a symbol of sorrow, repentance and mourning. Those not sprinkling ashes on themselves or marking an ash cross on their foreheads were regarded as unrepentant, and cursed aloud. As the ash tree has black buds children carried twigs in bud to symbolise mourning. On this day alms were given, and it was customary to eat fish. White clothing was never worn.

IRELAND Many ate only one meal today and drank only water. Palm saved from Palm Sunday last year would be burned and the ashes taken to church to be blessed. These would be used to mark the foreheads of all in the family.

Today, all utensils and implements used for meat were cleaned and put away.

Unmarried men and women were again taunted today, and ashes sprinkled on them or bags of ashes furtively pinned to their clothes. Even greater humiliation was exacted on them by tying them to logs and dragging them through the streets. In Ardmore, Co. Waterford, the latter 'punishment' followed unmarried women being made to dance round a stone to which tow was attached, and then to spin it while they danced.

Jedburgh Hand Ba' Game, Jedburgh, Scotland

ISLE OF MAN Baldwin Fair was held today at Keeill Abban, now St Luke's Chapel, until 1834. Kirk Marown Fair was held near the ruins of Keeill Pharick (St Patrick's Chapel) on the quarterland of Ballafreer. Also held today was Kirk Conchan (or Onchan) Fair, until 1834.

CORNWALL Jack-a-Lent figures were made and treated as scapegoats, the purpose of which was to take on everyone else's bad luck. They may have been based on effigies of an old winter god, or perhaps they might have been effigies of Judas Iscariot. Jack-a-Lent was dragged through the streets and ceremonially hanged.

BRITTANY Typical fare today and in Lent was thick pancakes, potato soup, fish and bread, with left-over cake to follow.

Thursday after Ash Wednesday

IRELAND In Dunmore, salt was sprinkled upon unmarried men and women to 'preserve' them until next Shrove Tuesday.

SCOTLAND

Jedburgh Hand Ba' Game, Jedburgh

Border

This game has been played for centuries, except when it was banned because it became so violent. One such occasion happened in 1704 following a number of fatalities. Another attempt to stop it occurred in 1848, but a High Court ruling in Edinburgh overturned the attempt. In the 18th century it was changed from a game of football to one of handball. The alternative name is Fastern's E'en Ba' Game (Shrove Tuesday Ba' Game), but here they believe Shrove Tuesday to be the first Tuesday after the first new moon after Candlemas, which is usually, but not always, the date as on the ecclesiastical calendar.

The Boys' Game starts at noon, followed by the main game at 2 pm between Uppies and Downies, representing the two parts of the town. The wooden ball is decorated with coloured streamers, and can be thrown, carried or passed, play even continuing into the icy River Jed. At the start the ball is thrown up at the Mercat Cross by the sports champion of the grammar school, elected Candlemas King.

TAKE THE A698 NORTH-EAST FROM HAWICK, THEN RIGHT ON THE A68.

First Sunday in Lent

IRELAND This was known as Chalk Sunday, which derives its name from the custom of marking the clothes with chalk of anyone eligible but still unmarried by this day. There was strong social pressure for everyone to marry, and this practice was continued into the 1930s in Munster and South West Leinster, usually on the way to or from church. Nowadays it is done in fun.

Another name for this day was Scowl Sunday (or Puss Sunday), after the popular view that those still unmarried walked around with scowls of disappointment and self-pity on their faces.

BRITTANY All memories of the Sunday of the Torches ceremony once held today appear to have disappeared in Brittany.

This was another day when farmers would inspect their fields for signs of germination.

First Monday in Lent

IRELAND In Ballinrobe they had the same custom today as in Dunmore on the day after Ash Wednesday.

Second Saturday after Shrove Tuesday

Cornish Hurling Match, St Columb Major   Cornwall

This is a rematch of the Shrove Tuesday match, starting at 4.30 pm.

Mothering Sunday Mid-Lent Sunday, Fourth Sunday in Lent, Laetare Sunday

CELTIC The Church custom of making donations to one's Mother Church on this day of relaxation from abstinence expanded to include honouring one's own mother, and young people such as servants and apprentices were given the day off to visit their mother and take gifts of food and spring flowers. The flowers were blessed in church first, and it was customary for the children to take on all their mother's chores for the day. The custom had lapsed by 1935, to be revived after World War II through the influence of United States servicemen whose own Mother's Day on the second Sunday in May had been instituted in the USA in 1907.

WALES In the Welsh border area, Mothering Sunday was recorded as a celebration in honour of Mother Church from the mid-17th century. Later, servants and apprentices had a day off to visit their mothers and take presents.

BRITTANY This is known as Refreshment Sunday, when children particularly indulged themselves. The day is personified as Madame la Mi-Carême (Mrs Mid-Lent), who arrives across the sky shaking sweets and other delicacies from her horn of plenty. In some places she is a riderless white horse that distributes codfish to everybody. Bread or hay was taken to her. Children were taken to the foot of a cross to see her pass, carrying a little hay as a present. Sometimes the hay was burnt there, possibly to attract her attention, and she rewarded good children with ribbons.

Carnival, Nantes   Loire Atlantique

Associated activities start on the previous Thursday.

NANTES IS ON THE N137 DUE SOUTH OF RENNES.

Carling Sunday Passion Sunday, Care Sunday, Fifth Sunday in Lent

CELTIC In ancient times beans were eaten at feasts commemorating the dead, and this may explain the custom of eating grey peas, called Carlings, on the news of the imminent death of Christ. In Roman times beans were also given as a dole, and in Lent they have always been an approved food. When eating them communally, the one getting the last carling in the dish will be the first to marry. Fig pies, when figs can be obtained, are also traditionally eaten, in memory of the alleged cursing of a barren fig tree by Christ when making his triumphal entry to Jerusalem, but Fig Sunday is celebrated on the 4th, 5th and 6th Sunday in Lent in different regions.

SCOTLAND This was called Car Sunday, and peas were eaten. They were roasted and tossed in butter, or grey peas were soaked overnight and cooked in butter with salt and pepper.

WALES This was called Pea Sunday (Sul-y-Pys), although peas would have been commonly eaten in Lent like other vegetables. Before cooking (usually boiling, but sometimes roasting) they were steeped overnight in water, milk, wine or cider, then dried. In Llansanffraid-ym-Mechain, Powys, roasted peas were taken up the hill Y Foel and eaten. Water from the local well was drunk.

BRITTANY The Passion was sung today, and Passion songs sung right up to Palm Sunday, normally just after nightfall. In some places the custom was to stop at Maundy Thursday, or Easter Eve. Young people go from house to house, and from village to village, one called the 'basket carrier' who collects the eggs normally given for their singing. Before starting they shout out, 'Shall we sing?', and if the reply is 'Yes!', or there is no reply, they do so. The passions were usually in the form of a chant, though some were more like plaintive ballads. If their request for a gift is denied they cut the cabbages growing on the land. In the district of Liffré a threat was uttered first, and if this was ignored a special song was sung which was full of likely unpleasant consequences.

Day before Palm Sunday

SCOTLAND Although palm parades were abandoned after the Reformation, in Lanark, Strathclyde and Speyside until the end of the 18th century decorated branches of willow were carried in Palm Saturday parades. In Lanark, schools held Palming Parades.

Palm Sunday   Sunday immediately preceding Easter

CELTIC When Christ entered Jerusalem on a donkey he was greeted by cheering people waving palms. In the Celtic lands, where palms will not readily grow, catkin-bearing willows like sallow (or Pussy Willow, *Salix caprea*) or other available greenery were used as symbols, decorations and buttonholes, and branches made into crosses. This custom dates from at least the 5th century. It was banned in many parts after the Reformation as idolatrous, but revived afterwards.

Pax Cakes or Buns ('Pax' is Latin for 'peace') were distributed after the church service. Fig pie or pudding is also traditionally eaten today.

Children used to make liquorice water by mixing liquorice with well water, which on this day was regarded as 'holy'.

IRELAND Sprigs of conifer served as 'palm' and were taken to church to be blessed, then worn in lapel or hat and hung up in house or byre. A sprig was also used to sprinkle holy water. Eggs due to hatch were marked with a cross made by a charred palm stem. Shredded palm was added to grain before sowing.

WALES As Care Week, the week before Palm Sunday, came to a close and Good Friday approached, family graves were cleaned and weeded, and fresh flowers supplied. This is still done in parts of Glamorgan, and is probably part of the pre-Easter custom of renewal after the privations of Lent, though it is done at Easter nowadays.

There were remnants of the pre Reformation re-enactment of Christ's entry into Jerusalem on an ass in South Wales in the 19th century. An effigy of Christ was made and fixed to a wooden donkey, decorated with flowers and evergreens. This was pulled along as part of a procession of people carrying posies of flowers, herbs and evergreens, which were valued afterwards for their protective power against malevolent forces.

CORNWALL Vegetation picked and taken into the family home will bring luck. At Our Lady of Nant's Well in Little Colan, near Newquay, people went in procession with a palm cross in one hand and vegetation in the other for a divination ceremony.

In Polperro, local apprentices were given a day's holiday to visit parents.

BRITTANY This was called Flower, Laurel or Box-wood Sunday.

Saining was done with crosses made of laurel or box, consecrated on Palm Sunday, and also divination.

There was a widespread belief that the wind which blows during the Gospel (L'Évangile) at the Palm Sunday service is that which will dominate the weather during the rest of the year, and sailors would go out and look at the weathervane on the steeple. In come places they believe the time to watch the wind is when the staff of the cross is knocked three times on the door. If there is a southerly or westerly during the Palm Sunday procession there will not be any apples.

If one did washing during this week one was liable to have a death in the household. If it rained this week groups went mourning from door to door singing the Passion, and householders gave them eggs as recompense.

✠ Pardon (Stations of the Cross), Callac

CALLAC IS ON THE D787 SOUTH-WEST OF GUINGAMP.

Maundy Thursday Passover Night

CELTIC This is the last day of Lent. Churches were often cleaned on this day, in readiness for Easter.

SCOTLAND In the Western Isles fisherfolk call this day Gruel Thursday and offered gruel and mead or ale to a local sea god in the hope that their supply of seaweed would not fail. It was collected and spread on the fields as fertilizer. This custom eventually died out at the end of the 19th century.

CORNWALL This was called Holy Thursday, and on this and the following two Thursdays girls went to St Roche's Well, Roche, East Cornwall, for marriage divination. They threw crooked pins or pebbles into the well and sought to read signs of the fidelity of their sweethearts in the bubbles rising to the surface. The chapel that used to be beside the well was originally a place of pilgrimage for those seeking a cure for disease.

BRITTANY On Holy Thursday bells were not rung as it was believed they had gone to Rome to ask the Pope for permission to eat meat. They return on Saturday, so they are then rung in full majesty. Children used to line the roadsides hoping to see the bells pass by on their return from Rome. No digging was done when the bells were in Rome.

Procession of The Wooden Ass on Palm Sunday

March customs

March with its lengthening days was a hard-working month for the Celts, and relatively little time was spent festively. Cold dry March winds were feared for their effect on shoots, as Isle of Man weatherlore tells us. The people there, and other Celts, started ploughing and sowing. Brittany had abundant weatherlore this month. The tides brought seaweed for food and fertilizer, and was much used by the Scots, Irish and Welsh. Apart from collecting seaweed for fertilizer, the type of seaweed called laver (*Porphyra umbilicalis*) was eaten. In Wales it was collected mainly on the south coast, and washed and boiled (for about five hours) to form a gelatinous purée called laverbread. **Laverbread with Oatmeal and Bacon** *(see p.197 for recipe)* was served for breakfast.

Variable Dates

 Edinburgh Folk Festival, Edinburgh   Lothian
   EDINBURGH IS THE PRINCIPAL CITY OF SCOTLAND.

Fixed Dates

1st March **St David's Day**

CELTIC St David is the patron saint of Wales who died this day in AD 589. He founded St David's Abbey in Pembrokeshire, known for its strict regime and life of austerity. He was said to have saved the monastery at Glyn Rhosyn from destruction by Irish invaders by converting them to Christianity. A daffodil is worn, and leeks are eaten. St David is known to have been a vegetarian, modelling his spartan existence on that of the desert monks of Egypt. Leeks are said to drive evil spirits away and to purge the blood, especially if eaten in March. This may explain their adoption as an emblem of Wales and by Welsh troops, the latter practice first recorded at the Battle of Meigen in the 7th century. It is said that St David gave the idea to the Welsh leader Cadwallader for his battles against the Saxons. King Arthur, whom the Welsh claim to be one of their own, was said to have insisted his troops wear a leek in their caps to be distinguished from their Saxon foe. St David was also the patron of flocks and ships. David's mother St Non adopted the daffodil as a symbol because it grew in the Vale of Aeron where her son was born. It became the Welsh national emblem in 1907, being championed by LloyGeorge.

Whuppity Stourie (or, wrongly, Scourie), St Nicholas' Church, Lanark Strathclyde

This is a centuries-old tradition after the resumption of bell-ringing after the layoff from October until February. There is a peal of bells at 6 pm, when boys run three times round the church, then fight each other with paper balls suspended on string while the bells sound. Until the 18th century the fight was with caps against rival youths from New Lanark, at a site at Wellgate Head. The victors paraded back singing a traditional victory song. Today, at the conclusion of the paper mace fight the Provost throws pennies at Hyndford Place for children to scramble for.

The bell-ringing and fighting may be a vestige of an ancient ceremony to drive out the dark forces of winter, or, more likely etymologically, to drive away the spirits travelling in clouds of dust (stour) that settle on crops in spring. The sound of the bells achieves the same effect as banging on pans and trays or whirling caps or paper balls. Going three times round a sacred object was a Druidic practice. However, there are other suggested derivations, none of which can be regarded as certain.

LANARK IS ON THE A73 SOUTH OF CARLUKE.

WALES There is a custom on this day called Cymhortha, the visiting of anyone in the village too ill to plough their fields. Neighbours took an ox, plough and a special stew made from leeks, of which Wales has several types, including **Leek and Ham Soup** *(see p.197 for recipe)*, **Leek and Potato Soup** *(see p.197 for recipe)* and **Cawl** *(see p.198 for recipe)*. Cawl is a stew/soup and was once a staple diet of rural Welsh families.

In soute-east Dyfed people rose early to sweep the fleas from their doorsteps.

3rd March St Winnol's Day

CELTIC St Winnol (or Winwaloe) was a Breton who became an abbot in Cornwall. The churches at Landewednack and Gunwalloe, both at Lizard Point, Cornwall, are dedicated to him, and he was also venerated in Norfolk.

Gathering wrack for manure

4th March St Adrian of May's Day

CELTIC St Adrian was an Irish missionary murdered by Vikings on this day in AD 875. The now ruined priory on the Isle of May in the Firth of Forth was dedicated to him. It was a place of pilgrimage for centuries. It is of interest to note that this island has Scotland's oldest coal-fired warning beacon.

5th March St Piran's Day

CELTIC This Cornish saint, a 5th-century hermit from Perranzabuloe, near Newquay, is the patron saint of Cornish miners, and they would not work on this day. The site of his hermitage is now marked by a Celtic Cross. Cornish village names beginning with Perran- are named after this saint. Tin miners invoked his blessing by leaving Piran dolls, or engravings of him, at mine entrances. St Piran is said to have died drunk, hence the Cornish simile 'as drunk as a Piraner'.

First Friday in March

CORNWALL Tin miners had a holiday for 'Friday in Lide', Lide being an old word for March. A comic custom was held on this day. A young man was sent on to the highest hillock of the mine works and told to sleep as long as he could. The length of this sleep was to be the length of the miners' afternoon nap for the next year.

6th March St Baldred's Day

CELTIC St Baldred was an 8th-century hermit on Bass Rock off the coast of Lothian.

9th March St Constantine's Day

CELTIC St Constantine was a Cornishman who was martyred on Kintyre in Scotland in the 6th century. Two places are named after him, Constantine village near Padstow, and the granite-walled Constantine Tunnel south-west of Falmouth. The latter is also known as Pixie's Hall as pixies were believed to inhabit it.

CORNWALL A tower of an old church dedicated to St Constantine stands near Padstow, East Cornwall. This saint's day was celebrated by eating limpet pies, holding a church service and then a hurling match. The ball for the match was presented by the owner of Harlyn, a manor house in the area. A fair was also held. The feast day was also kept at St Merran, as this and St Constantine are now one parish, where a hurling match is also played.

16th March

ISLE OF MAN This is St Abban's day, but it is not celebrated as such for it refers to an ancient site called Keeill Abban (Abban's Church), almost certainly pre-Norse and pre-Christian.

The Parliament for the south of the Isle of Man was near Keeill Abban in the 15th century, and that for the north was at Crork-Urley. They were subsequently merged into the Tynwald held at St John's for the whole island.

17th March St Patrick's Day

CELTIC St Patrick is the patron saint of Ireland. He was born in AD 389 at Bannavem Taburniae, a Roman village in Northamptonshire, near where Norton is now. He was the son of a Christian Roman father Calpurnius, a tax collector who became a town councillor and deacon, and a Celtic mother. When 16 years old Patrick was captured and sold as a slave to an Irish farmer. Six years later, in Armagh, he began the conversion of the Irish to Christianity. A shamrock is traditionally worn today, to commemorate St Patrick's use of the three-lobed leaf to illustrate the Holy Trinity to King Loigaire.

IRELAND This day has become an expression of nationalism, but in the past it was not as important as major Celtic and Church festivals. The cult of St Patrick was strongest in Ulster. Although the wearing of the shamrock has become the norm, this was once thought of as vulgar compared with making and wearing St Patrick's Crosses. Many regional designs existed, and some were for wearing on the person and others, made of sallow twigs, were to pin up inside the house. The first one goes above the door and each year the row is extended. Boys and girls made them out of paper, the boys' design differing from the girls', the former wearing it on the cap, the latter on the breast or shoulder. In the south of Ireland a cross was marked on foreheads with charcoal, with a prayer urging the recipient to keep faith in St Patrick.

The privations of Lent were relaxed today so there was much feasting, with meat, and drinking Pota Pádraig, or St Patrick's Pot. A shamrock is thrown into the final glass and picked out when it has been drained, then thrown over the left shoulder. This is called 'the drowning of the shamrock'.

SCOTLAND This was Buggle Day in Orkney and Shetland, when people sowed and tended a small patch of land to mirror the fate of the whole field. The corn from it was made into buggle-cakes, which were bannocks clipped round the edges to resemble the sun. In Orkney, before cutting the first spring furrow, urine was poured on the plough to ensure a fertile soil. Also, a thin round stone called a dian-stone, or sun-stone, was tied to the plough-beam and turned sunwards when the plough was turned; perhaps a relic of sun-worship.

21st March Vernal Equinox

CELTIC This day was celebrated by the Ancient Celts as the day when the Sun God Bran (alleged to be buried on Tower Hill, London) regains power over the forces of darkness and causes the days to lengthen thereafter.

25th March Old New Year's Day, Lady Day, Feast of the Annunciation of the Virgin

CELTIC As this was New Year's Day before 1752 in many parts of the British Isles, but not Scotland, many fairs were held today.

Lady Day was a quarter day, fixed for legal purposes, on which rents were due and contracts and leases came up for renewal. The tax year still starts near this day.

IRELAND This was a Holiday of Obligation at the time the Lenten fast was relaxed. There was no merry-making.

28th March Old St Patrick's Day

ISLE OF MAN St Patrick's Day Fair was held at Peel. This was a day to hire female servants at the fair, and they started work on 12th May. The fair ceased after 1872.

29th March St Gwynllyw and St Gwlady's Day

Uniquely, this saint day is dedicated to a married couple. They lived a life of piety in the 6th century at Stow Hill in Gwent, Wales. The Cathedral of St Woolos at Newport, Gwent, was built on the site of their hermitage.

Easter customs

Although Easter is now thought of as the period from Good Friday to Easter Monday it was usual in times past to refer to the whole week from Good Friday as Easter Holy Week. The solemnity of religious observance on Good Friday was followed by preparations at home and in church on the Saturday for the Easter Sunday service and family feasting and enjoyment afterwards. Devotions completed, Easter Monday was given over to sport, visiting markets and fairs, and general merry-making.

CELTIC Eggs are an ancient symbol of the life force, and rabbits and hares symbols of good luck and fertility. It was natural, therefore, that at a time of the renewal of life after the dormant period of winter, these symbols became universal. When the festival of the Anglo-Saxon goddess of the dawn and spring *Eostre*, equivalent to the Norse goddess *Frigga*, was held the hare was adopted as her symbol, as it was also for the moon goddess. The Easter Bunny is derived from the hare, and hare hunting became a traditional Easter activity, latterly on Easter Monday. The ancient Celts rolled eggs downhill at Beltane, in imitation of the movement of the sun, but the Church remodelled this custom to symbolise the rolling away of the stone in front of Christ's tomb, and took the theme of death and re-birth and superposed the death and resurrection of Christ. The Celts also decorated eggs.

Many of our Easter foods are derived from those eaten at Jewish Passover, such as lamb, eggs, cake, bread and wine, the period of Lenten austerity having passed. In keeping with the spirit of renewal, new clothes were often bought for Easter, including a new bonnet.

IRELAND As a preparation for Easter the women would clean the house inside and out, and even repaint it, while the men would tidy the land and animal houses.

Newly purchased clothes were customarily worn for the first time at the Easter Sunday service.

SCOTLAND Presbyterians in Scotland long regarded Easter egg customs as popish and superstitious.

Dyeing eggs and making decorated baskets to put them in was a popular pastime with Scottish children. Children went asking for eggs, although a sanctioned custom in the Highlands was for boys to take eggs unobserved from neighbours and hide them. Pace-egging was also done, and egg-rolling.

An Easter dish made from chicken was called Pesse (or Pasch) Pie, the name deriving from Passover, the Jewish feast on 14 April celebrating the liberation from Egypt.

WALES A surviving Easter Christ effigy-making tradition existed in Tenby, Dyfed, in the mid-19th century. It was made of reeds, and nailed to a cross in the corner of a field or barn.

Monday before Easter

WALES In North Wales there was a custom of 'clapping for Easter eggs'. This survives in Anglesey, with children going from door to door with wooden clappers (or bird scares) chanting for eggs. A favourite recipe for them was **Anglesey Eggs** *(see p.198 for recipe)*.

Good Friday

CELTIC On this day of commemoration of the crucifixion of Christ, solemnity, devotion and fasting were the rule in Catholic Ireland, whereas in other areas the mood varied from subdued to festive according to how far Catholic strictures had been relaxed since the Reformation. Generally no work was done except seed-planting, for which the day was auspicious. Church bells tolled at 3 pm, the reputed hour of Christ's death. Altars were cleared of all adornments and no decorations except yew were allowed in the church, yew symbolising mourning. Before the Reformation some churches even took down their crucifix, and replaced it on Easter Sunday. No meat was eaten, even in Protestant areas, but fish and shellfish were allowed. Until the 16th century every Friday and Saturday were fish-only days, after that it was Friday only by individual choice. The eating of hot-cross buns for breakfast occurred only in areas of English settlement or influence.

In former times Judas effigies were exhibited in the streets and then burned. It may be that this custom is a Church substitution for an older pagan ritual of the burning of a scapegoat. In contrast, there were also parades with effigies of Christ nailed to the cross, reminiscent of those in Catholic countries of Europe and in Latin America.

IRELAND This was a day of strict fasting on meagre rations, with the first food taken commonly at noon. Shellfish were collected and eaten. At the morning service shoes would be left in the porch, and afterwards graves were visited, and also wells as their water had enhanced powers today. Between noon and 3 pm, when Christ was traditionally on the cross, a respectful silence was kept, or was spent in prayer. If the weather was poor this was felt to be appropriate.

A few seeds would be planted to invoke a blessing on the crops, but otherwise no work was done on the farm, particularly not in the abattoir or workshop, for no iron implements were used. Fishermen stayed in port. The Easter cleaning would have been done in bare feet with hair loose, as a symbol of mourning.

There were many other devotional activities today. Males cut their hair, to keep away headaches in the coming year, and their nails. Anyone born today and baptised on Easter Sunday was thought to have the gift of healing, and anyone who died today and was buried on Easter Sunday was certain to go to heaven. It was also a propitious day for eggs to hatch, as the birds would have a healthy life, and for them to be laid. The latter were marked with a cross and shared out on Easter Sunday.

ISLE OF MAN Generally commemorated as elsewhere. No iron was put into the fire, nor tongs. A rowan stick was used instead. The griddle was also removed from the fireplace. A large bannock (soddag) was made, with three corners, and baked on the hearth. No ironing was done. Flitters (limpets) were eaten for breakfast, eggs and fish for dinner.

SCOTLAND Spiced hot-cross buns were eaten, normally made with a pastry cross, but were a recent introduction.

WALES In the past this was a solemn, church-going day, and transport and business activities were suspended. Some people walked barefoot so as not to disturb the earth. The custom of eating hot-cross buns in the past is mainly recorded in areas of English influence such as south-west Dyfed, where they were eaten after the morning church service. They were unknown in other parts of Wales until recently. Some were hung up in the kitchen all year as a protection against ill-fortune, while in some households a bun would be wrapped tightly and stored. There was also in this area a relic of the pre-Reformation re-enactment of the burial of Christ, called 'Making Christ's Bed'. An effigy of Christ was made from woven reeds and laid on a wooden cross placed in a corner of the garden or a field.

CORNWALL This was called Goody Friday, and was more of a feast than a fast. It was a holiday, and people indulged in walks and picnics. Winkles and other shellfish were gathered for cooking, a favourite source being the River Helford at St Constantine in West Cornwall, famous for the quality of its oysters, limpets and cockles.

St Day had a Goody Friday Fair, but it was moved to Easter Monday. There was also a Goody Friday Fair at Perranporth, near the oratory of St Piran called Perranzabuloe.

Hot-cross buns were made and sold today, some spiced and eaten hot with butter and sugar, others made with currants and saffron. A type unique to Penzance was made with currant paste covered with saffron. It was about 4 in across and ⅛ in thick with a cross dividing it into four segments. In farmhouses a hot-cross bun was hung up to protect family and cattle from disease. Sick cows were given a warm mash made from grated hot-cross buns.

BRITTANY On the evening of today, Holy Friday, in Paimpol, the ceremony of the Burial of Our Good God was held. A bier was placed in the church, covered with a black pall on which large silver tears were placed. Upon this pall was put a life-sized figure of Christ upon the cross. A service for the dead was held, and after the Absolution the figure was borne in a funeral procession to a crossroads where stood a painted wooden calvary on a granite pedestal, that served as an altar. The figure was laid at the foot of the altar on flowers. The procession returned, singing the Lamentations of the Prophet.

Eggs laid today must be eaten straight away to signal that Lent has ended.

At Bain there is a pool called The Huais, and next to it a ruined chapel dedicated to Saint Melaine. Each year on this day people made offerings of pig's feet in order to get favourable weather for their crops.

Easter Eve Holy Saturday

CELTIC Hard-boiled eggs (or Paschal (Passion Lamb) Eggs) are decorated today or rolled down slopes to see which will get furthest. It is a sign of good luck to come for those whose egg-shells remain intact. The Church adopted this custom of egg-rolling and taught that it symbolised the rolling away of the stone which closed Christ's tomb.

Well-worship, water spirits and water rituals are associated with Easter Eve and Easter Day, a pagan survival integrated into later Church blessings.

IRELAND Water was blessed in church today, and each parishioner took a little home as a protective and curative. Three sips (for the Trinity) were always taken, some was sprinkled around house and farm, and the rest kept. A cinder from the Paschal Fire was kept in the house to protect it from burning down.

The trade of butchers' suffered during Lent, of course, and today they celebrated the return to meat-eating tomorrow by staging today a symbolic funeral of a herring, called a Herring Procession. The fish was suspended from a pole, paraded, thrashed and thrown into a river with much invective. On the return march, a cut of lamb was hoisted up in its place, and this time the procession was joyful.

WALES Graves of loved ones were cleaned and fresh flowers supplied for Easter.

A custom today was the wearing by a girl of an earthenware crown, the points of which formed cups, which were filled with a drink called bragod. In between the cups candles were stuck on with clay. Those present took it in turns to try and drink the bragod without being burnt or causing the girl to be burnt. The custom was sometimes done on Easter Tuesday.

Well-water throughout Wales was believed to turn into wine during the time between 11 pm and midnight.

BRITTANY At the ends of aisles in churches pious women placed what they called 'tombs' behind black curtains. They kept a vigil and uttered prayers like lamentations. At the dawn hour when Mary Magdalen went to the Sepulchre to find the stone moved and the grave empty the curtains were drawn aside and the priest proclaimed 'Christ is risen!'

It was customary for groups of youngsters to go round singing an Alleluia urging the afflicted to rejoice that Christ will rise again. Sometimes they accompanied themselves on hurdy-gurdy and violin. As on other occasions they asked permission to sing first, and then they requested a gift, asking if the chickens had laid today, and were usually given eggs. If they received nothing they issued threats of retribution, such as to cut off cabbages. Some householders told the children to return for their gift tomorrow, but this merely brought a threat of more serious reprisals.

CELTIC Today was uniformly a joyful day. All over the Celtic lands this was a family day, and they rose early to go to a hilltop and see the sunrise. The sun was said to dance for joy at the resurrection of Christ, though the custom of observing this by looking at the sun's reflection in water made this certain, as the refraction and shimmering of the light caused the image to 'dance'. People bowed to the sun and danced themselves.

Eggs, which had accumulated in Lent, were given as gifts to children, so it was a natural step to do the same when chocolate eggs were made in the 19th century, or eggs of other edible or inedible substances. The Church adopted this ancient symbol of renewal as the symbol of resurrection. Lamb was a popular food for the main meal, and egg-decorating and egg-rolling were done after the church service, and afterwards a family picnic.

IRELAND Wells used to observe the rising sun were called Sunday's Wells and their water had extra curative powers.

A boy born today was thought to have a future in high office in the Church.

As no eggs were eaten during Lent everyone had a surplus of them by today, so they were used for food, to decorate, to play games such as egg-rolling, and as gifts to servants, workers and poor neighbours. A custom called clúdóg or clúideog exists, although no longer in the south of Ireland. Children would visit relatives or godparents, in their best clothes and carrying woollen stockings, and be given eggs to put in them, as well as other foods like cakes and sweets. They would then go out and find a place to cook the eggs and have a picnic. Country walks and picnics were popular with families today.

Easter Sunday dinner was a large meal of meat (lamb, veal or beef), cabbage and potatoes. **Salt Beef and Cabbage** *(see p.198 for recipe)* – called corned beef in Ireland – was a favourite. The piece of meat pinned up in Lent would be taken down and burned.

To colour eggs, they would be boiled in water with washing blue or with onion skins for a yellow to brown colour, then painted. After eating the eggs, people saved the decorated shells to hang on May bushes. Egg-rolling and playing 'marbles' with hard-boiled eggs exists only in the north among Presbyterians, so may have been a Scottish import.

After last mass today herrings were flung into the nearest lake, river or stretch of sea to celebrate the end of the monotonous Lenten diet. An evening dance, The Cake Dance, was popular today, with a prize of a cake (like barnbrack) for the pair adjudged best dancers – hence the phrase 'taking the cake' when you win. The prettiest girl would be elected Queen of the Feast, to cut and distribute a cake to the guests.

ISLE OF MAN This was thought an unlucky day. Many stayed inside for fear of accidents. Daffodils, whose Manx name meant goose-herb, were not brought into the house while geese were hatching as this brought bad luck. If the mother goose saw the daffodils she might look at the yellow colour of the flowers and think all her goslings had hatched, deserting the nest. Similarly, chickens hatching at Easter were a sign of bad luck.

SCOTLAND Watching the rising sun lasted longest in the Hebrides. After the Easter Sunday service hard-boiled eggs were rolled down slopes. Children also sailed empty shells as boats, but never left any pieces around as witches were thought to use them for magic.

Children stole eggs at the end of Lent and used them today to make omelettes and pancakes. These were often eaten at Easter Sunday picnics.

WALES At least one new item of clothing was worn today for the Easter service, especially if it was something brightly coloured. Easter carols would be sung. It was the custom for children to sing carols outside homes in order to receive Easter treats. They announced their presence to the householders with rattles.

Today was also a popular day to have children baptised, and their new clothes were regarded as suggestive of the new character they would assume after baptism.

In most parts of Wales eggs were eaten for breakfast and lamb was the preferred dish for the Easter main meal. None of the lamb was given to the dog (providing there was one) as it would be certain to make it go mad. On the Welsh borders until the end of the last century the Easter main meal was eaten outside in a wheatfield (Corn-Showing) as a picnic. Typical foods were plum cake, cider and **Welsh Toasted Cheese** *(see p.198 for recipe)*.

On this day married, childless women used to go to Whitchurch, Cardiff, and throw 12 white balls and 12 black balls over the roof. A crowd on the other side scrambled for them. How this helped conception is not clear, but it may be a relic fertility rite. It was repeated annually until a child was born.

CORNWALL Saffron Cake *(see p.198 for recipe)* was eaten, by tradition indoors only, with clotted cream at Easter.

Lostwithiel had a feast day today, presided over by an elected Mock Prince, who had a similar function to the Lord of Misrule and was elected by the local freeholders. Mounted, with crown on head, sceptre in hand, preceded by the sword-bearer, he rode through the streets to the church where the curate blessed him. After wards there was feasting and merry-making, with the Prince getting thoroughly spoiled, then all went home. This ceremony may hark back to the time when a real prince ruled from Restormel Castle nearby.

BRITTANY This day started with Mass, at which the Song of the Resurrection was sung. New clothes, coifs and shoes were worn.

Hard-boiled eggs were given as presents, in knotted handkerchiefs.

Easter Monday

CELTIC This was a day of enjoyment. There were many fairs, and families and villages played games and sports, such as egg-rolling and those mentioned under Shrove Tuesday. Sometimes hard-boiled, sometimes raw, eggs were rolled down slopes the object was to see which egg rolled the furthest without breaking. Any broken shell was gathered up so that witches could not use it to work malicious spells against the former owner. The same precautions were taken with any human debris such as nail clippings, hair trimmings and bits of discarded clothing.

IRELAND Traditionally there were many fairs and markets today, with games and sports widely played, but before 1829 it was a Holiday of Obligation, so people went to mass and did no work. Handball was popular, the Irish version being played with a gloved hand and hard ball, and also horse-racing, dog-racing, athletics and dancing. Children dyed eggs with the flowers of the whin or gorse bush and had competitions rolling them down slopes, a custom that is still to be found in parts of Northern Ireland. Fairs and markets were still held before 1829 on Church Holidays but were not the bustling commercial affairs that they were after this date. When it became an ordinary working day many of the private festivities, such as children's egg feasts, were transferred to Easter Sunday.

Traditional Easter Monday foods are **Dulse** *(see p.198 for recipe)*, **Sloke** *(see p.198 for recipe)* and **Willicks** *(see p.198 for recipe)*. Dulse is the reddish-brown seaweed *Rhodymenia palmata*, and sloke or sea spinach is *Porphyra vulgaris*. Other commonly eaten seaweeds are redware or sea-tangle (*Porphyra lacinata*) and Carrageen (*Chondrus crispus*). Willicks are periwinkles (*Littorina littorea*).

In Dublin, butchers and others in the meat trade dressed as guisers and held a procession in which there was an ass with a cloth on its back, a cross painted on it. Donations given compensated for the loss of trade in Lent.

ISLE OF MAN Tithes were paid to the Minister and Proctor today or tomorrow.

SCOTLAND Egg-rolling was traditional at Arthur's Seat in Edinburgh.

WALES In keeping with the tradition of alms-collecting on this day, children in North Wales went egg-clapping, attracting householders' attention with wooden clappers and asking for money or food.

Among the sports played today were stoolball and handball, the latter a variant of fives, in Tenby, both possibly of English origin.

Stoolball *This game originated well over 500 years ago in the south of England, probably in Sussex, where it is still thriving today as a women's or mixed sport. It is a precursor of cricket, and is said to have been played by milkmaids, hence the stool. A bowler bowls underarm at the 'stool' (today a square board stuck on a stake), and the batter tries to hit the ball with the roughly table-tennis-shaped wooden bat. There is a batter at each end of the pitch and their exchange of ends when the ball is hit scores a run. The rest of the scoring is similar to cricket.*

Handball was popular in Wales until it started to decline in the early 19th century when puritans sought to stop it being played on the north walls of churches. Public courts were built in many towns to try to save the game, but only two now survive. There is a disused court on the Jersey

Marine at Swansea, and the only one still in use is at Nelson, near Caerphilly, Mid Glamorgan. Welsh handball is played with the bare hand and a rubber ball on a court or space enclosed by three walls. Cock-fighting was also practised.

Lifting and heaving was practised in the border areas of East Clwyd and north-east Powys until the middle of the 19th century. Today the beribboned men went from house to house, accompanied by a fiddler, and lifted the women three times in a chair decorated with greenery, flowers and white ribbons. After kissing her the men expected a reward of money, food or drink. Lifting was not done after noon. Lifting was introduced from neighbouring English counties, but the Church imposed an explanation of the custom as a re-enactment of the raising of Christ on the cross.

In North Wales, around Bangor, Caernavon and Conway, the custom of stocsio (stocksing) turned the start of the day into one of mischief. Anyone still in bed by an appointed time was put into the stocks and humiliated before release.

An ancient Welsh dish, prepared since medieval times, eaten today is **Jugged Hare** *(see p.199 for recipe)*.

CORNWALL Today in Penzance householders used to set up stalls to raffle home-made gingerbread cakes and also crockery. They did so with a game called lilly-bangers which used cups and dice for the raffle.

St Day Fair was held today.

BRITTANY This is a public holiday. In the past, at St Malo and elsewhere, cock-fighting was held today. In Cesson and elsewhere owners of fine stallions used to parade them today, adorned with ribbons and flowers.

Easter Tuesday

ISLE OF MAN Tithes were paid today to the Minister and Proctor if not paid yesterday.

WALES Until the end of the 19th century lifting (*see above*)was done by women on this day, using a decorated chair. The men's shoes were taken off first, and then the women, living as they did in a male-dominated society, would enjoy a rare moment when irresistible tradition was on their side.

Women gathering seaweed on the Irish Coast

Hocktide customs

Hocktide is the Sunday, Monday and Tuesday after Easter, and combined the once serious business of paying rent to landlords and dues to creditors with the jollity characterising the end of Easter. The improving weather and longer duration of daylight added to the general sense of well-being and optimism for the growing season recently started. In addition to binding and lifting, money was raised for sport and festivities by fining those who were still in bed when the hockers called. By the end of the 19th century these customs had lapsed.

CELTIC It may be that it was English influence that introduced Hocktide customs into parts of Wales and Scotland. People were said to be 'in hock' if they owed tolls, rents and dues, and these were collected at this time, as this and Michaelmas were the two most important English rent days of the year. Any debtors not paying up were liable to be tipped upside down so that their money fell out of their pockets. This gave rise to the sport of 'lifting', done by men on women on Hock Monday and by women on men on Hock Tuesday. The lifters used a chair decorated with flowers and ribbons, or crossed their arms, grasping wrists, with the shoeless victim sitting in the 'cradle'. Either three lifts were done or the chair was turned three times. Afterwards a reward of a kiss, fine, food or drink was claimed. Fines were a modification of the custom to raise money for charity by 'tripping up and binding' passers-by and demanding money for their release. Women could 'buy' their release with a kiss. Surviving parish records show that women were very much more successful at collecting hock money than men, and this fact ties in with both the enthusiasm shown by women for the custom and the alleged commemoration of the capture and binding of invading Danes by Anglo-Saxon women. A play was once performed on the latter theme, but no historical records of this incident are known. It is of interest, though, to note that the 14th century poem 'Sir Gawaine and the Green Knight' refers to a game played by court ladies of exacting forfeits from aristocratic noblemen who overslept.

After the Reformation when binding was banned, ropes and chains were put across roads to stop passers-by. Hocktide generally was a period of feasting, fun and games, as it brought Easter to a climax and this has led to the suggestion that the name comes from the German 'hoch zeit' (high time). Indeed, attempts by the Church to stamp out what it saw as disgraceful forms of amusement were common in the 15th century, even though church repairs were often done with some of the money collected.

CORNWALL At this time, payment of rents and other dues, collectively called 'binding', was made. There were also a number of different sports played, particularly wrestling, which was particularly popular.

Cornish Wrestling *The object of this sport of Celtic origin is to throw an opponent so that he lands with two hips and one shoulder, or two shoulders and one hip, squarely on the ground. The wrestlers fight bare-footed, wearing canvas or sailcloth jackets. They shake hands at the start and finish of a contest, are not allowed to kick – although they can strike with the sides of the foot to unbalance an opponent-- or take hold below the belt. They stand apart initially, only taking hold of each other when the bout has in fact started.*

Variable Dates

Hock Sunday Low Sunday
CELTIC Low Sunday, the Sunday immediately following Easter, is so called because it contrasts with the 'high' festival of Easter Sunday.

BRITTANY This was called The Day of Quasimodo. In Le Croisic pots were smashed, and children did likewise in Pontaven, Finistère.

Hock Monday Monday after Easter Tuesday
SCOTLAND In south-west Scotland (the old county of Wigtownshire) men lifted women today.

WALES In north-east and east-central Wales, near the English border, men lifted women today.

Hock Tuesday Tuesday after Easter Tuesday
SCOTLAND In south-west Scotland (the old county of Wigtownshire) women lifted men today.

WALES In north-east and east-central Wales, near the English border, women lifted men today.

Cornish wrestling

April
customs

Once people had let off steam on April Fools' Day after the harsh winter privations, the reality set in that winter stores were low and spring growth not yet mature. No wonder the Manx called it the Hungry Month. But the cuckoo arrives to herald spring, and March winds change to April showers. In Brittany, this and September were the only months when washing was done. Everywhere, the grime and debris of sinter were cleaned out of house and farm, and perhaps there would be time for some outdoor recreation. Wrestling was a popular sport in April in Cornwall.

On the Isle of Man crabs were plentiful in rock pools from April to June, and bread rolls filled with dressed crab, known as **Manx Dressed Crab** *(see p.199 for recipe)*, were a favourite.

The month ends with one of the two most important Celtic festivals, Beltane, to welcome the summer sun and ensure fertility and abundance. Ritual and divination were religiously practised.

Variable Dates

SCOTLAND

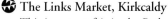 **The Links Market, Kirkcaldy**   Fife
This is a street fair in the Bethelfield district of Kirkcaldy around mid-April; originally an Easter feeing fair (hiring fair) and market.
TAKE THE A92 EAST FROM COWDENBEATH, THEN RIGHT ON THE A910.

Fixed Dates

1st April April Fools' Day
CELTIC The spring festival of the Celtic god of humour, Lud, involved a great deal of japery, coming as it did at the end of winter's privations. The first day, 25th March, and the last, 1st April, were the most important. A similar festival, Hilaria, was celebrated by the Romans. Further evidence of the complex origins of April Fools' Day comes from the festivities which once marked the end of the spring equinox, dating from at least the 2nd century, and the end of New Year celebrations on the Old Calendar, where New Year's Day was where 25th March is now. Another

contributory element may be the merriment which always accompanied the end of Lent fasting, and possibly another the mocking of Christ before his death.

A fool was commonly called a cuckoo, an allegedly foolish bird. The French term for an April Fool is Poissons d'Avril, which may come from the position of the sun at the spring equinox in the constellation Pisces. People are sent on fool's errands, or have pranks played upon them, but this must cease at 12 noon. The fool may thus have originally been a scapegoat or sacrificial victim.

IRELAND A common practical joke was to send someone unsuspecting to deliver a note that read, 'Send the fool further!'.

ISLE OF MAN A peculiarly Manx trick was to tell a farmer that you had seen a tarroo-ushtey (water-bull – a terrifying mythical beast) in his field.

SCOTLAND This day is known as Huntigowk Day or Gowking Day (gowk means cuckoo, or a gullible person). The gowk is sent on fool's errands, often with a sealed message to deliver, which is for the recipient, but actually directed at himself/herself, for example, 'Don't you laugh and don't you smile, hunt the gowk another mile!' On the Old Calendar this day was 13th April, the day when cuckoos were traditionally first heard.

CORNWALL Typical pranks played were sending someone for a penn'orth of pigeon's milk, for memory powder, for strap-oil, or with a note saying 'Send the fool further!'. A successful trickster shouts to the victim 'Fool! Fool! Guckaw!' (Cuckoo!).

BRITTANY Tricks are played on people and if they succeed one says to the duped, 'Poisson d'Avril! Poisson d'Avril!'. Children and the naïve are dispatched to neighbours on an impossible errand, such as to get a rope to turn the wind round, or a stone to make pigs do the St Vitus Dance. When the dupe returns, the pranksters run in front of him with a frying pan, making the motions of putting the fish in and cooking it.

2nd April

SCOTLAND This is Orkney's Fools' Day, and tricks can only be played after noon. Embarrassing items, or inviting messages of the 'Please kick me' variety, are pinned on victims' backs. Pig's tails used to be used, hence the name Tailing Day. In Fife, Taily Day involved tricks only concerned with backs or bottoms.

In some parts of Scotland all day on both 1st and 2nd April was for gowking.

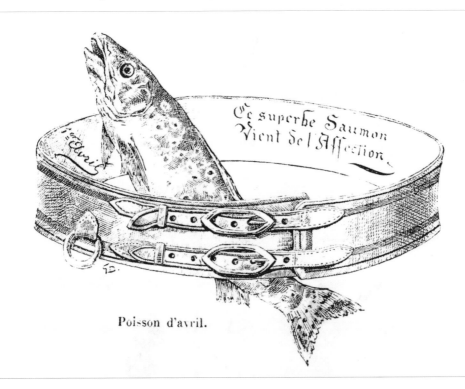

Ce superbe Saumon Vient de l'Affection.

Poisson d'avril.

5th April St Derfel's Day, Old Lady Day

CELTIC St Derfel was the 6th-century Abbot of Bardsey, who was originally Cadarn, one of King
Arthur's knights, until he took holy orders after fighting in the Battle of Camlann in AD 539.
King Arthur was killed at this battle. There was a shrine to St Derfel at Llandderfel, near Bala,
Gwynedd, which was destroyed in the Reformation.

ISLE OF MAN Jurby Fair was held, which was a hiring fair for female servants.

6th April Old Lady Day

SCOTLAND The Arbroath Pageant was held today in 1947 to recreate events leading up to the
signing of the Scottish Declaration of Independence today in 1320 (drafted in Arbroath) and
the Treaty of Northampton in 1328, both following the defeat of the English at Bannockburn in
1314. The Declaration by Robert the Bruce rejected interference by Edward II and his supporter
Pope John XXII in Scottish affairs, and this was endorsed finally by Edward II in the Treaty. The
pageant was held irregularly until 1981 when all the costumes and other effects were destroyed in
a fire.

7th April St Brynach's Day

CELTIC Little is known of the ancient Welsh king Brychan, who is thought to be the same person as
Brynach. A cross dedicated to St Brynach stands at Nevern, near Newport, Dyfed, traditionally the
perch of the first cuckoo to reach mid-Wales.

10th April or a Saturday in mid-April
SCOTLAND

✲ The Kate Kennedy Procession, St Andrew's University   Fife

There was an ancient pagan rite called Cath Cinneachaidh – the rebirth of spring – in the area,
and this seems to have evolved into the present procession. A Bishop Kennedy founded one of the
university's colleges, San Salvator's College, in 1450, and is said to have given the college church
a bell ten years later, which acquired the name Katherine, allegedly after the bishop's niece. No-one
in Bishop Kennedy's family is known to have been called Katherine, so this may be an attempt
to overlay the name of the pagan rite with an alleged devout person called Katherine Kennedy.

72 April customs

Alternatively, the bell may have been dedicated to St Katherine, or Kate may simply be a disguise for the goddess Bride.

The parade dates from the 1840s and is led by a first-year male undergraduate (or bejant) dressed as Kate Kennedy in a horse-drawn carriage accompanied by another student dressed as her uncle 'Bishop Kennedy'. Kate's page and footman are in the Kennedy colours of black and red, and the eight runners-up (in St Andrews' red gowns) for the honour of being Kate carry the eight shields of the university.

TAKE THE A91 EAST FROM CUPAR.

15th April

SCOTLAND In past times, on the south side of the island of Eigg, off Mallaig, there was a Dressil (or Deazil) ceremony at St Catherine's Well. Pagan islanders gathered there to worship, and walked three times sunwise (east to west, anticlockwise) round the well, in Druidic fashion. In the 17th century, a Catholic priest, Father Hugh, Christianised the ceremony by getting the people to bring stones to place at the source of the spring as a penance, then holding mass, and turning the Dressil into a candlelit walk. This custom is no longer held, but the water is never used to this day for boiling meat lest this should offend St Catherine.

16th April St Magnus' Day

CELTIC St Magnus was a 12th-century Norwegian Jarl who was martyred in the Orkney Isles when murdered by order of his cousin Haakon. He met his death by having his head split apart with an axe. Kirkwall Cathedral is dedicated to him, and in 1919 a skeleton with a cleft skull was discovered there.

SCOTLAND Today is the anniversary of the Battle of Culloden in 1746, when the Duke of Cumberland defeated the remnants of Bonnie Prince Charlie's army on Culloden Moor.

Sunday nearest 16th April
SCOTLAND

✚ **Culloden Memorial Service, Culloden Moor, near Inverness**   Highland

The service is held at the cairn on the site of the Battle of Culloden, to the south of the B9006. Old Leanach Cottage, which has a display about the events of the battle, is the only surviving building of the period.

TAKE THE A9 SOUTH FROM INVERNESS, THEN LEFT ON THE B9006.

17th April St Donan and his Companions' Day

CELTIC St Donan was a 7th-century Irish follower of St Columba on Iona, who left to found a monastery and commune on the isle of Eigg. At Easter AD 618 the members of the commune were all murdered by local people (traditionally by a chieftainess and her women followers) after a dispute about grazing rights. There is a loch on the island called Loch nam ban Mora – the Loch of the Big Women.

21st April St Beuno's Day

CELTIC St Beuno was a Welshman, from Gwynedd, who was reputed to be able to effect remarkable cures, often using the water from the well at Clynnog. He settled on land on the Gwynedd coast at Clynnog-fawr given by King Cadwallon, and built a church near the sacred well, which became known as St Beuno's Well. It was a site of ritual sacrifice of cattle, and this practice continued until the 17th century. Another well dedicated to St Beuno is Fynnon Beuno, near Tremeirchion, near Prestatyn, Clwyd.

23rd April St George's Day

ISLE OF MAN This day is not celebrated as St George's Day on the Isle of Man (St George is the patron saint of England), but there was a St George's Day Fair at Ballacleator Gate, Andreas, from 1813 until 1834. It was possibly instituted on this day as a compliment to King George III.

24th April St Mark's Eve
CELTIC This was a mystic evening, when a channel of communication opened to the world of the dead, when Satan and evil spirits were abroad, and divination was done for information about future partners and who would die in the next three years.

25th April St Mark's Day
CELTIC Divinations continued today. Farmers never ploughed on this day as it was feared that one of the horses would die within the year.

ISLE OF MAN After the first stroke of midnight ash, chaff or beans are scattered on the hearth. If a footprint appears in the morning and faces inwards then a child will be born in the house, but if the footprint points outwards then a death will occur in the household.

St Mark's Day Fair was held at Ballasalla, and one at Ballavarkish, Bridge on the old calendar.

BRITTANY On St Marc's Day in Ille-et-Vilaine the crayfish season used to start.

Barley should have been sowed by today. Some hemp was sown today in case the rest did not germinate, but was sowed in the morning because the birds would eat it if sowed in the afternoon. If all hemp were sowed today it would bolt.

Last Sunday in April
IRELAND In the north of Ireland cattle were put out to pasture, being brought in between dusk on May Eve and noon on May Day.

28th April St Vitalis Day
CELTIC On this day the Romans held their Floralia flower festival in honour of the Goddess Flora. The use of flowers and greenery in May Day decorations may have originated in Floralia, but is likely to be much older.

BRITTANY The village of Saint-Vaud is dedicated to Saint Vitalis, although 'he' was a woman. The rock on which 'he' rested is known as the Pierre Cantin, and is said to have the impressions of 'his' feet, head and stick. It was a popular place to visit.

Sunday nearest 28th April
CORNWALL The Cuckoo (or Crowder) Feast at Towednack, near St Ives, was held today, and a fair is still held. Allegedly, it started when a local man gave a feast and threw furze faggots on the fire. Out flew a cuckoo. It was caught and kept, and he resolved to have a feast annually. 'Crowd' means 'fiddle' and 'crowder' means 'fiddler'. On feasten day a crowder led the procession from the church door round the streets in Towednack.

29th April St Endellion's Day
CELTIC St Endellion was a 6th-century Cornish saint, and her shrine is at the hilltop church of St Endellion near Wadebridge. Nearby are two wells dedicated to her.

30th April May Day Eve, Beltane, Walpurgis Night
CELTIC To the Celts the winter sun Grianon reigned from sunset on 31st October (Samhain or Samhuinn) to sunrise on 1st May (Beltane or Bel), and today his daughter Cailleach Bheur (Scots Gaelic) or Cally Berry (Ulster) or Caillagh ny Groamagh (Manx – The Old Woman of Gloominess), the goddess of winter, turns to stone. The two great fire festivals of the Celts, Samhain and Beltane, in honour of the sun, are thus six months apart. Beltane may derive its name from the Celtic pastoral god Belenos, or it may be derived from the old Celtic for 'bright fire'. Certainly it has nothing to do with the Canaanite god Baal. At fire festivals the forces of nature were propitiated to ensure fertility, which meant sacrifice. This was originally human, but later animals and finally food were offered. People danced sunwise round the fires. Purification, often with the smoke from fires, of family, house, animals, animal houses and fields was done to protect from malevolence or mishap. Animals were driven through the fire or hoops of rowan, and pitchforks of blazing material carried round fields. The baking of oatcakes and their use in choosing someone to leap through the bonfire flames was a common feature, perhaps originally a scapegoat

or sacrificial victim. Ash and charred brands remaining were regarded as fertile and protective. House fires were put out and rekindled from a burning faggot from the bonfire.

At Samhain the animals were brought in for the winter and the crops harvested. Beltane fell when livestock were taken to their summer pasture and the planting of seeds had finished. The journey was called the Flitting, and ended with a feast of lamb.

Walpurgis Night is an important witches' festival. Malevolent fairies were abroad and people protected their houses with crosses made from rowan wood and with elder leaves. The latter also healed wounds. Talismans were used as protectors, examples being crosses or other objects made from rowan or iron, yellow flowers, salt and holy water. The period from sunset today to sunrise on 1st May was the most feared in terms of the actions of faeries, witches and supernatural forces. This became the most unlucky day of the year to be born on.

As befits a day signifying a change of season and pattern of life, divination customs were widely practised. Snails were commonly used in divination today.

In later times, in areas of English population or influence, the Celtic customs were gradually replaced by those of the English May festivities. This was particularly the case in Cornwall, south Dyfed, the Welsh Marches, and south and east Scotland. Houses were decorated with branches of rowan, birch, sycamore or more rarely may (hawthorn). This was called 'Bringing in the May'. Blackthorn was regarded as unlucky and was not touched. Certainly both traditions had always involved bringing in greenery and flowers of some kind.

IRELAND Bonfires were lit, a custom that survives in Limerick City. Another custom which almost survived in south-east Ireland was the driving of cattle through the flames and singeing their hair with pieces of burning material. The latter were also used to purify the fields.

Boys used to stroke or thrash people with nettles, possibly a custom based on an old cure for rheumatism, but similar to an English custom on someone who was not wearing an oak sprig on Oak-Apple Day (29th May).

The father of the house had the duty to bless and protect his family, which he did by lighting a candle and praying.

Marriage divination was common tonight.

ISLE OF MAN Gorse was burned on these high places, dollans (skin drums) were beaten and horns were blown through the night to scare away witches. No one gave fire today. The fires were sited so that the prevailing winds carried smoke over cornfields, cattle houses and dwellings for their purification, or the animals were driven through it. Housefires were put out and rekindled with a piece from one of these sacred fires.

Rowan (cuirn) crosses were made called Crosh Keirn by breaking rowan twigs (not cutting with anything made of iron) and binding them with sheep wool. The crosses were hung from front doors to protect the occupants from witches, evil spirits and other malevolent forces. They were also attached to cattle, hiding them in the long hair of the tail.

The well Chibbyr Baltane (Beltane Well) is on the moorside of Surby.

Elderflower Wine *(see p.199 for recipe)* was traditionally made today.

SCOTLAND Nine varieties of wood were used to make the hilltop bonfires, which were lit at dawn. Domestic fires were extinguished first. A circular patch of turf was removed, and two bonfires made, with a passage in between for people and livestock to pass through and be cleansed (sained) by the smoke. The people surrounded the fire, and had bannocks with nine knobs on. Turning their backs to the fire they broke off the knobs one by one and threw them into the fire as they propitiated. When the flames subsided women leapt through them to ensure eligibility and a good husband, and pregnant women to ensure a safe delivery. In Shetland the fires were kept alight for three days. In most of rural Scotland this custom lasted until the 18th century, but in Birse, Aberdeenshire, until the mid-19th century. There they lit a bonfire on a knoll, danced three times sunwise around it, then sained cattle and crops.

At Beltane, in 18th-century Callendar, Tayside, a mock sacrificial victim was selected. All the boys met on the moor, cut out a round patch from the grass and made a fire. They cooked and ate a type of custard – the **Beltane Caudle** *(see p.199 for recipe)* – of eggs, milk and a little oatmeal, and spilled some on the ground as a libation. Then they kneaded a cake of oatmeal and toasted it in the embers. The cake was cut into portions sufficient for one each, but one portion was blackened with charcoal. All portions were put into a bonnet and each drew one. The one drawing the black piece was the 'victim', who had to leap three times through the flames. Each put a marked stone in the fire, and next morning any not found meant the owner was 'fey', and would die within a year.

In the Highlands **Beltane Bannocks and Beltane Caudle** *(see p.199 for recipe)* were baked and served. On one side of the bannock was a cross representing life and on the other a symbol of death. They were rolled down a hillside three times. The side that was uppermost most times indicated the character of the year ahead, full of good tidings or woe. A similar custom in the Highlands to that in Callendar chose a mock sacrificial victim.

In Lowland Scotland 'Bringing in the May' was done, though the boughs brought into the house were usually of rowan or birch, not hawthorn or the unlucky blackthorn.

Beltane Fire, Edinburgh Lothian

Recently revived after dying out in the early 19th century, this bonfire next to the Acropolis on Calton Hill is the focus of general festivities from 10 pm.
EDINBURGH IS THE PRINCIPAL CITY OF SCOTLAND. CALTON IS AN EASTERN SUBURB ON THE A1 TO BERWICK-UPON-TWEED.

WALES Until the end of the 19th century Beltane fires were lit, combustible materials being gathered by someone with no metal on their person. Before the materials were piled up, a circle was cut from the turf and base sticks arranged crosswise. Sometimes two fires were built with a gap between for people and animals to pass. Nine types of wood were gathered, using no metal implements. Lighting was provided by a spark generated by two oak sticks or by drilling an oak augur into a log. The hill called Tan-y-bryn in south-east Dyfed is particularly associated with Beltane. **Welsh Oatcakes** *(see p.199 for recipe)* were made for the occasion and put into a bag, from which each chose; they are larger and thinner than Scottish oatcakes and were traditionally cooked on a bakestone. Those choosing a brown cake were scapegoats and had to jump over the flames three times or run thrice between the fires. This was a purification and fertility ritual originally.

In North Wales, a custom called Rhoddi Penglog ('skull-giving') was done today, which has certain similarities to Mari Lwyd. Young men of a village hung a horse's skull on the door of a woman they disliked. Her name was written on the skull. The custom has also been recorded in South Wales, for example in Glamorgan on Twelfth Night.

Another custom recorded was when a jilted man would put a straw effigy of his replacement under the window of his former girlfriend. A letter would be pinned to it, and the matter often concluded with a fight between the two men at the local fair.

Going a-maying is recorded from English-speaking parts of south-west Dyfed. May branches (usually rowan or birch, but later hawthorn; not unlucky blackthorn) were brought indoors and also put outside the windows. It was unlucky to bring any thorned plant into the house. Flowers would be strewn along paths and on steps, to welcome the new season of growth and abundance.

CORNWALL Maypoles were erected annually in several towns, Pelynt, Dulver, East and West Looe, and in Hugh Town, St Mary's, Scilly, girls wore garlands round their heads and even large wreaths of flowers down to their waists as they danced round the pole to fiddle and drum. Hayle children dressed in paper clothes adorned with flowers. The maypoles were garlanded and protected by a guard to stop neighbouring villagers from stealing them. If stolen they were returned next day.

Bonfires were lit in many places and bundles of oily rags set alight and rolled along the streets. Children sat up until midnight, and then, with musical instruments playing, went a-maying. The blowing of horns or conchshells commonly ushered in May Day. For every year a May horn was used a penn'orth of tin was fixed round it. Whistles, called 'feepers' or 'pee-weeps', made of green wheat stalks were blown in St Ives, whereas in Penzance fiddles and drums were the favoured accompaniment. Crowds of children went round collecting money or food. Houses were decorated with 'May', usually sycamore, whitethorn or other greenery.

If boys succeeded in fixing a May bough (of hawthorn, sycamore or whitethorn) above a farmer's door without being detected they could demand breakfast.

Millbrook, on the banks of the River Tamar, once had a procession featuring a gilded ship. This may hark back to the days, as in Padstow, when the town was a port before the silting up.

Preparations begin several days in advance, with dancing and singing practice on the quayside, bunting put up in the streets and the maypole erected in Broad Street.

The ceremony starts at midnight, when the whole town comes alive, to the strain of 'Unite and unite, let us unite, for Summer is a-cummin' in!'. The singers go to selected houses singing lines of verse suited to the occupant, who appears and acknowledges them. Each 'Obby 'Oss has its team of Mayers in white shirts and trousers, blue or red sashes and sailor's hats. Each team has a master of ceremonies in morning suit and top hat, and a Teazer bearing a club. The Mayers who are musicians lead the crowds in the song, the rhythm alternating between dirge (death) and upbeat (revival). The crowd shouts "Oss, 'Oss, wee, 'Oss!'

The two 'Obby 'Osses are the Blue 'Oss, representing the town's teetotaller group which contributes its funds to charity, and leaves from the Institute at 10 am, and the older Red (formerly Black) 'Oss whose supporters use contributions for jollification, which leaves from the Golden Lion Inn at 11 am. 'Oss and Teazer weave about, and any who dance with the 'Oss will be blessed with good fortune in the coming year. Any woman who gets caught under the frame of the 'Oss will become pregnant before the year is out. The Padstow May Carol is sung to welcome the Summer. Only in the evening do the two 'Osses meet at the maypole and dance together. The ceremony finishes at 8 pm.

In past times the 'Obby 'Oss was carried through the streets to Treator Pool, ¼ mile out of town, to 'drink'. Spectators were sprayed with water ('dipped'). Also, the 'Osses used to dab a chosen person with soot. Black, the colour of the 'Osses' capes, is traditionally symbolic of fertility, as with the inviting of chimney sweeps to weddings. The maypole was first erected in 1883.

TAKE THE A39 WEST OUT OF WADEBRIDGE, THEN RIGHT ON TO THE A389 PAST LITTLE PETHERICK.

BRITTANY There was a tradition of young people singing May songs in return for a reward of eggs.

The Padstow 'Obby 'Oss, c.1914

Rogationtide customs

These customs stem from pagan spring fertility rites. The Roman blessing of crops at Ambervailia and the beating of bounds at the May festival Terminalia, in honour of the god of boundaries, Terminus, provide the two themes which have been incorporated into the Church celebration of Rogationtide, starting five weeks after Easter. Rogation means 'beseeching', and the Rogation Days proper are the Monday, Tuesday and Wednesday before Ascension Thursday.

CELTIC On the Rogation Days the clergy and villagers visited fields, ponds, meadows and coastal waters to ask for Divine blessing on all growing things. After these devotions the clergy led a procession round the parish boundaries and beat the boundary markers, a possible survival of the pagan ritual to awaken the sleeping earth. In the past boys were actually beaten with willow wands, or otherwise mistreated, to instill in them where the boundaries were.

The blessing of material objects and the use of crosses as boundary markers led the more strident anti-Catholic churches to condemn Rogation processions as perverted and idolatrous. This caused their rapid demise in Scotland, and this and the changing use of the countryside, resiting hedges and fences, and the provision of better maps, all conspired to reduce the need for perambulation in Wales, the Isle of Man and Cornwall. Records do not confirm the extent of the custom in Ireland.

ISLE OF MAN On the Monday, Tuesday and Wednesday perambulation of the boundaries took place in parishes. Boys had their ears wrung at boundary points to help them remember them.

WALES The Rogationtide crop blessing at Llanfair Caereinion, Powys, was conducted from a train on the Welshpool and Llanfair Light Railway.

Variable Dates

Rogation Sunday Fifth Sunday after Easter, Sunday immediately preceding Ascension Day

Rogation Monday Monday before Ascension Day

BRITTANY The weather on the three Rogation days from Monday to Wednesday presages that which will reign when gathering in the crops: Monday for haymaking, Tuesday for the corn harvest and Wednesday for the harvest of grapes and apples.

To make butter with healing powers owners put their cows out before sunrise on Monday and Tuesday before going to mass. On Wednesday the butter was extracted before sunrise.

Rogation Tuesday Tuesday before Ascension Day
BRITTANY At Saint Jugon's Chapel, La Gacilly, buckwheat seeds were blessed today.

Rogation Wednesday Ascension Eve

Ascension Day Fortieth day after Easter, Thursday before Whit Sunday
CELTIC The Roman flower festival *Fontinalia* honouring the spirits of streams and fountains took place now, and the association of Ascension Day with giving thanks for the gift of water may come from the Church's efforts to eradicate water- and well-worship. Wells were rededicated to saints. The tradition of thanksgiving for pure well water dates back to the Black Death when villages were spared because of their pure water. Some perambulations and blessings also occurred today.

Children used to mix well water with sugar or liquorice before drinking it. Water from healing wells was thought to be especially potent today.

There was a general fear of mishap and accident today, and clothes were never washed lest someone dies as the clothes are drying.

IRELAND It was the practice in Co. Kildare, and probably elsewhere, to bring holy water home from church and sprinkle it on gardens and fields as a fertility rite.

Outdoor activities recorded are hurling, cricket and cock-fighting.

ISLE OF MAN Meat was eaten today, and wells visited.

WALES Miners at Penryn quarries, near Bangor, Gwynedd, took this day as a holiday because they feared accident if they worked. Generally, no work was done in fields and gardens today lest the crops grow weak and harvests turned out poor.

BRITTANY This is a public holiday.

✠ **Pardon of the Horses, Saint-Herbot Church**   Finistère
THE CHURCH IS SOUTH-WEST OF HUELGOAT.

St Ignatious Well at Strathglass, Inverness-shire, c.1928

May customs

With the grip of winter released and with shoots, buds and blooms sprouting forth it is easy to understand the reasons behind the temporary indulgence from hard work allowed in the old Manx custom of ritually gathering the first plants and flowers and strewing them around. After ploughing, and after May Day but before 1st July, the Manx cut the year's supply of peat for fuel. No peat stacks were allowed to remain by 1st October. At the end of May or in June tithes on lambs and on wool were paid.

At this time too the herring season started on the west coast. The fishermen would follow the shoals of glistening, fish southwards round the island's coasts throughout the summer months until they reached their east-coast spawning grounds in October. The first herring to come out of the nets was boiled whole and shared, to symbolise how the rest of the season's catch would also be shared equally between the fishermen. A few herring were always thrown overboard as an offering to the merman. **Grilled Manx Kippers** *(see p.199 for recipe)* are a favourite dish for breakfast, as are herrings which have been split, cleaned, washed in brine, and smoked by hanging over fires of oak shavings for several hours.

For everyone, as a new season began so it would be accompanied by its own new rituals with elements of thanksgiving for the fertility and supply of natural resources such as trees and water. More work meant more labour to hire, on farms and fisheries. Sheep are still sold at May fairs in the Welsh border area, such as at Knighton and Hay-on-Wye in Powys. Hiring fairs, where farm-hands and labourers would be employed for a year or half-year, were once common occurrences in Wales around May Day (13th or 14th May on Old Calendar). For sweeps it was the end of the season and time to look for other work elsewhere.

A growing sense of relief and optimism as the winter got further away led to more recreation, and even abandon. In West Cornwall any foolish activity is called a May-game (pronounced 'may-gum'). Many Cornish wrestling matches were held in May. In Brittany May marriages were thought to be unlucky, but baby girls who fed at the breast during the month of May would have a beautiful complexion. May kittens would be eaten by their parents, and jays hatched in May did not thrive because they had epilepsy. Hemp could safely be sown on all Thursdays in May. Cockchafers were in the oaks and elms. By now the ground would have been hard enough for children to take off their wooden sabots and go around in bare feet.

SCOTLAND

✵ **Eaglesham Summer Fair, Eaglesham**   Strathclyde
The royal charter from King Charles II granting a weekly market and annual fair dates from 1672.
The fair was then in August, and featured a feuars' mounted parade, which stopped regularly for
whisky and cakes supplied by inns and householders, a foot race round the square for a Kilmarnock
bonnet, and climbing the greasy pole for a leg of mutton. It became a biannual event in 1961 and is
now held on a Saturday in mid-May every two years. It features a children's fancy-dress parade, the
crowning of the Village Queen, sports and games, such as tossing the sheaf, with the last event being
the foot race.
EAGLESHAM IS ON THE B764 SOUTH-WEST OF EAST KILBRIDE.

WALES

✦ **Leek-Throwing Competition, Crickhowell**   Powys
This takes place near the limestone summit called Table Mountain.
TAKE THE A40 NORTH-WEST FROM ABERGAVENNY.

BRITTANY

✵ **Potters Fair, Lamballe**   Côtes-d'Armor
LAMBALLE IS ON THE N12 EAST OF ST BRIEUC.

✋ **St Michel Spring Folklore Festival, Mont-St-Michel**   Manche
MONT-ST-MICHEL IS ON THE D976 NORTH OF PONTORSON.

✋ **'Riv'Ages' Café-Théâtre Festival**

✋ **Festival en Arwen, Cléguerec**   Morbihan
There are four days of fest-noz. It is held in early May.
CLÉGUEREC IS ON AN UNCLASSIFIED ROAD SOUTH OF MÛR-DE-BRETAGNE.

❀ **Flower Festival, Combourg**   Ille-et-Vilaine
This is held in mid-May.
COMBOURG IS ON THE D795 SOUTH OF DOL-DE-BRETAGNE.

✋ **Le Mai Breton (Festival of Breton folklore), St Brieuc**   Côtes d'Armor
This takes place towards the end of May.
ST BRIEUC IS ON THE NORTH COAST, ON THE N12.

Fixed Dates

1st May May Day
 CELTIC As with so many customs the association of May Day with floral decorations may have a
multiple origin rather than being from just one easily identifiable source. Hawthorn was sacred to
Persephone, goddess of spring, and its flowering in ancient times signalled the time to start the
Celtic festival of Beltane. The use of greenery in May celebrations echoes pre-Christian tree and
nature worship and the commemoration of the resurrection of Attis, lover to Kybele, goddess of
flowers and fruitfulness. The crowning of the May Queen (and May King or Green Man) may possibly be a long-surviving relic of the myth of Kybele and Attis. Another possible origin of the May
Queen is the image of Flora the Roman goddess of spring. However, the election of a May Queen
(and King), the parading and erection of a maypole and the dancing and sports that followed may

owe more to English influence than to indigenous Celtic commemoration. The Celts saw this day as the climax of the ritual, annual combat between summer and winter, with the latter giving way. This may explain the habit of stealing maypoles and other paraphernalia from one's neighbours, as to steal their maypole was to steal their luck. This practice is known from the Isle of Man, Wales and Cornwall.

Prior to the Restoration the advent of the merry month of May was a time of great celebration to welcome the summer, but as ever the puritans soon toned things down. Girls rose early to bathe their faces in the May morning dew, which was held to have curative and beauty properties, and to grant wishes, and considered it lucky to draw the first water from the well this morning. People tended to be suspicious of happenings on May Day, lest they be portents of what the summer had in store for them, and guarded animals, produce and wells.

This was the start of summer farming jobs. Cattle were turned out to pasture, and from now on would be milked outside. Sheep were moved to higher ground and the tilling of the soil started. Labourers would be hired and land rented or tenants' rents collected. May Day was a Celtic quarter day.

IRELAND This was a so-called 'gale day', when tenancies began or ended. At the beginning a half-year's rent fell due. Hiring fairs enabled farmers and householders to hire labourers and servants. They lined up with trade symbols. Lettings of grazing and meadow land were available. Turbaries would be available for rent so that turf-cutting could start. In Ulster these activities were done on 12th May for a time after 1752 when the rest of Ireland adopted the Gregorian calendar.

Farmers who still had hay and winter feed left, and wives who had eked out the flour, felt proud. **Hasty Pudding** *(see p.199 for recipe)*, or stirabout, was made.

Most May customs were devoted to the welcoming of summer, but the Church tried to Christianise them by redirecting them towards the honouring of 'Our Lady'. Before dusk on May Eve or before dawn on May Day people picked flowers and decorated inside and outside house and animal quarters, including strewing them along paths.

In Munster particularly branches in leaf were brought in and set up as May Boughs. In Cork the preferred tree was the sycamore, called the Summer Tree. In Leinster people set up a May Bush, usually a large branch of whitethorn, outside the doors of house and byre, decorating it with yellow flowers, ribbons, candles and painted pieces of Easter egg-shell. After dark a bonfire and the candles would be lit and a fiddler played for dancing. At the end of the festivities the Bush was burned. To steal someone's May Bush was to steal their luck. May Balls, decorated hurling balls, were often hung on May Bushes in the south and east of Ireland, and also given as gifts. In Co. Waterford and Co. Kilkenny newly married couples gave silver or gold May Balls to unmarried men in their villages, a custom that often led to quarrels and fights over them, or to disputes by those young men who preferred to receive gifts of money or whiskey instead. Gold and silver balls may have originally represented the sun and moon. The May Bush ceremony may be the result of English influence.

Various processions were organised, with music, conviviality and collection of money, such as garland parades, processions by farm workers displaying their tools in the hope of an abundant harvest, and also for the carrying of a May female effigy (May Baby) in Counties Louth, Meath and Monaghan. The latter may have originally been an effigy of the Roman flower goddess Flora, as it was adorned with flowers and ribbons upon its pole. Some records refer to a hobby-horse in these parades, and others to performances and antics by gaudily dressed mummers. Two other characters sometimes accompanied the May Baby, a strawman and strawwoman, dancing in a lewd manner. Childless women would try to touch them as they thought it would help them conceive.

More in Leinster and east Ulster than elsewhere, the May Boys, men in white linen shirts adorned with knotted ribbons, cut and erected a maypole, collected donations and danced round it. A May King and Queen were elected, a tradition surviving longest in Belfast. Before 1820 there were great celebrations around maypoles in Dublin, and after similar activities to those above the pole was greased and a prize offered to anyone who could climb it. Typical sports played were foot races, hopping races, sack races, leaping events, wrestling, ass races, blindfolded men trying to catch a man ringing a hand-bell, dancing competitions, gurning through a horse-collar, and trying to grab a greased pig's tail.

ISLE OF MAN This was St Philip's and St James's Day, though all celebrations were of pagan origin.

The battle of summer against winter is a theme in some May Day customs. When a Queen of the May was elected, attended by maids of honour and a boy as captain, a Queen of Winter was also elected in opposition to her. This was a man in women's clothes, warm woollens, with a similarly dressed entourage. The Queen of the May walked in procession with violins and flutes playing, while the Queen of Winter was accompanied by the clatter of tongs and cleavers. They met and engaged in a mock battle. If the Queen of Winter won, then the Queen of the May was ransomed. Then the Queen of Winter retired and everyone feasted.

Beltane Fair was held at St John's, at least until 1872. There was also a Beltane Fair at St Patrick's Well in Kirk Lonan until 1834.

On this day people would also set off for the turf grounds to begin cutting the year's supply of fuel. They took as sustenance a thick gruel called **Cowree** *(see p.199 for recipe).*

SCOTLAND Schiehallion Mountain, near Loch Rannoch, Tayside, is said to have a faerie kingdom. On May Day locals visit Schiehallion Well and leave offerings.

At Arthur's Seat in Edinburgh dew gathered at dawn on May morning has strong curative powers and can grant wishes. Wells were visited today, and Cloutie Well on Culloden Moor, near Inverness, still is.

Beltane food in Scotland included egg-custard (Beltane Caudle), nipple cakes, which were eaten at outdoor fireside parties, and sheep's-milk cheese. Plain bannocks were baked and rolled down a hillside three times at Kingussie. If one broke then whoever baked it would die first in the coming year.

Traditional Beltane festival sites are Arthur's Seat, Edinburgh; Dechmont Hill, Cambuslang, Glasgow; Kinnoul Hill, near Perth, Tullybelton (Beltane Hill), north of Perth, Tayside; and Tarbolton (Beltane Hillock), near Mauchline, Strathclyde. At Tulbelton, a good year is assured if you walk nine times round sunwise, then nine times sunwise round the standing stones nearby.

Like some other festivals, Beltane lasted eight days, or an octave, but the Calvinists succeeded in banning it in 1555.

Gradually, through English influence mainly, Druidic rites were replaced by maypoles, elections of May Kings and Queens, May dances and games. An 'Abbott' was elected to preside over these festivities. Before dawn youngsters collected rowan, birch and other greenery, decorated the

maypole (originally a branch) and paraded with great merriment before erecting the pole. The King and Queen went through a mock marriage, a vestigial fertility rite. The May King was also known as Robin Hood, but this may be a misnomer for Robin the pagan wood-sprite (Robin Goodfellow or Puck), as mentioned in the Helston Hal-an-Tow song in Cornwall. Dancing and games (Barley Brakes was popular) followed.

Greeting the Rising Sun, Arthur's Seat, Edinburgh
Lothian

This is done from the summit, after which there is a short service. Gathering dew and bathing the face in it (for beauty, health and happiness), and making wishes, is done at St Anthony's Well below. These customs are a recognition that fire and water are needed for the renewal of life.

EDINBURGH IS THE PRINCIPAL CITY OF SCOTLAND.

WALES True to the Celtic tradition this day was regarded as the beginning of summer, just as 1st November was seen as the start of winter. Farm workers were hired today on a half-yearly or yearly basis, or it was done on Old May Day. Hiring Fairs were held. House and farm tenancies would often expire today.

May carollers rose early and went round the village greeting everybody and singing to them. The carols were locally written, and accompanied by local musicians such as fiddlers or harpists. Food and drink would be offered to them. The tradition survived longest in Clwyd and north Powys. Maypole customs were different in North and South Wales but both died out by the beginning of the 17th century, to be reintroduced from English border counties. The birch tree is often associated with love in Welsh poetry, and this tree provided the pole. Morris dancing was also done. In South Wales the pole was painted in different colours, possibly also decorated with flowers and greenery, and sometimes paraded first. Each dancer fixed their ribbon, then the pole was raised, and the dancers began from those positions. Afterwards less formal dancing by couples took place. Youths from one village would try to collapse a neighbouring village pole, or even steal it. In North Wales youths dressed in beribboned white clothes, similar to those worn by the entourage of Mari Lwyd, except there was 'the Old Fool' and 'the Old Cadi', similar to Pwnsh and Siwan – Punch and Judy – in Mari Lwyd. The Old Fool was ridiculously dressed and carried a flag. The Cadi had a mixture of male and female clothing on, and either had a painted face or wore a mask. The pole or branch, decorated with objects of silver and pewter, was carried by the 'garland bearer'. These shiny objects may be a relic of sun worship. The procession set out in the morning to go from door to door. It was led by the Cadi, with broom and collecting ladle, then came the garland bearer, musicians and dancers. The pole was held erect at a stopping place and the Fool entertained householders while the others performed. This Cadi ha' custom ended in the evening with feasting, paid for by the collection.

84 May customs

The ritual combat between summer and winter was symbolised in Defynnog, Powys, by the Carrying of the King of Summer and the King of Winter. Two boys were dressed all over with birch branches, only their faces showing. Summer was crowned with ribbons and Winter with holly. A villager with drawn sword led a procession through the village, collecting money and ale, to the churchyard where a dole of money was given to the boys, but less to Winter than Summer.

In Anglesey and north-west Gwynedd rejected lovers went to the homes of their former sweethearts and placed a straw effigy outside. There are records of rival suitors fighting at fairs.

At Edern, Caernavonshire, people collected and broke the eggs of magpies and other crows and blackbirds.

May Day was referred to as the 'opening of the village green', as it was a day of festivities and games, including dancing, wrestling, bowling, and throwing the stone or beam.

CORNWALL Having breakfast or supper outdoors on May Day was called going a-junketing, as **May Junket** *(see p.199 for recipe)* was eaten as a sweet.

At Hayle, children put on paper clothes, adorned themselves with flowers and sang through the streets. In the evening bonfires were lit, torches carried, and balls of petrol-soaked rags lit and kicked around. Another name for May Day was Dipping Day, and being sprinkled with water today was lucky. In Polperro and Pelynt, anyone not carrying or wearing a May bough or sprig or flower was liable to be sprayed with water. Looe boys used to carry their water in bullock horns, collecting money to spend at Looe Fair on 6th May.

There was a tradition of May songs in Cornwall.

Maypole Raiding, Lanreath, near Fowey   Cornwall

This is an ancient surviving custom of stealing neighbouring villages' luck. People from nearby villages try all sorts of tricks to steal the annually erected stripped young trunk and prevent the locals from pursuing them. After the festivities the trunk used for the maypole is always chopped up and made into skittles.

TAKE THE A390 EAST FROM ST AUSTELL, RIGHT ON THE B3359, THEN RIGHT ON AN UNCLASSIFIED ROAD.

BRITTANY This is Fête du Travail (Labour Day), a public holiday. It is St Philippe's Day.

There was until the end of the 19th century a tradition of boys secretly placing a decorated may branch in the ground outside the house of an eligible girl. In Berry, they were placed outside the houses of honest girls. It is essential that the girl is unsuspecting, and if a girl does not receive this symbol there is the suggestion that she either is not loved or is not virtuous. The branch must be a whitethorn without flower or bud, as the presence of flowers indicates that the girl is no longer

'Clooties' at St Boniface Well, Black Isle, nr. Inverness, Scotland

a virgin. There were other floral symbols used in May, a sort of language of flowers. Honeysuckle was for a dear girl, but cabbages were for the ugly and thyme for a whore. In Iffiniac and Langueux a way of insulting a girl was to place outside her door a crudely misshapen clay figure instead of a May branch.

First Sunday after May Day
IRELAND In Co. Cork and Co. Kerry cattle were put out to pasture today, the malevolence of May Day having passed. Syllabub, such as **Irish Whiskey Syllabub** *(see p.199 for recipe)*, was made in the morning, family walks or excursions taken in the afternoon and celebrations held in the evening.
SCOTLAND A May game, though more of a mumming play in character, involving the characters from the Robin Hood legend was staged today in Edinburgh.
CORNWALL Families from Penzance visited Rosehill, Poltier and other nearby villages to picnic. On the way they would call in at farm dairies and make **Fuggan** *(see p.200 for recipe)* from their own ingredients.

May Bank Holiday
This is usually the first Monday in May.

First three Sunday mornings in May
CORNWALL People in East Cornwall bathed in the sea. In West Cornwall children were taken before sunrise to holy wells, for example St Maddern's Well (Madron's), to be dipped and cured.

First three Wednesdays in May
CORNWALL People visited the holy well at Chapel Euny (St Uny), near Sancred.

2nd May Elevation of the Cross
CELTIC Hiring Fairs for agricultural and other labourers to do summer work were held today and lasted about a week. The labourers would display a symbol or implement of their trade, and hoped to get a retainer when terms had been agreed.
SCOTLAND Some Beltane fires were kept alight for three days, that is until today. Rams were also sacrificed, their blood allowed to drip on to the soil to fertilise it and ensure a good harvest.
   In the Highlands this is Rood E'en, and saining was done.
CORNWALL There was a hurling match today as part of the marking of the annual renewal of the town bounds. The teams were players from two streets against the rest.

3rd May St Helena's Day, Rood Day, Roodmas, Discovery of the Holy Cross
SCOTLAND People in Buchan would rise before dawn to collect a pailful of water, put on the right-hand side of the hearth, and an armful of grass, put on the left-hand side of the hearth. These remained until the first Sunday in the Beltane octave, to ensure food and water in the coming year.
   This was Avoiding Day in the Highlands. Malevolent faeries were out to make mischief, so people avoided marrying, travelling, new ventures, and counting livestock lest some are missing – taken by faeries.
   On this day, or in Rogation Week, Dundee used to hold its Perambulation of the Marches.

First Sunday in May
SCOTLAND Today is the traditional time to visit Scotland's three remaining Clootie (Cloutie) Wells, or Rag Wells, all near Inverness: St Mary's Well near the site of the Battle of Culloden, Craigie Well on the north shore of Munlochy Bay on the Black Isle across the Moray Firth, and St Boniface's Well between Munlochy and Tore on the Black Isle.

Beltane rites, St Mary's Cloutie Well, Inverness   Highland
Near Culloden Moor are springs whose waters go to wells traditionally visited on quarter days on 1st May, but nowadays today.
CULLODEN MOOR IS TO THE EAST OF INVERNESS.

8th May St Michael's Day, St Indract's Day

CELTIC The Feast of the Apparition of St Michael is celebrated in Cornwall where St Michael is the patron saint of Helston. He is said to have fought the devil for possession of the town, and the Devil threw a huge stone at him (Hell's Stone) which landed where the Angel Hotel is now and is incorporated into one of its walls. As his most powerful weapon missed St Michael, the Devil gave up the fight, and the town, named after the stone, celebrates St Michael's victory each year on its Furry Day, formerly today but now moved to the nearest Saturday.

St Indract was an Irishman who lost his life in Somerset in AD 700 while on route back to Ireland with grain for those starving after an especially poor harvest. Saxon raiders thought he was carrying valuables.

SCOTLAND This is the last day of the period 30th April to 8th May called Between the Beltanes. Anyone born in this period is strong of body and mind, and is said to have the power of influence over all creatures.

BRITTANY This is VE Day (1945), a public holiday.

✠ **Pardon de Notre-Dame-de-Déliverance, Quintin**   Côtes d'Armor

This sometimes takes place on the second Sunday in May.
QUINTIN IS ON THE D790 SOUTH-WEST OF ST BRIEUC.

Nearest Saturday to 8th May
CORNWALL

❀ **Furry Day, Helston**   Cornwall

This was traditionally held on 8th May, but takes place on the preceding Saturday if 8th is on a Sunday or Monday. Furry is thought to derive from the Old English 'fery' meaning feast day of a patron saint. The streets are decorated with flowers. The Early Morning Dance is performed after the Mayor starts the proceedings at 7 am from the Guildhall. The alternative word Faddy may be from the Cornish for sycamore, as branches of this are waved in the Hal-an-Tow which starts at 8.30 am from St John's Bridge with its mumming song. Alternatively, the verb 'to fade' means 'to dance from country to town'. This may be a surviving example of a crop fertility dance, but has some features of mumming. The Furry Song accompanies the parade. The Children's Dance starts at 10.15 am from the secondary school. The main Furry Dance starts at the Guildhall at noon, and is for couples in formal dress. The line of pairs of dancers weaves in and out of houses, bringing the occupants good luck. The last dance is at 5 pm and is for everyone to join in.

Cornish Furry at Helston, Cornwall, c.1900

In former times, during the preceding week, every house in Helston was spring-cleaned. Also, if anyone was discovered going to work on this day they had to leap over the Cober stream, which is quite wide, or pay a fine towards the festivities.

Traditional foods eaten on this day include saffron cake, crab salad, Cornish splits with butter and cream and **Helston Pudding** *(see p.200 for recipe)*.

HELSTON IS ON THE A394 BETWEEN FALMOUTH AND PENZANCE.

9th May

CELTIC On this day was the Roman festival of Lemuralia, when the spirits of the dead walked the earth. It was similar to Hallowe'en, and elements were once seen in May commemoration, to be removed by the Church. Its legacy was an enduring fear of marriage in May.

First Sunday after the first Tuesday in May

CORNWALL Lanivrey Feast was held. Fatted oxen were decorated with garlands and paraded the day before, then slaughtered for the feast.

11th May Old May Day Eve

ISLE OF MAN As many on the island resolutely stuck to the old calendar, Beltane rituals were performed today.

12th May Old May Day, Garland Day, Flitting Day

CELTIC Many people moved to a new job at this time (Flitting Day), possibly acquired from a hiring fair, so it was a holiday in many areas.

In east Cornwall the English custom of garland-weaving was done. Wild flowers were arranged on a framework supported by a pole.

Monday on or after 12th May

ISLE OF MAN Servants hired on 28th March started work today. This was also a day for letting of houses, paying half-yearly rents and taking in grazing cattle for a fee.

There are records kept of sheep, horses, calves and cocks being sacrificed on this day for the prosperity of the rest.

Old May Day Fair was held at St Mark's, Kirk Malew, and a similarly named fair at St Patrick's Well, Lonan.

14th May Pag Rag Day

CELTIC In some areas this was a similar day to Flitting Day, when seasonal workers packed their belongings into a handcart or backpack and moved to their next job.

15th May St Dympna's Day

CELTIC St Dympna was the daughter of a 6th-century Celtic monarch, who fled from him when he pressured her to take her mother's place in his bed after the death of her mother. Her chaplain, St Gerebernus, took her to Antwerp in Belgium, where she is said to have cured the mentally ill and epileptics. Her father traced her there and killed both her and her chaplain. She became the patron saint of the insane, and her shrine is at Gheel, Belgium, which is now a centre for treatment of the mentally ill.

17th May St Madron's Day

CELTIC St Madron was a Cornish saint from the village near Penzance that bears his name. His well at Madron is a place of pilgrimage for those seeking cures or to reveal the future by studying its reflections. Lunatics and sick children are said to be cured if they sleeps inside the ruined chapel by the well, on 'St Madron's Bed'. Rags are left on the hawthorn nearby.

18th May

ISLE OF MAN This day was connected with the Hospitallers, or Order of St John of Jerusalem, and was called the Summer Feast Day of Hospices (Hospitals), on which the Spitlhin Souree Fair was held at St John's. It was discontinued at the end of the 19th century.

19th May

BRITTANY This is Saint Yves' Day. He was the much venerated patron saint of barristers, known as St Yves of the Truth. When referring a dispute for judgement, one of the two individuals who cannot agree would throw a sou (a small-denomination coin) on the ground in front of the other. The one who is in the wrong, or who has lied, will die within the year. In some districts of Côtes-du-Nord those who cannot retrieve money from a debtor say a mass to St Yves. By this means their money will be repaid in a year or the debtor will die. In the chapel of Saint-Yves-de-Vérité the standard entreaty to him is to say, 'You were just in your lifetime, show you are still.' Then one can be sure that the perpetrator will die within the year.

Third Sunday in May
BRITTANY

✪ **Pardon de St Yves, Tréguier**   Côtes-d'Armor

St Yves is the patron saint of lawyers. This sometimes takes place on 15th May.

TRÉGUIER IS ON THE D786 EAST OF LANNION.

✪ **Pardon de St Yves, Bubry**   Morbihan

BUBRY IS ON AN UNCLASSIFIED ROAD SOUTH-WEST OF PONTIVY.

Third week in May
WALES

✪ **Knighton Fair, Knighton**   Powys

This is now a stock and pleasure fair, but it was formerly a hiring and mop fair. People lined up with trade symbols and prospective employers would treat them to a drink and hope to hire them for less than the going rate. They gave 'earnest money' as a way of sealing the deal. Some labourers took the money and disappeared, others took their chances. The earnest money was often spent on drink, leading to drunken brawls and a movement to ban this and other hiring fairs, which was eventually successful.

KNIGHTON IS ON THE A488 NORTH-EAST OF PENYBONT.

Beating the Bounds, Carmarthenshire, Wales, 1948

21st May St Collen's Day

CELTIC St Collen was a 7th-century hermit who lived in a cell at the foot of Glastonbury Tor. He is said to have founded the churches at Llangollen, Clwyd, and at Colan, Cornwall.

22nd May

CORNWALL To cure sciatica and rheumatism crawl under the Cornish Pebble, a large stone balanced on two others, at Perranarworthal, near Falmouth.

Late Spring Bank Holiday This is usually the last Monday in May.
WALES

Boundary Walk, Laugharne   Dyfed

This walk takes participants round the 26-mile boundary of the town, and starts at 6 am. It is tradition to beat children playfully who cannot remember the names of the boundary stones. The same tradition existed at Newport, Dyfed.
LAUGHARNE IS ON THE A4066 SOUTH OF ST CLEARS.

Last week in May
SCOTLAND

Landimare Day, Rutherglen   Strathclyde

This takes place every three years, on the appointment of a new Provost.
TAKE THE A724 SOUTH-EAST FROM GLASGOW.

24th May

SCOTLAND The two-day Inverness Mod (Gathering) and Horse Races first began today in 1662, lapsed during the 18th century, but after a brief revival towards the end of the 19th century they were abandoned.

Last Saturday in May
SCOTLAND

Piping and Dancing, Drumnadrochit, Inverness   Highland
DRUMNADROCHIT IS ON THE A82 SOUTH-WEST OF INVERNESS.

Last Sunday in May
SCOTLAND

 **The Atholl Gathering and Parade, Blair Athol, near Pitlochry** Tayside
The parade is led by the Atholl Highlanders, which was founded as a private clan army in 1777 to fight for Britain in the American War of Independence. The traditional bagpipe tune 'The Atholl Highlanders' is played. Highland games feature at the gathering.
TAKE THE B8079 NORTH FROM PITLOCHRY.

BRITTANY

✚ **Pardon, St Brieuc** Côtes d'Armor
ST BRIEUC IS ON THE NORTH COAST, ON THE N12.

28th May
CORNWALL At St Germans in East Cornwall there was a festival starting on this day centred around the walnut tree at the foot of Nut-tree Hill. Children erected a basket-swing in the afternoon.

29th May Royal Oak Day, Oak-apple Day
CELTIC In areas of English settlement Charles II's enthronement day in 1660 was celebrated, houses being decorated with oak branches, and lapels on those loyal to the crown sported an oak leaf. This symbol, which may have distant echoes of ancient tree worship, commemorates his escape from the Roundheads by hiding in an oak tree on 6th September 1651 after the Battle of Worcester. Only in Cornwall did this commemoration survive into the 20th century.
CORNWALL In St Germans, East Cornwall, a Mock Mayor was elected. Anyone without an oak sprig was drenched and deemed disloyal. In Looe and other parts of East Cornwall people wore an oak leaf for Oak-apple Day, or risked being spat upon ('cobbing'), a protection against bad luck.

Right and left: Oak Apple Feast Day at St Neot

Whitsuntide customs

Whitsuntide, Whit Week or just Whit, starts seven weeks after Easter Sunday, and is the week running from Whit Sunday until the day before Trinity Sunday. The Jewish feast of Pentecost, 50 days after Easter, commemorates the giving of the Ten Commandments by God to Moses on Mount Sinai and lies on the same day as Whit Sunday. Whit was a joyous occasion for Christians, originally celebrating the inspiration of Christ's apostles by the Holy Ghost. 'Whit' may be derived from 'white', the customary colour of baptismal robes, or alternatively perhaps from the giving of 'wit' to the disciples. The traditional religious parades, pageants, and monetary donations gave way in time to Church Ales and May games, the degree of solemnity being much reduced everywhere except in devout Catholic areas.

CELTIC In areas of English settlement (mainly Cornwall and the south and east of Wales) the Church used to organise an outdoor feast for parishioners, to take advantage of the generally fine weather at this time of year, which came to be called the Whitsun Ale after the specially brewed ale that was provided. A Lord and Lady of the Ale would often be elected to preside over the festivities, which included music, dancing, sports and games, miracle plays and much more. Fairs grew up around them and organisations held parades.

As Whit Monday and Tuesday became public holidays this occasion tended to be the start of a whole week of activities, culminating in the Whit Walks on the Friday. Originating probably in Rogationtide Beating the Bounds ceremonies they were adopted by Benefit Clubs and Friendly Societies as healthy alternatives to the excesses of the Whitsun Ales. These Societies, which also had Sick Clubs, for which members paid an early form of health insurance, were teetotal, and outlived the general Protestant opposition to Whitsun Ales in the 17th century.

Surviving Whit celebrations have mostly been moved to the Late Spring Bank Holiday at the end of May.

SCOTLAND The feasting, dancing, music and games associated with the Whitsun Church Ales did not survive the Reformation in Calvinist Lowland Scotland.

WALES A custom once held at Lleyn had an apparent sexual motive, where couples desiring happiness tried to pass through a divided tree called Y Pren Dedwydd ('The Blessed (or Happy) Tree'). Also in this town women used to hold their hands behind their backs and try to hold a lamb between their teeth. The successful woman was known as the Lamb Queen, and was toasted with beer, which was called Cwrw Oen or Lamb Beer.

As on Easter Monday, stocsio was done in Bangor, Caernavon and Conway at Whitsuntide. Whitsun Church Ales were held, and in Tenby there was the procession and annual dinner of the Benefit Club.

Morris dancing was seen at Whitsun, especially in Glamorgan. The dancers had bells on their knees and blackened faces, and were accompanied by a Fool and Megen (or Marian), a man dressed as a woman, to entertain and collect money. The style of dancing seems to resemble that in Cheshire and Derbyshire more than in other English regions.

CORNWALL Whitsun was a time for relaxation and enjoyment. Polperro children used to go to farms and beg for milk and cream. To refuse them was considered unlucky.

Whitsun fairs are held at Helston, Lanreath and Truro.

Variable Dates

Whit Saturday

WALES This was the last day to ensure that family graves were cleaned and provided with fresh flowers for Whit.

BRITTANY

⊕ **Pardon, Moncontour**   Côtes d'Armor
This pardon continues into Whit Sunday.
MONCONTOUR IS ON AN UNCLASSIFIED ROAD SOUTH-WEST OF LAMBALLE.

⊕ **Pardon de Saint Gildas, Penvénan**   Côtes d'Armor
This pardon continues into Whit Sunday, and involves the blessing of the horses.
PENVÉNAN IS ON AN UNCLASSIFIED ROAD NORTH-WEST OF TRÉGUIER.

Whit Sunday Fiftieth day or seventh Sunday after Easter, Pentecost

CELTIC Open-air services were common, at which those who were to be baptised and confirmed wore white, in memory of the appearance of a white dove to the new apostles. The wearing of white also became customary during processions and Whit walks. For indoor services the church would be decorated with greenery and flowers and rushes would be strewn on the floor. After the service Whitsun Ales were organised, as already described, and it became traditional for men to do women favours or give them treats.

Children born on this day were thought likely to die very soon, hence the practice of putting the baby through a mock burial a few days later, and resurrecting it, and changing the birthday, so the baby would not be known as a Whitsun baby and so not suffer an early demise.

IRELAND This was regarded as an unlucky day, so strenuous efforts were made by everyone in order to avoid travelling, or doing any other potentially hazardous activities, particularly if they involved water, such as sailing or swimming. This was in strong contrast to Easter which was generally regarded as lucky.

Anyone cursed with ill-luck could transfer it. For example, to be born today meant you had the evil eye, or you would die a violent death or cause death. The spell could be released by killing a small creature, so a chicken would be killed in the child's hands.

CORNWALL Cornish folk never went out today without wearing something new, lest birds mess on them. **Squab Pie** *(see p.200 for recipe)* was a traditional Whitsun dish made with pigeon, nowadays replaced by pork.

BRITTANY

✿ **Fête de Toulfouen, Quimperlé**   Finistère
This Festival of Birds continues tomorrow.
QUIMPERLÉ IS JUST TO THE NORTH OF THE N165 BETWEEN QUIMPER AND LORIENT.

✠ **Pardon de La Trinité, La Trinité-Porhoët**   Morbihan

LA TRINITÉ-PORHOËT IS ON AN UNCLASSIFIED ROAD NORTH WEST OF PLOËRMET.

Whit Monday

CELTIC After the decline of the Whitsun Ales this became a day for picnics, fairs, games and sports, although some organised events were much like the Ales of old. Latterly these events tended to move to the Late Spring Bank Holiday.

The Church originally set aside Whit Monday and Tuesday as holidays, and the warm weather combined with the fact that Whit lay conveniently between the ploughing of fields and their sowing, and the forthcoming hay-making, led to these two days becoming ones of open-air enjoyment. This allowed freedom from winter restrictions of church and barn accommodation, the only large buildings available to villagers and both difficult to heat and make comfortable. The drunkenness and revelry associated with Whit was of course not welcome in churches anyway, and many of these occasions deteriorated into disorder and violence. This fact led to a variety of alternative entertainments and distractions being instituted on Whit Monday. The Lord and Lady of Misrule, formerly appointed to preside over the festivities, evolved into an elected mock-King and Queen, perhaps having a link with the election of Summer Queens today in Scotland. It may have been the reluctance to abandon the tradition of May or Whit games that brought about the creation of a formal summer holiday, taken, if at all, before the corn harvest, but not necessarily in one's own community. Soon popular travel was to see the demise of the organised communal events, save perhaps for village fêtes.

IRELAND As with Easter Monday, this was a Holiday of Obligation before 1829, with fairs, patterns and devotions at wells, but became an ordinary working day afterwards.

CORNWALL This was a holiday, and picnics were popular. Typical foods were 'heavy cream cake' and a **Junket** *(see p.200 for recipe)* with clotted cream.

Church Ale feasts were held. Two men had been elected the previous year to collect money and organise the feast for the parishioners.

Methodists arranged an open-air service at an earth-round called Gwennap-pit at Carn Marth, near Gwennap, near Redruth. A fair was held at Redruth to coincide, and it was usual for most of those who took the special-service excursion trains to go to the fair rather than the service!

BRITTANY This is a public holiday. Today is a traditionally rainy day. It was said that every time the Veni Creator was sung in church today the week would be rainy.

The Pardon de Saint-Mathurin de Moncontour used to be held today, and it was the best-attended in Brittany because Saint Mathurin was so greatly venerated. It was said that he would have been able to supplant the Good Lord if he had wanted, but he refused as it would have hindered his good work. Pilgrims offered beef to him, and some went to the church on their knees. Later they became content to embrace the glass plaque on the front of a silver bust containing a fragment of his head. An older bust of bronze was said to have several times been carried off by pilgrims wanting to take the saint's power into their homes, but he only works for this church, and the thieves always discovered this and returned it. On sale were lead busts of the saint with a pimply surface, cast from an ancient mould. Purchasers would wear it in their hats or on their clothes, attached with ribbons, and it gave protection from mad dogs, serpents and many evils.

✠ **Pardon de Notre-Dame-de-Callot, Carantec**   Finistère

CARANTEC IS ON AN UNCLASSIFIED ROAD NORTH OF THE D58, NORTH-WEST OF MORLAIX.

Whit Tuesday

CELTIC The significance of this day was really only as an overspill from Whit Monday.

Whit Friday

CELTIC Through English influence this was the most popular day for Whitsun walking. Walkers dressed in their best clothes with coloured sashes, rosettes and top hats, with members of clubs carrying their banners or flags.

Trinity customs

Trinity is the two days, Sunday and Monday, starting on the eighth Sunday after Easter Sunday, the first Sunday after Whit Sunday. The celebration of the mystery of the Holy Trinity did not long survive the Reformation except in Brittany, and those customs that did persist on these two days soon had little of their original religious character left, as they were mainly devoted to feasting, drinking, dancing, sports and fairground amusements, instead of the former church services, processions and plays.

CELTIC Only vestiges of Trinity customs survive, and these not normally on their original date. Originally, preparations began on Trinity, and even the Saturday before Trinity Sunday, and events continued until Trinity Tuesday. Before the Reformation the doctrine of the Trinity, that God reveal himself in 3 persons, God the Father, God the Son and God the Holy Spirit to the other two persons of the Trinity that led to the schism of the Orthodox and Roman Catholic Churches in the 11th century. The cult of the Trinity was introduced into the British Isles at the time of the Norman Conquest, and was devotedly followed until the Reformation, when all church Trinity ceremonial ceased in the Protestant areas. Some Trinity symbolism survived for a time. The equilateral triangle was a common symbol, and in Ireland the 3 leaves on a stem of clover were used, allegedly after St Patrick's illustrative use of it in his teaching. The all-seeing eye of God was also employed, drawn as an ordinary human eye, as was the Fleur-de-Lis. John Wesley and his Methodists used the analogy of 3 candles in a room giving overall only one light. Others resorted to a more dramatic representation, owing to the popularity of Trinity plays, of an actor playing 3 parts in a play, wearing a different mask for each part. A further reminder of the Trinity lies in the inclusion of 'Holy, holy, holy' in hymn texts.

Variable Dates

Eve of Trinity Sunday
BRITTANY

✦ **Pardon de Notre-Dame-du-Crann Chapel**   Finistère
THE CHAPEL IS ON AN UNCLASSIFIED ROAD SOUTH OF SPÉZET.

Trinity Sunday First Sunday after Pentecost, fifty-seventh day after Easter, eighth Sunday after Easter

CELTIC The performance of mystery plays today was widespread before the Reformation. A tradition existed of dressing the pews of the local church with hay on this day, perhaps as a way of expressing gratitude or wishes for a successful hay-making.

WALES In Caernavon there was an old Trinity custom surrounding calves and lambs born with a certain natural mark on the ear, called the Ned Beuno, or mark of St Beuno. They were led to the church, formerly to the monastery, of Clymog-fawr on Trinity Sunday and delivered to the church wardens, who sold and accounted for them. The money earned was deposited in a great chest, called Cyff St Beuno, and made of one oak and secured with 3 locks. From this practice comes the Welsh proverb about attempting to do any very difficult task, 'You may as well try to break open St Beuno's chest'. The money resulting from the sacred beasts, and any casual offerings was applied either to the relief of the poor or used for church repairs. See 21st April for further details about St Beuno.

BRITTANY A custom in former times at La Trinité was for farmers to take their landlords a roll of butter and some curds, and the farmers in turn were invited to sit at the landlords' table.

✠ Pardon de Notre-Dame de Rumengol (or Pardon of the Trinity),   Finistère
Rumengol Le Faou

This event sometimes takes place on 5th June. Rumengol Le Faou is a traditional place of pilgrimage in the Forêt de Cranou. There are associated elements on the eve.

RUMENGOL IS ON AN UNCLASSIFIED ROAD NORTH EAST OF LE FAOU.

Trinity Monday

CELTIC No traditions appear to survive in the Celtic areas.

The Tuesday after Trinity Sunday

ISLE OF MAN A fair was held at Lezayre, and one at Sulby

Pardon de Notre-Dame-de-Rumengol, Brittany

Corpus Christi customs

Corpus Christi is the Thursday after Trinity Sunday when Christians celebrate the presence of Christ in the bread and wine of the Eucharist, and the doctrine of transubstantiation.

Variable Dates

Corpus Christi Eve
CORNWALL Corpus Christi Fair, Penzance, started today and finished the following Saturday.

Corpus Christi **Thursday after Trinity Sunday**
CELTIC Before the Reformation Corpus Christi brought the Easter Cycle to a climax through the bearing of the Host through the streets in procession and the performing of biblical dramas. Records from larger Scottish burghs tell us how elaborate these processions were, and although they ceased in their original form in the early 17th century the legacy of the dramas lived on longer. They were miracle or mystery plays performed by guilds from high partitioned carts called *pagiante* (hence pageant) in wealthy religious centres. They were performed by town guilds, and featured the biblical cycle from creation to doomsday. Each guild was responsible for one scene or act and was fined if it defaulted. The Corpus Christi carol is no longer sung.

Corpus Christi fairs were held in many parts.

IRELAND The pre-Reformation pageants, plays and fairs ceased long ago. In the 19th century churches started to organise processions, but on a very modest scale compared with earlier times.

Today was a favourite day for the elderly to entertain the young with stories.

BRITTANY This was called Le Sacre or Le Sac, and was a very solemn festival with a procession of crosses, banners, litters and statues, including Notre-Dame. The priest was in a golden chasuble with a gilded canopy; he carried the monstrance. After him came dignitaries, men, women and children, in that order. Beggars, blind people and cripples lined the route with mugs for coins. In Upper Brittany bystanders held up sheets adorned with flowers and strew gladioli on the ground. At Morieux there are records of children running in front of the blessed sacrament and blowing discordantly, into whistles of lead or wood. In Lower Brittany women spread rushes, reeds and flower petals of white, yellow, blue and red in radiating patterns outside their houses.

June
customs

The lightest month of the year was a time of great activity, and the bonfires of St John's and St Peter's Eves late in the month signalled the turn of the agricultural season. Hay-making began, the fruit-pickers were out in force, herring fishermen set sail for their season until October, and the sheep-shearers, particularly in Wales, began a period of furious activity which ended in riotous celebration. Welsh sheep-shearers would fortify themselves on **Shearing Cake** *(see p.200 for recipe)*.

Summer is the time when cockles were collected on Welsh beaches, and still are on Llanrhidian sands, West Glamorgan, most mornings. Either marsh ponies and carts or donkeys and baskets were taken down to the mud-flats or sands. The cockles are found about 1 in below the surface, using a sickle-like implement to cut up the sand, scooping it up and sieving. Once cleaned and washed they can be boiled, pickled or fried in butter. They were sold daily in Swansea market. Favourite dishes include cockles, leeks and bacon, or **Cockles, Laverbread and Bacon** *(see p.200 for recipe)*.

The Scottish Ridings, mainly in Border burghs, start in early June, and there are many outdoor events with sports, games and competitions of all kinds, including those staged at stock fairs.

At the end of June the tanneries closed at the culmination of their season of bark stripping and processing. This would be marked with feasting and festivities. At the end of the cherry-growing season, towards the end of the month, there were festivities and fairs.

Variable Dates

SCOTLAND

⚙ **Children's Gala Day, Cockenzie**   Lothian
This takes place on a Saturday in June, during which the elected Summer Queen sails on a fishing boat from Port Seton to the now disued Cockenzie harbour, where she endures a mock attack by local boys dressed as pirates.
COCKENZIE IS ON THE B1348 EAST OF MUSSELBURGH.

⚙ **Election and Crowning of Summer Queen, Carnwath**   Strathclyde
TAKE THE A721 SOUTH-EAST FROM CARLUKE.

Walking the Holyrood Marches, Edinburgh
Lothian

This takes place every two years in mid-June.

HOLYROOD ROAD IS A LEFT TURN FROM THE A7 COMING SOUTH FROM WAVERLEY STATION. DUDDINGSTON IS A SOUTH-EASTERN SUBURB OF EDINBURGH, BETWEEN THE A7 AND A1.

Riding of the March Stones, Aberdeen
Grampian

This takes place on two days in mid-June, near the 12th.

ABERDEEN IS AT THE JUNCTION OF THE A90, A92 AND A93.

Dundee Highland Games, Dundee
Tayside

This takes place on a Saturday in late June.

DUNDEE IS AT THE JUNCTION OF THE A90 AND A92.

Kirkcaldy Youth Pageant Week, Kirkcaldy
Fife

This takes place in late June.

TAKE THE A92 EAST FROM COWDENBEATH, THEN RIGHT ON THE A910.

BRITTANY

Festival Arrivée d'Air Chaud (Arrival of Warm Air), Douarnenez
Finistère

This takes place in late June.

DOUARNENEZ IS ON THE D765 NORTH-WEST OF QUIMPER.

Fête de Musique Gallèse, Monterfil
Ille-et-Vilaine

This takes place during the last weekend in June.

MONTERFIL IS ON AN UNCLASSIFIED ROAD TO THE NORTH OF THE N24, WEST OF RENNES.

Fixed Dates

First Tuesday in June

SCOTLAND On this day, or Whitsun Tuesday, Glasgow used to hold a Riding of the Marches and Fair. It was originally a perambulation, but the Riding ceased in 1726.

4th June St Petroc's Day

CELTIC St Petroc was a 6th-century Cornishman who founded the monasteries at Padstow and Little Petherick. His head-reliquary can be seen in the parish church at Bodmin.

ISLE OF MAN Trinity Fair at Sulby was held.

5th June St Boniface's Day

SCOTLAND St Boniface is associated with Cloutie Well, a rag well close to Munlochy, north of Inverness, Highlands. The ritual at the well is to sprinkle well water three times on the ground, then tie a rag to one of the shrubs, cross yourself, and drink some well-water.

First Friday in June
SCOTLAND

The Whipman Play, West Linton
Borders

This event lasts for at least a week, and began in the early 19th century as an annual outing of carters, ploughmen and other horsemen, who formed their own benevolent society. Its origins are in the Common Ridings, done to reassert boundaries in the Lowlands each year. The Whipman rode to all local landowners and afterwards there was sport, feasting, tests of horsemanship, ploughing and horse-decorating competitions, and a drama called the Whipman Play. Only the ride now survives.

WEST LINTON IS ON THE A702 SOUTH OF EDINBURGH.

Common Riding at Hawick, Roxburgh, Scotland, 1935

The Weavers' Parade and Govan Fair, Govan   Strathclyde

The procession of weavers was led by the bearer of the Society of Weavers' emblem, a sheep's head on a pole. Today the Queen of the Fair processes round the town with a sheep's head sceptre.

GOVAN IS A WESTERN SUBURB OF GLASGOW, ON THE A8.

BRITTANY This was named White Friday, and the next day became known as Gone-to-Seed Saturday. If buckwheat is not sown by today it will go to seed. The first week of June was called the White Week.

First Friday and Saturday in June
SCOTLAND

Folk Festival, Aberfeldy, Perth   Tayside

PERTH IS ON THE A90 WEST OF DUNDEE.

First Saturday in June
SCOTLAND

Lilias Day, Kilbarchan, near Paisley   Strathclyde

This is a pageant in honour of the local piper Habbie Simpson (1550–1620) who was well known in the area for his playing at weddings and other functions, and as a sportsman. It was formerly held on the third Saturday in August.

KILBARCHAN IS WEST OF PAISLEY, ON THE A737.

Newland Day, Bathgate   Lothian

This celebration is in honour of John Newland, who left some money on his death in 1799 to found a free school in Bathgate in 1833, the street of his birth.

TO REACH BATHGATE TAKE THE A89 EAST FROM COATBRIDGE.

Day before the first Thursday on or after 6th June
SCOTLAND

The Lanimer Riding, Lanark   Strathclyde

This may be the oldest surviving instance of Border Riding, during which a bell dating from 1100 is rung. A lanimer is a march separating adjoining lands. Lanimer Day is the day after the traditional date of the Old Beltane Fair, the last Wednesday in May on the Old Calendar. The ride is followed by a week of events.

LANARK IS ON THE A73 SOUTH OF CARLUKE.

Thursday of the first full week in June (or the Friday after the second Monday in June)
SCOTLAND

Hawick Common Riding, Hawick
Border

HAWICK IS ON THE A7 SOUTH OF GALASHIELS.

7th June St Meriasek's Day, St Colman's Day

CELTIC St Meriasek was a 6th-century Cornish saint from Cambourne, whose protection was traditionally sought by tin miners. They put clay images of him at mine entrances and at the entrances to each level of working, even as late as this century. St Colman was from Ulster.

Second week in June

CORNWALL In mid-Cornwall, at St Roche and nearby parishes, the annual feast on this day featured a local dance called The Snail's Creep.

The Snail's Creep *The dancers, in a serpent, led by a band, dance in an ever-narrowing circle, forming a coil going inwards. Then the band takes a sharp turn about, and retraces the circle, the dancers uncoiling with it.*

There was also a game played by Sunday School children in West Cornwall which was similar. This was called Roll Tobacco.

Roll Tobacco *Children hold hands in a line, the tallest at the head. One on one end remains still and the others move round in an ever-decreasing circle until coiled in a tight bunch. Then the one in the centre turns round and leads the others out, uncoiling as they go. A similar game, called Row Chow Tobacco, has been recorded in Scotland.*

First Tuesday after the second Thursday in June
SCOTLAND

Riding of the Marches, Linlithgow
Lothian

The date for this Riding, which started in 1389, arises from the pre-Reformation custom of using Rogation Days.

LINLITHGOW IS TO THE SOUTH OF JUNCTION 3 OF THE M9.

8th June St Columba's Eve

ISLE OF MAN In the 16th century the King's Forester climbed the highest hill on the island, sounded his horn three times, and repeated the forest laws. He then inspected the husbandry on the farms three days later and took any appropriate action. Stray animals were marked and sold.

SCOTLAND Oblation cakes were made for St Columba's Day.

Riding of the Marches, Edinburgh
Lothian

This is irregularly held nowadays, being transferred to this date in 1946 from Hallowe'en.

HOLYROOD ROAD IS A LEFT TURN FROM THE A7 COMING SOUTH FROM WAVERLEY STATION.

9th June St Columba's Day

CELTIC St Columba (Columcille or Colum), an Irish missionary, established the first monastery on the Scottish island of Iona in the 6th century. Exiled from Ireland, he and 12 companions landed on Iona in AD 565, and began the conversion of the Picts. He died on 6th June AD 597. Visitors can see the old monastery, the church, the cemetery of the Kings and the Street of the Dead.

SCOTLAND Traditionally St Columba's Day was the Thursday of the second week in June.

Oblation cakes were made the evening before, toasted over a fire of rowan, oak, yew or other sacred wood. One would have had a silver coin in it. This morning the cakes were cut up by the man of the house into as many pieces as there were children and the pieces put into a bee skep. The children, blindfolded, picked out a piece, and then the one to find the coin was given this year's lambs.

11th June St Barnabas' Day, Feast Day

CELTIC Before the calendar change this was the longest day of the year.

ISLE OF MAN Another name for this day was The Summer Feast Day of the Cross. Before 1748 the King's Forester could mark stray sheep and other animals on this day and then sell them afterwards. After 1748 the key date was 21st June.

CORNWALL

⚙ Menheniot Fair, Menheniot   Cornwall

MENHENIOT IS ON AN UNCLASSIFIED ROAD SOUTH-EAST OF LISKEARD.

BRITTANY On this St Barnabé's Day one should not sow buckwheat, but it is a good day to sow 40-day turnips. If the sweet chestnuts are good so will the buckwheat be.

Saturday nearest the 12th June

SCOTLAND

⚙ Aberdeen Highland Games, Aberdeen   Grampian

ABERDEEN IS AT THE JUNCTION OF THE A90, A92 AND A93.

Second week in June

SCOTLAND A Scottish children's game played in summer is called Green Grass.

Green Grass *A multi-versed song accompanies this game. All children save one stand in a line. The lone child stands facing them, and sings the first verse. Afterwards he/she co-opts one from the line to join him/her and the two sing the second verse. Another is co-opted for the third verse, and so on.*

⚙ Riding of the Muir, Brechin   Tayside

The craft guilds used to ride the boundaries, part of which is an old cattle raik, which have large march stones, at both the Trinity and Lammas Fairs. Today, the Provost and Council ride them by bus.

BRECHIN IS ON THE A90 NORTH OF DUNDEE.

⚙ Guid Nychburris Day (Good Neighbours Day), Dumfries   Dumfries and Galloway

TAKE THE A75 WEST FROM GRETNA GREEN.

⚙ Huntsman's Ride and Gala Day, Penicuik   Lothian

The Penicuik Huntsman's Club has replaced the original Whipmen's (Carters') Club, and they, with the Children's Gala Day Association, organise the week.

TAKE THE A702 SOUTH FROM EDINBURGH, THEN LEFT ON THE A703.

CORNWALL There was a feast held at Roche. The Snail Creep dance was done. Children played Roll Tobacco (Wind Up the Bush Faggot). Another game, Troy Walls, was popular in West Cornwall.

Troy Walls *A maze is drawn on paper or on a slate and competitors have to draw their way out.*

Second Wednesday in June

SCOTLAND

⚙ Trinity Tryst, Trinity Muir, Brechin   Tayside

What was once a three-day horse and cattle market with a Magistrates' Court at Justice Hall is now a two-day fun fair, although the Magistrates and Councillors still attend on the second day.

TRINITY IS JUST NORTH OF BRECHIN.

Second Saturday in June
SCOTLAND

Gala Day, Biggar
Strathclyde

This has its origin in the 16th century St Peter's or Midsummer Fair. There was a Ba' game, a foot-race for a pair of white gloves donated by Lord Fleming, and The Society of Whipmen's annual horse parade. The election of a Fleming Queen, after the local family of that name, comes from the Twelfth-Night appointment of Mary Fleming as Queen of the Revel at Holyrood House in 1563.

BIGGAR IS ON THE A702 SOUTH OF EDINBURGH.

The Lockerbie Ride, Lockerbie
Dumfries and Galloway

Until the early 20th century there was a sheep and lamb fair on Lamb Hill on this day.

LOCKERBIE IS ON THE A709 EAST OF DUMFRIES.

Second Sunday in June
SCOTLAND

Riding the Marches, Biggar
Strathclyde

BIGGAR IS ON THE A702 SOUTH OF EDINBURGH.

Thursday and Friday after the second Monday in June (or the third full week in June)
SCOTLAND

Crying the Burley and The Common Riding, Selkirk
Border

The prelude on the eve of this 400-year-old Common Riding involves the participants being summoned by the Burgh Officer and a fife and drum band. Burleymen or bylawmen are common right inheritors.

SELKIRK IS ON THE A7 SOUTH OF GALASHIELS.

16th June
SCOTLAND This was St Columba's Day on St Kilda. As on St Brendan's Day the community's milk was shared out among the inhabitants.

17th June St Nectan's Day

CELTIC St Nectan was a 6th-century Devonian, who was allegedly mortally wounded at Hartland Point, near Stoke, Cornwall. He staggered half a mile to the well, and foxgloves are said to have sprung up where drops of his blood fell. Today, children parade to the well carrying foxgloves, and a service is held. Another myth associates St Nectan with St Nectan's Glen, Trethevy.

Third week in June

SCOTLAND

🏰 Summer Festival Week, Melrose, near Galashiels — Border

TAKE THE A609 SOUTH-EAST FROM GALASHIELS TO MELROSE.

🏰 March-Riding and Beltane Festival, Peebles — Border

This week-long festival includes horse-racing for a prize of a bell, possibly derived from the choice of the word Beltane for the event, which is not connected with May Day.

PEEBLES IS ON THE A72 WEST FROM GALASHIELS.

Third Friday in June

SCOTLAND The Salmon-fishers' Boat Race is no longer held in Newburgh, Fife. Each salmon-cobble was manned by two fishers, and they had to row around a marker boat anchored along the River Tay, starting at 11 am.

20th June St Alban's Day, St Govan's Day

CELTIC St Alban was the first Celtic Christian martyr, having been put to death at Holmeshurst Hill, Verulamium, under the orders of Diocletian at the beginning of the 4th century because he renounced Roman gods.

St Govan, who lived in a tiny chapel on St Govan's Head, near Bosherston in Dyfed, Wales, is said to be Sir Gawain of King Arthur's Round Table and to have come to the chapel after the dissolution of the Round Table, hiding from his pursuers in a cleft in the rock wall of the chapel.

21st June Summer Solstice

CELTIC Today the sun is at its zenith, its highest point in the sky, and the Druids led the ancient Celts in ceremonies of homage to the sun. A later variant of one of their rituals was the wrapping of a cartwheel with straw, setting it alight, and rolling it downhill to typify the beginning of the sun's declination. In order to redirect these devotions the Christian Church transferred the tradition to 24th June and rededicated them to St John the Baptist.

ISLE OF MAN After 1748 The King's Forester could mark stray sheep and other animals on this day and then sell them.

23rd June Midsummer Eve, St John's Eve

CELTIC Many surviving customs have their origins in ancient sun worship and purification rites, intended to encourage the sun to keep shining, and were mainly a feature of Anglo-Saxon and Scandinavian settlement or influence, such as Cornwall, Lowland and eastern Scotland, Orkney and Shetland, but spread to other areas. Bonfires are lit in memory of the Druid Beltane fires, though Druidic and Scandinavian customs have become entwined today. As with all cusps in the folk calendar, protective and preventative measures were called for. Prayers and pleas were uttered while walking sunwise round the fire. Children joined hands and leapt through the embers to symbolise growth of corn and harvest abundance. Farmers drove animals through the embers to protect them from disease and carried brands sunwise round fields to purify the crops. Ancient druidic divination practices survive in midsummer rites. Rural people associated the night with faeries, spirits and ghosts of the past. A garland of St John's Wort picked at dawn was fixed to the door to protect the household from faeries, and other sacred plants had magical properties, such as yarrow, mugwort and elder. The morning dew was credited with the same healing and beautifying powers as May morning dew.

As on St Mark's Eve (24th April) it was thought that divination ceremonies tonight could reveal who would soon die, or a future lover.

IRELAND Midsummer fires are still lit in a few places, traditionally at sunset, and in some places after sprinkling it with holy water, to encourage the sun to keep shining. People leapt through the flames for luck in a new venture or marriage, when trying for a baby, for good health and self-purification, and struck each other with hocus leaves to protect against illness in the coming year. Farmers leapt high so their crops would grow tall. The oldest woman in a village would go three times sunwise round the fire on her knees, saying prayers, to ward off disease. A dish called 'goody' was made in Connaught, in a large iron pot hung over the fire.

In addition to the communal bonfires householders lit smaller ones as a centrepiece for their merry-making. Children collected combustible materials from their neighbours, stealing it if a request was refused, and putting ashes on the step afterwards. There was rivalry and sabotage among fire-builders. When the fire was well alight boys would throw burning sticks into the air. Sometimes an effigy was burned, of whom it was not always clear.

✠ Pilgrimage to St Patrick's Well, Struel — Co. Down

This place, where St Patrick built a chapel, was once the scene of a large pattern, although not strictly classifiable as such because it was not on the saint day.

STRUEL IS 1½ MILES EAST OF DOWNPATRICK.

ISLE OF MAN It was the custom to hang rowan crosses up.

SCOTLAND The solstices were important times to the Norsemen, less so to the Celts, so this festival was more significant in north-east Scotland, Orkney and Shetland. Baldur, God of Light, starts his descent from Asgard, the Home of the Gods, to the lower world as the sun passes its zenith. It was a time when lovers clasped hands and leapt through flames. At Bigswell, lovers drank together then held hands through the Stone of Odin to plight their troth. A similar stone at Stennis, Orkney, was in use for the same purpose. Several stone circles have evidence of sun worship at midsummer. To mimic the decline of the sun, wheels bound with straw were set alight and rolled downhill, carrying everyone's bad luck with them, especially if they plunged into water at the bottom.

A bone placed in some fires may have been a relic of former sacrificial rites. Midsummer Eve practices survived until 1945 in Cairnshee, near Durris, Kincardineshire.

The Battle of Bannockburn, which took place today in 1314, is still commemorated.

St Patrick's Well at Struell, Ireland

Midsummer Fire, Cairnshee Hill, Durris

This fire in the Mearns is the last surviving midsummer bonfire, and traditions accompanying it were kept from prehistoric times until 1945. It was traditionally lit by the oldest inhabitant at sunset, latterly by the youngest herd-laddie. There was dancing round it to the pipes, and a supper of ale, bread and cheese. Local herd-laddies were given silver sixpencees.

TAKE THE B9077 SOUTH-WEST FROM ABERDEEN.

WALES The 'summer birch' was erected this evening in Glamorgan, probably moved here from Midsummer Eve. This was a pole trimmed smooth so that pictures could be painted on it. As if in solar imagery, it was then decorated with gilded, beribboned wreaths, with a gilded, beribboned weather-cock on the top. It was guarded with pride against attempts by outsiders to steal it. Some villages did not paint, or even decorate, the birch. Like all maypole customs in Wales this died out at the end of the 19th century.

Bonfires were lit this evening, and there was divination for future lovers. Ffatio was done.

Today or tomorrow was usually the day when the lime-kiln owners of Gwendraeth Fawr Valley, Dyfed, held a feast for their loyal workers.

CORNWALL In the afternoon in West Cornwall girls would gather flowers for head garlands or shoulder wreaths. They wore white dresses, and their frocks were decorated with laurel leaves.

In Penzance and other parishes of West Penwith, after nightfall, tar barrels were lit in the streets and bonfires were lit on cairns and hills around Mount Bay. People danced round them as protection against witchcraft, then leapt over them when the flames were lower. The Town Crier of Penzance announced 'No Fireworks!', but this was largely ignored as squibs and crackers were popular. Torchlight processions followed, the torches being made of canvas dipped in tar and fixed on poles. Youths fixed torches to chains and whirled them round their heads. An organised firework display took place in the square (The Green Market), attended by the Mayor.

In Mount Bay youngsters played 'Threading the Needle' through the streets.

Threading the Needle *The children stand in two rows, each holding the hand of the child opposite. The last two form an arch. While singing the song 'Thread the Needle', the chain goes under the arch. When all have passed under, the first two make an arch and the process is repeated, each pair having a turn to make the arch.*

Midsummer Eve bonfires have long been traditional in Cornwall. The general pattern was of a pole with a large bush on top and fuel heaped around its base. The Old Cornwall Movement reinstated the lightings in 1929. In former times the first fire to be lit was at Garrick Sans (Holy Rock) near Sennen, followed by Carn Brea, Castle-an-Dinas, Bartinney, Sancreed, St Agnes, Carn Galva, Tregonning, Godolphin, Carn Marth, etc. The Federation of Old Cornwall Societies now lights a chain of bonfires across the county as a revival of the custom of lighting hilltop fires. The chain goes from Chapel Carn Brae, near Lands End, to the River Tamar in Devon, through St Agnes Beacon; Four Burrows; Carn Brae, near Redruth; Castle An Dynas, near St Columb; St Breok Downs, near Wadebridge; Bodmin Beacon; and Kit Hill, near Callington. After a short thanksgiving ceremony at each, children and young couples leap through the flames for luck, a survival of an ancient purification rite. Flowers are thrown into the flames. On some a broomstick is placed to ward off evil, and an oak-handled sickle for fertility.

One old bonfire custom was for young people to link hands around the fire, dance round, and try to pull each other across the fire without breaking the chain. If it broke the 'weak hands' would have ill luck in the year. Otherwise, all would live out the year happily.

St Cleer Bonfire, Liskeard   Cornwall

This fire is crowned with a broomstick and is lit to keep witches away for the year. A sickle with a newly cut oak handle is thrown into the flames to ensure fertility for farmers and fields alike. Also thrown in are bunches of herbs (cinquefoil, clover, restharrow, tormentil, vervain) tied with ribbons (coloured red, blue, green, yellow and white). St John's Wort wreaths adorn the village to banish witches.

TAKE THE A38 WEST OUT OF LISKEARD.

Lighting the first Midsummer Bonfire, Carn Brea   Cornwall

Carn Brea is a granite tor between Camborne and Redruth, and is the signal for the others to be lit in a chain through Sennen, Sancreed Beacon, Carn Galver, St Agnes Beacon and St Cleer to the River Tamar. Each fire is blessed by a local clergyman in the Cornish language, and herbs and wild flowers are burnt. People leap across the embers for good luck and to drive away evil.

CARN BREA IS JUST TO THE SOUTH-WEST OF REDRUTH ON AN UNCLASSIFIED ROAD.

BRITTANY On Saint Jean's Eve, bonfires (called rieux or raviers) were lit on hilltops and saining of cattle was done by driving them through the smoke. It is said the custom started when St Jean lit a fire at night to protect his party from wolves, but the tradition is much older. In many places by the mid-19th century the custom had ceased, even in villages like Ercé-près-Liffré in Ille-et-Vilaine where Saint Jean was the patron saint. Some villages had several fires. Gifts of bundles of gorse or heather were made to the bonfire builders by each family, and these gifts could not be refused. It is said that the Man in the Moon is carrying a faggot, which flew off a bonfire. The kindling was heaped up and around a pole, on top of which was a bunch of flowers or a crown woven on with rushes. This was normally furnished by someone with the name Jean or Jeanne, and someone of one or other name lit the fire. At that moment everyone cried 'Jump!', and similar cries were heard from other villages. As the fire burned people sang and danced round it, leaping through it when it died down somewhat. Boys grabbed girls and swung them by the arms and legs over the embers nine times (ober ar wakel). Brands were taken home for protection from thunder and lightning, and to throw into the well to purify the water.

In the area around Mené volleys of gunfire saluted the lighting.

The custom of 'stretching the rushes' was done. A copper basin is placed on a tripod, and a key put in the basin, which is then sprinkled with vinegar or sour cider. Rushes are stretched over the basin like the strings of an instrument. As the hands are drawn over them, backwards and forwards, the vibration is transmitted to the basin and a sound like that of a hurdy-gurdy is produced. It can be heard from afar, and was done before the bonfire was lit. The different sounds from villages near and far were a distinctive feature of this evening.

Moving house was often done today, and servants left one service for another.

Tonight there are many Fest-Noz (Night Festivals) held in Brittany.

Pardon, St Jean du Doigt, near Morlaix   Finistère

The village displays its famous relic of the index finger of St John the Baptist, brought here in 1437. It is dipped into water in a basin to make the water holy. This ritual sometimes takes place on the last Sunday in June.

ST JEAN DU DOIGT IS ON AN UNCLASSIFIED ROAD NORTH OF MORLAIX.

Standing stones of Callanish, a Hebridean stone circle, Lewis, Scotland

Saturday evening and Sunday before 24th June
BRITTANY

✠ **Pardon, St Tugen**   Finistère
ST TUGEN IS DUE WEST OF AUDIERNE.

24th June Midsummer Day, St John's Day, Nativity of St John the Baptist

CELTIC St John's Day was always associated with water and communities celebrated this day by dressing their wells.

St Bega, the 7th-century Irish saint, was once associated with this day, but is now thought not to have existed. She was alleged to have travelled to Cumbria and established an abbey at St Bees. A bracelet was kept at her shrine, and as the Anglo-Saxon for bracelet is *beag* this is thought to be the source of the invention.

The fears of the eve having passed, this was a day of outdoor jollification. Wells were dressed, house exteriors decorated with greenery, and fires lit as a focus for feasting and festivities. Men jumped through the flames for good luck, and other bonfire rituals followed. The ashes of the midsummer fire were used to tell fortunes and foretell the future. Many fairs were held.

St John's Wort, or Chase Devil, was traditionally picked today to protect from evil and disease. Midsummer Day was a quarter day.

IRELAND It was felt that swimming was no longer an inherently dangerous practice from today onwards.

In cities like Limerick and Galway, tradesmen and fishermen used to hold processions. For fishermen it was the day when they did repairs to their nets and gear, and had them blessed before the start of the summer fishing season.

Many St John's Day fairs were held. The centre of the fairground was marked by a craebh, a decorated pole. Patterns were organised for visitors to wells dedicated to St John.

ISLE OF MAN At Barrule, well into the 19th century, bundles of grass were laid down for the Celtic God of Man & Arran, Manniman-beg-mac-y-Lear, who appeared as a heron and would be seeking women to court.

This was John the Baptist's Feast Day or Little Trinity. Midsummer Fair (or Little Trinity Fair) was held at Sulby Claddaghs, Lezayre.

SCOTLAND Birch branches were hung over doors and archways.

🎧 **Visiting the Callanish Stones, Lewis**   Western Isles
It is traditional on this day to view the sunrise on the leading stone, called The Shining One, of this cruciform group. The stones are said to animate, particularly if a cuckoo heralds the sunrise. In ancient times St Ciaran built a church here.
CALLANISH IS ON THE A858 WEST OF STORNOWAY.

WALES The 'Summer birch' custom was held in Glamorgan, a custom more important than May Day customs. Bonfires were lit in the Vale of Glamorgan.

In the Dyfed village of Pendine people went from door to door asking for milk to make Midsummer Pudding. This was similar to Hasty Pudding.

CORNWALL This was a holiday. Tin miners blew up boulders with gunpowder in celebration: indeed, it was considered unlucky to work today. They placed a green bough on the shears of the engine-houses in commemoration of St John's preaching in the wilderness.

Pelynt Fair, East Cornwall, which had a large bonfire, was held today. Quay Fair was held on the Old Quay in Penzance. Hiring a rowing-boat was a popular attraction, as was the row of stalls set up by strawberry growers to sell their fruit.

BRITTANY Today, or in some areas 29th June, for example at Rennes where there was a hiring fair on this day for labourers, the Hay Harvest normally began, but in the warmer parts of Brittany it was possibly earlier. The reapers carried their stone for sharpening the scythe in a horn (couyé) suspended between their legs. During their breaks they used the stone to knock on the blade in a tuneful way. The best hay is that cut before La Madeleine on 22nd July. The hay reapers feared being stalked by the devil, and if they saw eddies in the hay they thought it was the devil trying to abduct one of them. They threw a knife or pitchfork into the eddy. The loading of the hay into haylofts was a time for fun and frolics of a sort that will not be entered into here. Music, dancing and feasting attend the conclusion of the harvesting.

Week including 24th June
SCOTLAND

♔ **Dumfries Riding**   Dumfries and Galloway

TAKE THE A75 WEST FROM GRETNA GREEN TO DUMFRIES.

Saturday nearest Midsummer Day
SCOTLAND

❀ **Bannockburn Day Rally, Stirling**   Central

Bannockburn is 3 miles south of Stirling, and is the site of the defeat of Edward II's English army by Robert the Bruce on 24th June 1314.

STIRLING IS TO THE EAST OF JUNCTION 10 OF THE M9.

25th June St Non's Day

CELTIC St Non was from Altarnum, Cornwall, and his well is by the 14th-century church. Lunatics were plunged in and out of the water to cure them, a process known as Bowsenning.

26th June St Anne's Day

CELTIC St Anne is said to have lived in the 1st century BC and to have been the mother of Mary and the wife of Joachim.

BRITTANY St Anne is the patron saint of Brittany, but there this is St David's Day. St Anne's Day is 26th July.

Parents plunge their children into St David's fountain at Landébià, near Plancoët, to give them strength and vigour. Today is an auspicious day to so 40-day turnips.

28th June St Peter's Eve, St Peter's and St Paul's Eve

CELTIC This was also a fire festival like St John's Eve, but, in some places, instead of retaining the ritual content of the latter the occasion became mainly used for merry-making. The fires survived longest in Cornwall and the Sutherland area of Scotland, but all have now ceased.

IRELAND This is the third fire festival of the year, and on St Peter and St Paul's Eve (or Old St John's Day and Little St John's Day) mid-summer fires were lit in the east of Ireland, from Monaghan to Wexford, possibly influenced by Anglo-Norman settlements in south Leinster. These celebrations may once have been like those at St John's Eve fires, but latterly they were purely merry-making.

SCOTLAND As St Peter was patron of fishermen, who lit fires in front of their homes this evening. Their colleagues in the Hebrides always used to put to sea today, whatever the weather, as they felt protected by the saint.

CORNWALL St Peter is the patron saint of fishermen and in fishing villages today the church towers were illuminated and bonfires, tar barrels and fireworks lit. The bonfires were a strong tradition around Mounts Bay in particular. Effigies of disliked characters were borne through the streets and thrown on to the fires. In Wendron and other mining villages around rock-cannons, or 'plugs', were fired.

BRITTANY On the Feast of St Pierre and St Paul some villages whose patron is St Pierre had a bonfire instead of on St Jean's Day, and others had fires on both days. A record from 1912 on Croaz-Houarn in Motreff tells us of the events that used to happen on the Night of the Fires. This hilltop was a pagan site and a calvary was erected there to purify it. A pole was erected and a wreath of flowers put on top by the prettiest maiden. The first gorse sheaf was held aloft on a pitchfork and blessed, then it and others were stacked around the pole. The oldest inhabitant of the Croaz-Houarn clan lit the fire (called Tan-tad) with a pine candle, igniting the blessed faggot first. Mothers held up their babies to be blessed by St Peter. The Fire Song was then sung. When the fire died communal prayers were said, ending as the last spark died. When the fire died they walked three times round the ashes, pausing on each circuit to ask God to pardon the souls of the dead, and to take a stone, mark it with the thumb in the sign of the cross, and place it round the perimeter. The stones served as seats for returning souls, who have the remaining hours of darkness to be their former selves. The ashes were then auctioned, to bidders who had contributed faggots; the highest bidders removed their faggots after dawn. Each unsuccessful bidder was given a compensatory handful, prized for its curative powers, and scraps of burnt wood were taken as talismans. As they returned home they looked up to the sky. Each shooting star was thought to be a redeemed soul going from Purgatory to the Realms of the Blessed.

Last week in June (or first week in July)
SCOTLAND

⬭ Riding of the Marches, Kirkcudbright   Dumfries and Galloway
During the ride, six stakes called stobs are used as boundary markers, and stone and earth collected at each point.
TAKE THE A75 SOUTH-WEST FROM CASTLE DOUGLAS, THEN LEFT ON THE A762.

Last Saturday in June
SCOTLAND

⬭ Ceres Festival and Games, Ceres   Fife
Ceres soldiers played a part in the Scottish victory over the English at the Battle of Bannockburn, fought near Stirling on 24th June 1314. Robert the Bruce granted the town a charter for a market and games in recognition, and they were held on the village green called Bow Butts. Possibly the games are the oldest continuously held in Scotland, and include Highland games and a horse-race, the Ceres Derby.

The walk of the Ceres soldiers back from Bannockburn is sometimes re-enacted on the day.
TAKE THE B939 WEST FROM ST ANDREWS.

Last weekend in June
SCOTLAND

⬭ Galashiels Gathering, Galashiels   Borders
This is a Riding dating from 1930, and led by the Braw Lad and Lass. It commemorates the founding of the burgh in 1599, but there are no common lands. There is a mounted parade held here
GALASHIELS IS ON THE A7 SOUTH-EAST OF EDINBURGH.

Last Sunday in June
BRITTANY

✦ **Pardon de Sainte Barbe (Summer Pardon of St Barbara), Le Faouët**   Morbihan
LE FAOUËT IS ON THE D769.

✴ **Théophile-Malo Corret Festival, Carhaix-Plouguer**   Finistère
The festival, sometimes held on 27th June , includes ends with traditional Breton games including
Bazhig Kamm (French 'crosse') or Breton hockey, Palet or Breton quoits, Sevel ar Berchen or
lifting the pole (tossing the caber in reverse!) and Ar vell or Breton rugby. Also Gouren or Breton
wrestling, played barefoot with hemp shirts, may be seen. The aim is to throw the opponent
down with both shoulders to the ground, and a ram was traditionally awarded to the winner of
a contest.
CARHAIX-PLOUGUER IS ON THE N164.

✦ **Pardon of Saints Peter and Paul ('Procession of the Little Saints')**   Plouguerneau
PLOUGUERNEAU IS ON AN UNCLASSIFIED ROAD NORTH OF LANNILIS.

29th June St Peter's Day, St Peter's and St Paul's Day
SCOTLAND In Loudon, Ayrshire, the Beltane rituals were transferred to this day.
CORNWALL St Peter is the patron saint of Polperro. A Mock Mayor was elected today and wheeled
round in a cart, dressed in tinsel and escorted by his 'constables'. After speeches at each inn,
guaranteeing to increase pay, reduce hours and give every man a beer allowance, he was dumped in
the sea. At Four Lanes, near Wendron, the Mock Mayor was also elected today, and presided over
a Cuckle's Court. Was this originally 'cuckold's' perhaps? 'Victims' were selected, especially
strangers, and tried and sentenced to have their faces blackened.
BRITTANY In Ille-et-Vilaine hiring fairs for servants were held.

30th June
ISLE OF MAN This was the last day of peat digging, by law, in public turbaries.

Right: The Bandsmen's Race, 1950 Left: Putting the ball at Ceres Games, 1950

July
customs

In this month much of June's activity continued. With the hay stored and cherries picked, eyes were on the weather portents for the coming harvest. Oysters were almost ready for gathering, and in Cornwall the pilchards were at their best. But in rural Ireland in past times there was anything but abundance. The month there was known as Hungry July, because landless people had often run out of stores put by during the previous harvest. Their problem got worse during the period from the second half of the 18th century until the mid-19th century when landowners ploughed up as much land as possible for crop-growing, leaving little to rent out to landless labourers. Potatoes were the staple food, but the variety they grew was of poor eating quality in July, leaving them with a monotonous diet of cabbage, oatmeal, and anything they could gather from the wild. Summer potatoes were generally not ready until after Garlick Sunday, the first Sunday in August. A further problem was the shortage of work in the period before the harvest.

Pilgrims and other devotees took advantage of the fine weather to make their journeys, and those whose propensities were more secular continued to enjoy outdoor sport and recreation.

Variable Dates

IRELAND

✚ Pilgrimage to Croagh Patrick
Co. Mayo

This takes place at the end of July and is an ascent to the place where St Patrick was alleged to have banished snakes from Ireland. It marks the end of summer and the beginning of harvest.
CROAGH PATRICK IS SOUTH OF LECHANVY, WHICH IS ON THE R395.

ISLE OF MAN

◉ Peel Longboat Races
Peel

In July, the Viking Longboat Races at Peel replace the now defunct, but much larger, Viking Festival, the date depending on the tides.
PEEL IS ON THE A1 NORTH-WEST OF DOUGLAS.

SCOTLAND In early July, chapmen (merchants who travelled on horseback with their goods in pack saddles), carters and farmers held their summer festivals, including the Chapmen's or Pedlar's Tournaments at which Tilting the Ring was popular.

Tilting the Ring *The rider has a lance, and rides towards a post with cross-beam from which is suspended a ring. The ring is elevated slightly above the rider. He tries to pierce and carry off the ring.*

Carters' (or Whipmen's) Societies were like Friendly Societies, holding an annual procession as well as a festival. Descendants of the Carters' Plays are seen at Irvine and West Linton, and in other burghs with no Ridings. The summer festival at Kelso includes a Whipmen's Ride.

Farmers, in their parades, adorned their hats and clothes with ribbons, flowers and ornaments.

♛ Douglas Day, Castle Douglas   Dumfries and Galloway
This takes place on a Saturday in mid-July.
CASTLE DOUGLAS IS ON THE A75 SOUTH-WEST OF DUMFRIES.

◉ Durness Highland Games, Durness   Highland
DURNESS IS ON THE NORTH COAST ON THE A838.

◉ Inverness Highland Games, Inverness   Highland
INVERNESS IS AT THE JUNCTION OF THE A9, A96 AND A82.

◉ Mull Highland Games, Tobermory, Isle of Mull   Strathclyde
TOBERMORY IS AT THE NORTH END OF THE A848.

❋ Eyemouth Herring Queen Festival, Eyemouth   Border
This takes place on a Saturday in July (normally the 3rd).
TAKE THE A1 NORTH FROM BERWICK-UPON-TWEED, THEN RIGHT ON THE A1107.

❋ Summer Festival, Moffat   Dumfries and Galloway
The festival takes place in mid-July.
TAKE THE A74 NORTH FROM LOCKERBIE, THEN RIGHT ON THE A701.

Right: Tossing the caber, Left: Throwing the iron ball, both part of The Scottish Highland Games

🎡 **Highland Games, Fort William**   Highland

These games include the 13-mile foot-race up and down Ben Nevis (4,406 ft high). They take place in mid-July or in August.

FORT WILLIAM IS ON THE A82, BY LOCH LINNHE.

WALES

🎡 **The International Eisteddfod, Llangollen**   Denbighshire

This takes place in early July. It is a distinct festival from the National Eisteddfod, which is held in a different town each year.

LLANGOLLEN IS ON THE A5 NORTH-WEST OF OSWESTRY.

CORNWALL A carnival and games was held on Halgaver Moor, near Bodmin. A Lord of Misrule presided over a mock court, making trumped-up charges and giving equally ridiculous and often humiliating punishments.

BRITTANY

✳ **The Nantes Fête, Nantes**   Loire-Atlantique

This is an arts festival, with a carnival, and takes place in early July.

NANTES IS ON THE N137 DUE SOUTH OF RENNES.

✳ **Fêtes du Bocage, in 30 villages around Vitré**   Ille-et-Vilaine

Street theatre, story-telling and folk-tales, and workshops, taking place in early July.

VITRÉ IS ON THE D178 SOUTH OF FOUGÈRES.

✳ **Fête du Livre Vivant, Fougères**   Ille-et-Vilaine

This festival includes drama, pageants and a floodlit spectacle.

FOUGÈRES IS ON THE N12 NORTH-EAST OF RENNES.

✳ **Festival of the Crêpe, Gourin**   Morbihan

This is a two-day festival with music, dance, folk art, displays of everyday life in the past in the Black Mountains, and pancakes cooked on a wood fire.

TAKE THE D769 NORTH-WEST FROM LE FAOUËT, THEN LEFT ON THE D1.

In Upper Brittany a pancake is called a galette and is made with buckwheat flour. A staple food of the early Bretons, **Galettes** *(see p.200 for recipe)* are made simply from buckwheat, salt and water. They were eaten spread with butter or jam, or cut into strips and soaked in fresh or soured milk. Later a variety of fillings was made, and a mix of buckwheat and plain flour or all plain flour used.

Crêpes *(see p.201 for recipe)* – the word for a pancake in Lower Brittany and the rest of France – is sweet and made with wheat flour (ordinary plain flour) or a mix of buckwheat and plain flour with the former a minor constituent. A 50/50 mixture is easier for beginners to prepare and cook. Traditionally it was spread on the griddle with a rozell, and turned with a spanell, both wooden implements.

✿ Fêtes du Clos-Poulet, St Malo
Ille-et-Vilaine

ST MALO IS ON THE NORTH COAST AT THE END OF THE N137.

✿ Festival of Kann Al Loar, Landerneau
Finistère

This is a week-long celebration of living Breton culture. There are workshops on puppetry, pottery, painting on slate, and sailors' crafts such as tying knots and building a ship in a bottle, seafood to eat and sea-shanties to sing. On the River Elorn is a procession of 30 old sailing boats.

LANDERNEAU IS JUST TO THE EAST OF THE D770, EAST OF BREST.

✿ Thursdays on the Port
Brest, Finistère

This takes place each Thursday in July and August. There is a variety of entertainments from both Breton and international artists.

BREST IS AT THE END OF THE N12, ON THE COAST.

✿ Fête des Remparts, Dinan
Côtes d'Armor

This lasts a weekend and takes place in mid-July, or at the end of (or early in) September every two years. It has a medieval theme, with jousting, feasting, a medieval market, a medieval army in encampment, jesters and other costumed characters, knights, soldiers, serfs and strolling players. There are similar events in Vannes and Moncontour.

DINAN IS ON THE N176, SOUTH OF ST MALO.

✿ The Festival of the Abbey, Redon
Ille-et-Vilaine

Events feature theatre, music and dance. It takes place mid-July to mid-August.

REDON IS ON THE D775, EAST OF VANNES.

✿ Festival du Musique Sacrée (Festival of Sacred Music), St Malo
Ille-et-Vilaine

This takes place mid-July to mid-August.

ST MALO IS ON THE NORTH COAST AT THE END OF THE N137.

✿ Assemblées Gallèses, Concoret
Morbihan

This takes place in the second half of July.

CONCORET IS ON AN UNCLASSIFIED ROAD SOUTH-EAST OF MAURON.

✚ Procession of Notre-Dame du Mene-Guen, Guenin
Morbihan

This takes place at the end of July.

GUENIN IS ON AN UNCLASSIFIED ROAD NORTH-EAST OF BAUD.

✚ Pardon de Sainte Anne, St Quay-Portrieux
Côtes d'Armor

This takes place at the end of July.

ST QUAY-PORTRIEUX IS ON THE COAST, ON AN UNCLASSIFIED ROAD NORTH OF ÉTABLES-SUR-MER.

✚ Pardon de Loïc, Sizun
Finistère

This takes place at the end of July.

SIZUN IS ON THE D18 NORTH OF LE FAOU.

✠ **Pardon de la Sainte-Anne-de-la-Bosserie**   Romagné
  This takes place at the end of July.

❀ **Summer Festival, St Brieuc**   Côtes d'Armor
  This takes place in July and August.
  ST BRIEUC IS ON THE NORTH COAST, ON THE N12.

❀ **Les Mercredis de Morlaix (The Wednesday Fêtes), Morlaix**   Finistère
  This takes place in July and August.
  MORLAIX IS ON THE N12.

✋ **Festival International de Folklore, Concarneau**   Finistère
  This takes place in late July and early August and features Breton and other Celtic music and folk
  costumes.
  CONCARNEAU IS ON THE D783, ON THE SOUTH COAST, SOUTH OF THE N165.

Fixed Dates

1st July St Serf's Day
  CELTIC St Serf was a Scottish saint, one of whose pupils was St Mungo or Kentigern.
  SCOTLAND At Culross, Fife, the local burgesses used to stage a parade in honour of St Serf. Eleven
  green branches were carried. The parade ceased in the 1860s.
  BRITTANY This is St Lunaire's Day, and when sailors passed Décollé, a dangerous point that lies
  between Saint-Lunaire and Saint-Briac, they would invoke the saint and asked him to save them
  from otherwise certain shipwreck. In the market town of Saint-Lunaire the fountain was a place
  of pilgrimage for those seeking cures for eye complaints. Similarly at Saint-Lormel, near Plancoët,
  a well under the pulpit in the church was visited and the eyes washed with its water. He is similarly
  invoked at Quiou in the district of Evran. Some people believe that this association between
  the saint and eyesight comes from the similarity between Lunaire and the French word for an
  eyeglass – lunette.

First Sunday in July
  BRITTANY

✠ **Pardon of Notre-Dame de Bon-Secours, Guingamp**   Côtes-d'Armor
  This lasts for three days, with elements of the celebration taking place on the previous Friday and
  Saturday. It is sometimes held on 2nd July.
  GUINGAMP IS ON THE N12, WEST OF ST BRIEUC.

❀ **Brittany Children's Festival, Guingamp**   Côtes-d'Armor
  There is a parade in national costumes, Breton wrestling and workshops in cookery and dance.
  GUINGAMP IS ON THE N12, WEST OF ST BRIEUC.

First Monday of July (or the Monday of the first full week in July)
  SCOTLAND

♟ **Reivers Week, Duns**   Border
  Today is the start of a week of Ridings and other festivities. Rides are held all week, led by the
  Reiver carrying the burgh flag, and his Lass. On Tuesday evening on Duns Law there is a service
  commemorating the gathering of the Covenanting Army of General Leslie in 1639.
  TAKE THE A6105 WEST FROM BERWICK-UPON-TWEED.

First Tuesday in July
  SCOTLAND The Farmers' Parade at Kilwinnoch, Renfrewshire, was held today.

First Friday in July
CORNWALL

🍺 **Bodmin Ale-tasting** Bodmin

As a prelude to Heritage Day in the town, ale-tasters visit local houses to invite the residents to taste a locally made ale (made the previous October) and make a donation towards the festivities.
BODMIN IS WEST OF LISKEARD AT THE JUNCTION OF THE A30 AND A38.

First Saturday in July
SCOTLAND

✷ **St Monan's Sea Queen Festival, St Monan's** Fife

TAKE THE A917 SOUTH-EAST FROM ST ANDREWS ALONG THE COAST TO ST MONAN'S.

☻ **Annan Ridings, Annan, near Gretna Green** Dumfries and Galloway

TAKE THE A75 WEST FROM GRETNA GREEN.

✷ **Children's Gala Day, Linlithgow** Lothian

LINLITHGOW IS TO THE SOUTH OF JUNCTION THREE OF THE M9.

✷ **The Galloway Pageant, Newton-Stewart** Dumfries and Galloway

This area was used by Sir Walter Scott as the setting for his novel 'Guy Mannering', and in commemoration of this the pageant was established in 1932.
NEWTON-STEWART IS ON THE A75 BETWEEN CASTLE DOUGLAS AND STRANRAER.

CORNWALL

🍺 **Bodmin's Heritage Day** Bodmin

The highlight of Heritage Day is the Bodmin Ride, when riders carry garlanded poles through the town. This originated as an annual tribute to the monks of St Benet's Priory, Lanivet.

First week in July
BRITTANY

🖐 **Les Tombées de la Nuit – Création Bretonne, Rennes** Ille-et-Vilaine

This is a series of night-time concerts and tableaux, first held in 1980, to celebrate Breton culture.
RENNES IS ON THE N137 BETWEEN ST MALO AND NANTES.

4th July Old Midsummer Eve, St Martin o' Ballymus' Day, Bullion Day

CELTIC St Martin o' Ballymus was a Scottish saint, perhaps a counterpart of St Swithin, as similar weather lore appertains. Ballymus is a Shetland corruption of Bullion-Mass, 'bullion' being a corruption of the Old French 'bouillant', meaning 'boiling hot' – what they hope the weather will be.
ISLE OF MAN Rituals were as on Midsummer Eve. The height of the next harvest was determined by how high men could jump over the flames.

People sat up all night to watch, some in church porches in order to see the souls of those who would die that year – as on St Mark's Eve and Hollantide Eve.

5th July Old Midsummer Day, St Morwenne's Day

CELTIC St Morwenne (Morwenna) was a 7th-century Irish saint, daughter of Christian King Brychan of Brecknock, who travelled through North Wales and became a hermit in Burton-upon-Trent, Staffordshire. Childless couples sacrificed a pig to her. She is said to have founded churches at Morwenstow, near Bude, Cornwall, and the church at Marhamchurch, also near Bude.
ISLE OF MAN Cheese-making was done on Old St John's Day for Harvest Home and rain wished for. Bonfires were lit on hills and blazing cartwheels rolled down, to typify the sun's decline.

Tynwald (Isle of Man Parliament) Ceremony, Tynwald Hill, St John's

Isle of Man

This takes place on 5th July or, if that is a Saturday or Sunday, on the following Monday. Dating back to Viking times, the Tynwald preserves the Old Norse custom of publicly announcing all new laws, in both Manx and English. Unfortunately Manx passed away as a vernacular language with the death of the last native speaker Ned Maddrell in 1962. The promulgation of new laws in Manx and English is necessary before they can be enforced. In the distant past the Tyn (from the Old Norse 'Thing' meaning public assembly) was also the place to settle disputes, so it was both parliament and court. One reason to hold it on this day was that all evil influences had been driven out the previous evening.

Tynwald Fair is also held today, which was a public holiday. If the 5th July is a Sunday, then both are held the next day. Tynwald Hill is between Douglas and Peel, but in former times there were assemblies for the North and South regions of the island. Tynwald Hill for the South was at Keeil Abban (now St Luke's Chapel), and that for the North was at Reneurling (now Cronk Urley or Urleigh).

The Tynwald is the last of a four-stage process of law creation. First, the laws are decided by the legislature in Douglas, formerly at Castle Rushen, Castletown. This body is called the Keys (from Old Norse 'kuid' meaning jury) and its members are chosen by popular vote. Second, the laws go to the Council for further scrutiny, and, third, to the monarch for ratification. Only then are they promulgated next Midsummer Day.

TAKE THE A1 WEST FROM DOUGLAS.

On the green at St John's the Tynwald Fair, following the Norwegian custom of holding a fair when their Parliament (Thing) was in session, has stalls, shies, bands, dancers and other entertainments. A speciality sold is home-made **Tynwald Fudge** *(see p.201 for recipe).*

6th July

SCOTLAND This is the traditional date of the lapsed Glasgow Fair, held since 1197 on this date or on the octave of St Peter and St Paul.

7th July St Thomas à Becket's Day

CORNWALL The once widespread remembrance of St Thomas à Becket was proscribed in 1538.

First Monday and Tuesday after 7th July

CORNWALL The Bodmin Riding was held on these two days, instituted in honour of Thomas-à-Beckett, until the early 19th century. Elected 'wardens' went with the Town Crier and a fife-and-drum band to householders to greet them and offer a specially brewed ale. The Town Crier saluted each house and invited them to come out and taste the beer. This was made the previous October, and if the householder liked it they paid for it. The band played 'The Riding Tune'. Next morning all went in procession to the Priory, St Benet's Abbey, some mounted on horse or ass with whips, and two large garlanded poles were collected. These were taken to the sports field and placed on the edge. The Riding Games were held there, with wrestling, foot-racing, jumping in sacks, cudgel-playing, bell-ringing, gurning (face-pulling through a horse-collar), and other events. The proceedings ended with a servants' ball. There was also a minor merry-making with this special brew at Whitsuntide.

A similar event was once held at Liskeard.

8th July

SCOTLAND The Riding of the Marches was held in Arbroath today (on the Old Calendar) in 1734, the day after St Thomas's Market.

9th July Old St Peter's Eve

CORNWALL St Peter is the patron saint of Polperro, and his church is on the seaward hill. His festival was held on 10th July (Old Calendar) with feast and fair. Today, on the eve, a bonfire was lit, and fishermen went from house to house begging for money or food for the festival. At night a pile of faggots and tar barrels was built on the beach, lit and danced round. When the flames were low the fishermen jumped through them.

10th July Old St Peter's Day

CORNWALL At St Peter's Fair, Polperro, which was held over three days, the 'standings' (stalls) with 'fairings' were on Lansallos Street. There were strolling Thespians, ballad-singers, gamesters drawing youngsters into weighted games of 'chance', penny-peep shows, jugglers and tumblers. Fiddlers charged twopence a reel. On the second day there was wrestling and a boat race. On the third day a Mock Mayor was chosen and paraded through the town in a cart decorated with green boughs. He made a speech full of extravagant promises, then was wheeled into the tide!

Friday before the second Saturday in July
SCOTLAND

✸ **Jethart Callant's Festival and Border Games, Jedburgh**　　　　　Border

On the Friday afternoon before the festival is a ride-out to Redeswire, commemorating the spot where Jedburgh callants helped the villagers defeat an English raiding party in 1575, the last time in Scotland that bows and arrows were used in combat. A mounted cavalcade also goes to the 16th-century Ferniehirst Castle, to the south of Jedburgh, for a ceremony at the Capon Tree. This area was once the ancient Jed Forest and this tree is a survivor. The castle is known for its spiral staircase, built the 'wrong way round' so that it can be defended by left-handed swordsmen.

The day after the festival,is the Border Games, founded in 1853. A cannon is fired at the Mercat Cross to start the Race Round the Town, which opens the proceedings, the games proper being held in the Riverside Park.

TAKE THE A698 NORTH-EAST FROM HAWICK, THEN RIGHT ON THE A68.

Second Saturday in July
SCOTLAND

◐ **Highland Games, Tomintoul**　　　　　Grampian

Tomintoul claims to be the highest village in Britain.

TOMINTOUL IS ON THE A939.

Second weekend in July

BRITTANY

Folklore Festival of the Ajoncs d'Or (Golden Gorse), Lamballe — Côtes-d'Armor

LAMBALLE IS ON THE N12 EAST OF ST BRIEUC.

Fête des Brodeuses (Embroiderer's Festival), Pont L'Abbé — Finistère

This sometimes takes place on 9th July.

PONT L'ABBÉ IS SOUTH-WEST OF QUIMPER, JUST OFF THE D785.

International Summer Festival — Nantes

NANTES IS ON THE N137 DUE SOUTH OF RENNES.

Musiques Mosaïques Festival — Quimperlé

QUIMPERLÉ IS JUST TO THE NORTH OF THE N165 BETWEEN QUIMPER AND LORIENT.

Journées Médiévales (History Festival), Vannes — Morbihan

VANNES IS ON THE N165.

Second Sunday in July

BRITTANY

Petite Troménie (annually), Locronan — Finistère

This annual pardon, sometimes held on 10th July, is a 7½ mile (12 kilometre) procession following the route to St Ronan's hermitage. Locronan is a centre for the weaving sailcloth, and St Ronan, the Irish saint, is said to have invented weaving. He lived here in the 5th century. The event is also known as the Fête des Collines Bleues.

LOCRONAN IS ON AN UNCLASSIFIED ROAD EAST OF DOUARNENEZ.

Grande Troménie, Locronan — Finistère

This is held every six years. The next will be on the second and third Sundays in July 2001.

12th July

IRELAND On this day in Ulster Orange Men march in commemoration of the Battle of the Boyne in 1690, when William of Orange defeated the ousted Catholic King of England James II. The Orange Order was founded in 1795 to symbolise the nationalist cause of the Protestants, who adopted William as their honorary emblem. This day has become a sectarian and political occasion rather than a folk custom. among Protestants.

Petite Troménie, Locronan, Finistère, Brittany

✿ **Scarva Parade, Scarva, near Portadown** Co. Down

This parade is a prelude to tomorrow's Sham Fight; see below for details.

TAKE THE A51 EAST FROM ARMAGH, THROUGH TANDRAGEE.

SCOTLAND Orangemen commemorate the Battle of the Boyne. See Ireland for details.

13th July
IRELAND

✿ **Sham Fight, Scarva, near Portadown** Co. Down

Scarva was the site of William's camp before the Battle of the Boyne. On this day or the next, there is a symbolic re-enactment by Orangemen of the battle, in the form of a combat between two horsemen, one dressed as William of Orange and the other as James II, and William of Orange is always the victor.

ISLE OF MAN This is St German's Day. He was a former, some say the first, Bishop of Man, in AD 447. Tynwald Hill is in the parish of St German.

14th July
BRITTANY Today is Bastille Day, a public holiday marked by firework displays. It is also St Bonaventure's Day, when weavers took a holiday and had their festival. Bonfires were lit in the 19th century in Upper Brittany, or on the nearest Sunday to the Fête de la République.

15th July St Swithin's Day
CELTIC By tradition, whatever the weather is on this day, it will last for 40 days. St Swithin, Bishop of Winchester, died in AD 862. On 15 July AD 971 his remains were removed to a shrine in the Cathedral. A torrential thunderstorm broke and lasted for 40 days. It was said that he was weeping at the moving of his bones. So began the legend, which went from England to the Celtic lands.

Sunday evening before the 16th July
CORNWALL Taking Day at Crowan, West Cornwall. Young people went to a church service, then to Clowance Park where villagers from Leeds-town, Carnhell-green, Nancegollan, Blackrock and Praze gathered. Young men chose a partner for the forthcoming fair from among the women.

16th July

ISLE OF MAN By a law passed in 1610, herring fishing began today. Later on it started much earlier.

CORNWALL Praze-an-beeble Fair was held today.

17th July
BRITTANY

⚙ Fête des Pommiers (Festival of the Cider Makers), Fouesnant   Finistère
FOUESNANT IS ON THE D44 WEST OF CONCARNEAU.

Weekend nearest 17th July
SCOTLAND

⚙ Aikey Brae Fair, Old Deer   Grampian
Curiously, in a formerly strongly religious area, this used to be a Sunday fair. It is said to have originated when a wandering packman dropped his goods in a burn (stream) one Sunday in mid-July, and spread the retrieved items on a bank to dry. People returning from church asked if they could buy them, and the salesman was so pleae with the trade that he came back each year at that time, starting a new tradition.
TAKE THE A950 WEST FROM PETERHEAD, THEN LEFT ON THE B9030.

Third week in July
SCOTLAND

⚙ Festival of the Herring Queen, Wick   Highland
The original gala lapsed in 1953, but the town holds a Gala Week, and crowns the Gala Queen.
WICK IS AT THE NORTHERN END OF THE A9.

A week in mid-July (usually the third)
SCOTLAND

⚙ Yetholm Ride and Civic Week, Kelso   Border
Since 1937 Kelso has held a summer festival which has included a ride through Yetholm and Kirk Yetholm, the latter being the traditional site of the largest gypsy camp in Scotland.
KELSO IS ON THE A698 SOUTH-WEST OF COLDSTREAM.

Friday and Saturday of the third week in July
SCOTLAND

⚙ Cleiking the Devil and St Ronan Games, Innerleithen, near Peebles   Border
These Games were started in the early 19th century. James Hogg, the poet and 'Ettrick Shepherd' were the first captains. The inaugural events were foot-racing, leaping, archery, heaving the stone, throwing the hammer, and wrestling. It starts with a ride to the town's saline well, St Ronan's Well, to drink its waters, famous for their curative properties towards eye and skin complaints. On the Friday evening Cleiking the Devil, or the Cleikum Ceremony, is staged, re-enacting the alleged fight between St Ronan and the Devil over possession of the well. Later the Devil, having been cleiked (hooked) by St Ronan's crozier, is ceremonially torched on a bonfire on Caerlee Hill.
INNERLEITHEN IS ON THE A72 EAST OF PEEBLES.

Third weekend in July
BRITTANY

⚙ Salon du Livre Maritime (Maritime Book Festival), Concarneau   Finistère
CONCARNEAU IS ON THE D783 SOUTH-EAST OF QUIMPER.

Third Sunday in July
BRITTANY

✴ Fêtes des Terre-Neuves et des Islandais, Paimpol — Côtes d'Armor
This celebrates the fishing links with Newfoundland and Iceland.
PAIMPOL IS ON THE NORTHERN END OF THE D7.

✚ Pardon de la Saint-Carantec, Carantec — Finistère
This starts at 10 am, with a Breton Mass at 11.15 am.
CARANTEC IS ON AN UNCLASSIFIED ROAD NORTH OF THE D58, NORTH-WEST OF MORLAIX.

✚ Pardon de la Sainte-Anne and Festival de Musique Celtique, Le Relecq-Kerhoun — Finistère
A Breton Mass is held at 11.30 am, and the Festival of Celtic Music starts at 14.30.
LE RELECQ-KERHOUN IS JUST EAST OF BREST.

✚ Petit et Grand Pardon de Sainte-Anne and the Fête des Pommiers, Fouesnant — Finistère
This is cider country and the festival is dedicated to the apple trees. It is sometimes held on the Sunday after St Anne's Day.
FOUESNANT IS ON THE D44 WEST OF CONCARNEAU.

✴ Fête des Mouettes (Festival of Seagulls), Douarnenez — Finistère
DOUARNENEZ IS ON THE D765 NORTH-WEST OF QUIMPER.

20th July St Margaret's Day
BRITTANY St Marguerite is invoked by women in labour, and by mothers whose children have difficulty sleeping. She also protects children from snakebites.

Third Saturday in July
SCOTLAND

✴ The Honest Town's Festival, Musselburgh — Lothian
Dating from 1936, Friday's preparations include the kirking of the Honest Lad and Honest Lass. The term 'Honest Town' was coined by the nephew of Randolph, Earl of Moray and Regent of Scotland after Moray fell ill here in 1332 – the townsfolk who nursed him refused to accept payment.
MUSSELBURGH IS ON THE A199 EAST OUT OF EDINBURGH.

22nd July St Mary Magdelene's Day
BRITTANY This was St Madeleine's Day. Hay cut after this date will blacken and the horses dislike it. Farmers say that if a horse eats hay cut after today its dung will sink in water rather than float.

23rd July
BRITTANY

✚ Pilgrimage to the Chapel of the Seven Saints, Le Vieux-Marché — Côtes-d'Armor
The saints referred to are the seven founding saints of Brittany.
LE VIEUX-MARCHÉ IS ON AN UNCLASSIFIED ROAD EAST OF PLOUARET.

25th July St James' Day, Grotto Day
CELTIC St James is buried at Santiago de Compostella in Spain, and pilgrims used to carry scallop shells as drinking vessels on their journey. Shell grottoes have been built in his honour, on 5th August which is Old St James' Day.

Oysters are traditionally eaten today: it is said that those who do so will not want for money during the year. It marks the beginning of the oyster season.

John Knill's Charity procession, Worvas Hill, St Ives, Cornwall

SCOTLAND

 St James' Day Fair, Kelso   Border

Traditionally this fair attracted many gypsies, and they still come and camp in the grounds to assert their ancient right to be present.

KELSO IS ON THE A698 SOUTH-WEST OF COLDSTREAM.

WALES Scallop shells (*Cragen Iago*) were used as cake tins in Aberffraw, Anglesey, to cook cakes known as **Teisen 'Berffro** *(see p.201 for recipe).*

CORNWALL

25th July, John Knill's Charity   Cornwall
(Dancing round John Knill's Needle), Worvas Hill, St Ives

This is held every five years (due 2001, etc). It was formerly called the Knillian-games. A pyramid on Worvas Hill near St Ives was erected in 1782 by John Knill, who was a Collector of Customs, then a resident at Gray's Inn, London, until his death in 1811. It is called Knill's Mausoleum, although he is, in fact, buried in St Andrew's Church, Holborn, London. Mr Knill left a detailed bequest with money for the needy and to ensure his memory was properly and festively commemorated on St James' Day by dancing, singing and competitions to find the most worthy wives of working men and to find the most skillful exponents of sea and fishing crafts.

At 10.30 a procession from the Guildhall to the Mausoleum of ten daughters in white (whose function today is to dance) of local fishermen and tin workers, led by a fiddler, begins the proceedings.

TAKE THE A3074 NORTH FROM LELANT OR THE B3311 NORTH FROM PENZANCE.

26th July St Anne and St Joachim's Day

CELTIC Anne and Joachim are said to be Mary's parents. Anne seems to be synonymous with the ancient Earth Mother Anu, and this saint may be a Christian invention to help eliminate the memory of the pagan worship of Anu. Among wells dedicated to her are those at Llanfihangel, South Glamorgan, and at Trellech, Gwent, the latter a wishing well.

BRITTANY St Anne, the patroness of Brittany, was much venerated, and pilgrims went in procession to her fountain near Gevezé, Ille-et-Vilaine, to immerse themselves at the foot of the cross. Formerly the same happened at Saint-Martin's fountain near Niort, and at the fountain of Saint-Grès-en-Champ-Saint-Père at Vendée, near to which had been raised a menhir long ago. It was recorded in 1870 that at Euré-et-Loir a procession plunged the cross into the fountain of Champrond. At Pommeret there was a procession of unmarried girls and women who appealed to St Anne to tell them if they would find a husband. Widows would join the procession and selflessly say that they had had their share. On St Anne's Day turnips were traditionally planted. If bees swarm today their hive is considered to be the hive of the king, and if they swarm on a day dedicated to the Virgin Mary their hive is of the queen.

✠ Pardon de Sainte Anne, Sainte Anne D'Auray   Morbihan

This is a very large two-day pardon, in honour of the patron saint of Brittany, with elements of the celebration on 25th July.

AURAY IS ON THE N165 WEST OF VANNES.

Last week in July (or 18th to 24th July, or the week before the fourth Sunday in July)
BRITTANY

🖐 Goueliou Kerne (Fêtes de Cornouaille), Kemper (Quimper)   Finistère

This is the largest folk festival in Brittany. Events continue for some 80 days. Many women will be in their giz or folkdress, usually black and ornamented with bands of velvet. They wear coifs (lace headdresses), aprons (satin or velvet, brocaded, embroidered or edged with lace) and embroidered chupens (velvet waistcoats), characteristic of their home village or region. Men may wear knee-breeches, or wide breeches called bragou braz, embroidered waistcoats and felt, beribboned hats. Wooden sabots are worn on the feet. There are solo singers and musicians, folk groups, choirs, plays in Breton, dancing, and a variety of street entertainment.

Breton instruments seen may include the two types of Breton bagpipe, the Biniou Coz and Biniou Braz, the Bombarde, the Telenn or Celtic Harp, the Batterie or drum, the Bouëze or accordion, the fiddle, and the hurdy-gurdy. The latter three are more likely to be played by Bretons from Haute Bretagne where there is more French influence on the music. The Biniou Braz is used in Pipe Bands (Bagadou), the Biniou Coz often playing duets with the Bombarde. Listening to duets of sacred music played on a church organ and a bombarde in local churches is a moving experence.

Traditional Breton dances to be seen are the Breton Gavotte (not the classical Gavotte) from Haut-Cornuaille and Pontivy, the Lariden from Vannes, the Plinn from Carhaix and the Fisel from Carhaix. Kan ha diskan (song and descant) is nasal singing, an accompaniment to dancing in which two singers alternate lines. The overlap at the end of each verse gives the impression of continuity. The fast, heavily stressed rhythm gives the beat for the gavotte.

The main stadium is in the Place de la Résistance. The morning's Grand Procession is a clockwise tour round Brittany, with music and costumes from Quimper, Brest, St Malo, Rennes, Nantes, Vannes, Lorient and back to Quimper. Bands led by flag-carriers and dancers alternate

Pardon of St Anne D'Auray, Morbihan, Brittany

through the stadium, with people carrying symbols of local crafts and industry. In the afternoon is the Abadenn Veur (Great Assembly). This starts with the presentation of the Reine de Cornouaille (Queen of Cornouaille), then a display of Breton dancing, ending with the Danse des Mille (Dance of a Thousand) in which all join hands and snake around the platform. In the evening at the Soirée de Lauréats the winners of events are presented, in the presence of the Reine de Cornouaille. After this it is non-stop festivities in the town as the Fest-Noz (Night Festival) begins.
QUIMPER IS ON THE N165 BETWEEN BREST AND LORIENT.

Last Saturday in July
SCOTLAND

⊕ **The Riding of the Marches, Wigtown**　　　　　　　　　　Dumfries and Galloway
WIGTOWN IS ON THE A714 SOUTH OF NEWTON-STEWART.

Last Sunday in July
SCOTLAND

⊕ **The Blanket Preaching, St Mary's Kirk of the Lowes,
Yarrow Valley, Yarrow, near Selkirk**　　　　　　　　　　　　　Border
This is an open-air service in commemoration of the Presbyterian covenanting preachers who were barred from churches in the time of Charles I and forced to hold services outside. Parishioners huddle together under blankets as in the days of 17th-century services held by the Covenanters.
YARROW IS ON THE A708 WEST OF SELKIRK.

BRITTANY

⊕ **Pardon, Île de Batz**　　　　　　　　　　　　　　　　　　　Finistère
THE ISLAND LIES OFF THE COAST AT ROSCOFF, WHICH IS AT THE NORTH END OF THE D58.

⊕ **Pardon, Le Folgoët**　　　　　　　　　　　　　　　　　　　Finistère
This pardon is in honour of St Christopher and includes the blessing of motor cars.
LE FOLGOËT IS ON THE D788 SOUTH OF LESNEVEN.

⊕ **Pardon of Ste Anne, Le Relecq**　　　　　　　　　　　　　　Finistère
There is a Breton Mass at 11.00 am and a Festival of Celtic Music at 15.30.
LE RELECQ IS ON AN UNCLASSIFIED ROAD OFF THE D769, SOUTH OF MORLAIX.

Last Friday in July
IRELAND The Friday before Lammas was regarded as one of the most beneficial days to visit the Struell Wells, near Downpatrick, Co. Down, for cures. It is said that St Patrick blessed the four wells – a Drinking Well, an Eye Well, and two bath houses, one for males and one for females.
SCOTLAND The Gilmerton Play was staged. It started as a Carters' Play on 6th May, but was moved to this date after World War I. There was a mounted costumed parade, horse races, and a dinner and barn dance in the evening. This lasted until 1935. From 1920 until 1938 there was a Children's Day, including the crowning of a Summer Queen.

⊕ **Langholm Riding, Langholm**　　　　　　　　　　　　　　Dumfries and Galloway
LANGHOLM IS ON THE A7 SOUTH-WEST OF HAWICK.

Last weekend in July
BRITTANY

⊕ **Pardon de la Sainte-Hélène, Bubry**　　　　　　　　　　　　Morbihan
BUBRY IS ON AN UNCLASSIFIED ROAD SOUTH WEST OF PONTIVY.

Last Saturday in July (or the first Saturday in August)
SCOTLAND

♛ The Common Riding, Lauder
Border
TAKE THE A68 NORTH FROM JEDBURGH.

Last Saturday in July
SCOTLAND

🐟 World Flounder Tramping Championships, Solway Firth mud-flats,
near Palnackie, south of Dalbeattie
Dumfries and Galloway
There is an old technique for catching flouder by treading gingerly in bare feet through the mud until you feel a flounder lying on the river bed. Reaching down quickly you pull it out of the water. Another old technique was to spear them with a leister, but this technique is not allowed in the championship. There is a prize for the heaviest catch. The championship started in 1972.
TAKE THE A711 SOUTH-WEST FROM DALBEATTIE.

WALES

🌟 St Margaret's Fair, Tenby
Dyfed
At noon the Mayor leads a procession around the walls of the town, and then the fair opens. This fair was traditionally held on 31st July.
TAKE THE A477 EAST FROM PEMBROKE, THEN RIGHT AT KILGETTY ON THE A478.

Last Sunday in July
IRELAND This is called Lammas (or Garland, Height, Bilberry) Sunday, and old Lammas celebrations were moved here. It was a first-fruits festival at the beginning of the harvest, and flower and fruit offerings were made at wells. Butter was thrown into streams and loughs, and cattle driven through for their good health in the year ahead.

Garland Sunday refers to unmarried girls taking garlanded hoops to church, then to the graveyard to dance around them to honour the dead. Homage to the dead is another aspect of Lammas.

Height Sunday and Bilberry Sunday refer to the celebratory gatherings on hilltops, where bilberries were collected in rush baskets. Until recently people assembled on Slieve Croob, Co. Down, though they still collect bilberries. .

✠ Pilgrimage up Croagh Patrick, Clew Bay
Co. Mayo
This hill overlooking the southern shore of Clew Bay is said to be the site of St Patrick's fast for 40 days and nights. Services are held at the summit, though the harvest celebrations are now a thing of the past.
CROAGH PATRICK IS SOUTH OF LECHANVY, WHICH IS ON THE R395.

29th July St Olaf's Day
CELTIC St Olaf was a Christian King of Norway, who lived from AD 995–1030. He was venerated particularly in the areas of Britain formerly settled by Norwegians, such as Orkney, Shetland, and down the east coast to East Anglia. St Olaf's Well at Cruden Bay, Grampian, was visited by fisherfolk for healing and good luck.

31st July St Neot's Day, Lammas Eve
CELTIC Little is known for certain about the life of St Neot, who gave his name to the village in Cornwall.
ISLE OF MAN This is Maughold's Feast Day of Summer, his first feast day, the other being on 26th November (or 15th). Maughold, or Machutus, has many legends attached to him. He is said to have been a former Bishop of Man, but his existence cannot be proved. There may have once been a St Maughold's Fair at Ramsey today.
SCOTLAND Saining rites, as on Beltane, were carried out.

August
customs

This month opens with the Celtic Harvest Festival of Lughnasa, or Lammas, and the harvest and sheep fairs were two important events for the Celtic farmer. The fairs allowed a welcome break for recreation. Sadly, mechanisation has caused most of the harvest rituals to be abandoned, and made harvest a relatively speedy affair, but this month used to be one of tiring, back-breaking work. If this month was fine in Brittany then the approaching winter would be good one. Children born there this month are quarrelsome and pedantic, and if a couple marry in August their children will be lazy. There was pressure on young couples not to marry this month unless the harvest was finished, as they would be needed by their parents as workers.

Variable Dates

SCOTLAND August is the month when those seeking the curative waters of St Fillan's Well, west of Crieff, Tayside, pay it a visit. According to custom the well used to be on the hill near the rock formation known as St Fillan's Chair, whose power is said to cure rheumatism. On its present site, the well-water is only effect if the supplicant walks, or is carried, three times round it, then drinks it and bathes in it. Then a rag or pebble is placed on St Fillan's Chair and the sufferer must be pulled down the hill feet first.

Quoits *Quoits are circular metal rings or horseshoes and they are cast at a peg (or hob), of which there are two, 18 yards apart, in clay. The quoit is cast so as to land either pierced by the hob or as near as possible to it. A narrow angle of flight enables it to embed in the clay. Players have two quoits, and score one point for the one nearest the hob (two points if both are nearer than the opponents' two) and three points for a quoit around the hob.*

⚫ Red Hose Race, Carnwath   Strathclyde
This is the oldest foot-race in Scotland, dating from before 1500, now a 1-mile event at the Agricultural Show. The stockings awarded today are a pair of red locally knitted woollen stockings, not blue as originally. In the past there were other events such as leaping, putting the stone, throwing the hammer, quoits, and tilting the ring, the final one being a steeplechase on foot.
TAKE THE A721 SOUTH-EAST FROM CARLUKE.

🌀 Highland Games, Portree, Isle of Skye   Highland
PORTREE IS ON THE A850.

🌀 Highland Games, Isle of Arran   Strathclyde

🌀 Highland Games, Perth   Tayside
PERTH IS ON THE A90 WEST OF DUNDEE.

🌀 Highland Games, Crieff   Tayside
CRIEFF IS ON THE A85 WEST OF PERTH.

🌀 Highland Games, Kinloch Rannoch   Tayside
KINLOCH RANNOCH IS ON THE B846, BY LOCH RANNOCH.

🌀 Highland Games, Nairn   Highland
NAIRN IS ON THE A96 BETWEEN ELGIN AND INVERNESS.

🌀 Highland Games, Luss   Strathclyde
LUSS IS ON THE A82, ON THE WEST SHORE OF LOCH LOMOND.

🌀 Highland Gathering, Glenfinnan   Highland
GLENFINNAN IS ON THE A830 WEST OF FORT WILLIAM.

🌀 Birnam Highland Games, Dunkeld   Tayside
DUNKELD IS ON THE A923 WEST OF BLAIRGOWRIE.

🌀 Cowal Highland Games, Dunoon   Strathclyde
These games take place in mid-August.
DUNOON IS ON THE A815.

Cowal Highland Games, Dunoon, Strathclyde, Scotland

BRITTANY

✿ Fête des Vieux Gréements, Douarnenez   Finistère
    This is an international tall ships parade and takes place in mid-August.
    DOUARNENEZ IS ON THE D765 NORTH-WEST OF QUIMPER.

✿ Fête de la Moisson, Corlay   Côtes d'Armor
    This is a traditional harvest festival, with folk music, and crêpes and cider to buy. It takes place in
    mid-August.
    CORLAY IS ON THE D790 SOUTH-WEST OF QUINTIN.

✿ Fête de la Mer, St Cast-le-Guildo   Côtes d'Armor
    This takes place in mid-August.
    ST CAST-LE-GUILDO IS ON AN UNCLASSIFIED ROAD NORTH OF MATIGNON.

✿ Grand Pardon et Journées Culturelles Bretonnes, La Baule-Escoublac   Loire-Atlantique
    The celebration of Breton culture lasts a whole weekend in mid-August.
    LA BAULE-ESCOUBLAC IS ON THE N171 WEST OF ST NAZAIRE.

✿ Medieval Festival, Moncontour   Côtes d'Armor
    This takes place in mid- to late August.
    MONCONTOUR IS ON AN UNCLASSIFIED ROAD SOUTH-WEST OF LAMBALLE.

Fixed Dates

1st August Lammas

CELTIC This festival appears to have multiple origins. Lugh was the grandson of the Celtic summer sun, and he slew him that the autumn sun would rise and oversee the harvest. This gave rise to the festival of Lughnasad, where the first fruits of the soil were sacrificed. Lugh also battled with a more primitive agricultural god Crom Dubh to win the corn for the people. In Irish folklore St Patrick came to be substituted for Lugh, possibly also in Man. The Christian Church took over the festival as a thanksgiving for the harvest, and it became known as Harvest Festival or the Festival of First Fruits. The word Lammas is thought by some to mean *Loaf* Mass, the bread being made from the first corn harvested. There was once a Lamb Mass involving feudal tenants, held at the Cathedral of St Peter in Vinculis, York, and some believe this gave rise to the name Lammas. At Lammas in Ireland there were patterns and devotions at wells and shrines, with the eating of first fruits on hilltops. The latter custom was recorded in the Isle of Man and parts of Scotland.

    Lammas was a term or rent day and a quarter day in the Celtic Year. Like all quarter days it was full of omens. Land tenure and rights of pasture were often settled on this day. Some grazing lands were given over to common use from Lammas to Candlemas.

    At Lammas Fairs, which were principally sheep fairs, couples used to agree to have a trial marriage for the duration of the fair, which was usually 11 days, and then to part if they proved incompatible after that time. Matchmaking and the baking of bride cakes was common. Some Lammas fairs were also used as hiring fairs, when farm labourers lined up with a trade token and offered their services.

    If couples suspected that faeries had snatched their child on May Day and replaced it with a changeling then the process could be reversed at Lammas.

IRELAND This was the Festival of Lúnasa and the first day of autumn, but celebrations were often transferred to the last Sunday of July or the first Sunday of August so that a working day was not lost. The harvest began today, even if all crops were not ready, and the first produce was used to make a celebratory meal that day. Records from the 18th and 19th centuries detail many open-air gatherings on hilltops throughout Ireland to celebrate the opening of the cereal or potato harvest, with a high concentration in Ulster. Colcannon was made with the first available new potatoes and **Mutton Pie** *(see p.201 for recipe)* was baked in the Dingle peninsula, Co. Kerry.

The old, wasteful practice of controlled burning of corn to release the grain was banned in 1634 because cattle needed the straw. On the Sunday family walks to hilltops and picnics, dancing and games round a fire were traditional, with many a match being made at popular sites. Trips to lakes and riverbanks were popular, too, where farmers drove their animals into the water, believing their health would be better for it. Horse-racing in the water, and swimming races, were held. Another name for this day was Lewy's Fair.

As a critical time for harvesters there was much weatherlore today.

At events today a special cake, called a **Barm Brack or Bairín Breac** *(see p.201 for recipe)*, was baked and divided up for guests by a betrothed couple.

In Ulster until the early 20th century Lammas festivities were held at a pagan site in Favour Royal Forest, near Altadaven, Co. Tyrone, called St Patrick's Well and Chair. The tenuous connection with St Patrick was probably a Christian substitution to try and give a deeply rooted pagan custom a claimed Christian origin.

Lammas was a popular time for patterns at wells and shrines, especially on hilltops, and for fairs. Some great fairs of the past, called Oenacha, were patronised by the nobility and high officers of the Church as well as merchants and traders, and took on the character of regional assemblies. Examples were at Carman and Tailtiu (Teltown) in Co. Meath. The Tailltenn Fair (Tailtiu was Lugh's foster-mother, who was buried, according to tradition, at the fair site) had bonfires, races, games, a marriage-market, and plenty of newly harvested food to buy. Trial marriages, lasting until the next Fair, were entered into.

The Mayor of Cork also has the title of Admiral of the Harbour. On this day, the Mayor and officials used to convene the Admiralty Court, and to assert their authority over the harbour they sailed to its entrance and threw a dart into the sea.

🎧 Offerings of fruit and flowers at the Strickeen on Knockfeerina   Co. Limerick

This was the seat of the God Donn Fírinne, where an annual Lughnasa assembly was held.
KNOCKFEERINA IS EAST OF BALLINGARRY.

🎧 Garlanding of the largest pillar stone (Rannach Chrom Dubh) in the great stone circle at Grange   Lough Gur

This is the site of the Lios, the largest stone circle in Ireland, and of other stone circles and a court-tomb.
LOCH GUR IS ON THE R512 JUST TO THE NORTH-EAST OF HOLYCROSS.

ISLE OF MAN The Feast of Lugh or Luan (Luanys's Day), the corn god, was on this day. Legend has it that Lugh spent his boyhood on the Isle of Man as Mannanan's foster son. Lugh and Crom Dubh battled for the personification of corn in a woman (called in Gaelic Eithne – grain or kernel). There was once a great fair in his honour in Santon parish. Visiting high hills and sacred wells on this day was done in ancient times to scare witches away as it was considered Midsummer Day. Moreover, harvest was seen as the climax of the year by farmers, who would also take the opportunity from on high to view their land with thankfulness, pride and not a little relief. The Church tried to eradicate the profane activities by changing the date to the first Sunday in August, replacing Lugh by St Patrick and substituting bible readings about Jephtha's daughter (replacing Eithne) and her companions going up the mountains to bewail her virginity. The Church also referred to it as the first Sunday of Harvest and steered the celebrations accordingly. In some cases the tradition degenerated to an outing to pick blueberries.

The time between now and Old Lammas on the 12th August was the favoured time to cure herrings.

SCOTLAND A Lammas Fair was held at Kirkwall, Orkney, and it attracted people from all over the islands. Makeshift sleeping quarters were prepared by spreading straw on the floor. Men and women often paired up as sexual partners for the 11 days of the fair, being referred to as Lammas brothers and sisters. These 'handfast marriages' were widely accepted as trial unions for a longer period, and either partner could, without any lasting stain on their reputation, agree to end them after a year. The fair survives, but not these customs.

The Stone of Odin at Stenness, Mainland, Orkney, was the last surviving handfasting stone, but was destroyed in the 19th century. Couples joined hands through the hole and vowed to live as man and wife for a year and a day. If the union survived this period they became truly man and wife, otherwise the marriage was dissolved at the next Lammas fair. **Orkney Bride Cakes** (*see p.201 for recipe*) were made and eaten on the wedding day, and when the bride entered her new home for the first time one would be held over her head and broken. She had to eat all the pieces to be sure of a long, happy and lucky marriage.

In Orkney and Shetland the fishermen and their wives ended the whitefish season with a feast and dance called the Lammas Foy.

At Lammas hiring fairs in Scotland cowherds used as their trade token a straw held in their mouths. This formed the basis for a Scottish children's game called Lammas. 'Handfast' or trial marriages also took place.

Lammas *Grip a straw between the chin and bottom lip, then try to say the following rhyme as many times as possible without dropping the straw. 'I bought a beard at Lammas Fair, It's a' awa' but ae hair – wag, beardie, wag!'*

Lammas cheese or curds were made and given by the farmer to those who helped lead the cattle down from their summer pastures in the hills. The boys who looked after the herds held a feast and followed it with games such as quoits and horse-racing. This was called the Herds' Festival and the horses were ridden along the beach and in the sea, a relic of the pagan cleansing-of-horses rites.

✴ Lammas Market and Fair, Kirkwall   Orkney
KIRKWALL IS THE PRINCIPAL TOWN OF ORKNEY.

WALES In Cardiganshire shepherds held their meets today in upland pastures.
CORNWALL In 1843 the Reverend R S Hawker of Morwenstow revived the Lammas Thanksgiving Service, for the harvest.

Sunday nearest to 1st August
CORNWALL Morvah Feast was held to commemorate an old tradition here of wrestling, throwing quoits and other games. On the following Monday there was a fair.

2nd August St Uniac's Day
BRITTANY A little distance from the town of Saint-Uniac is a found dedicated to him. It is called the Fountain of the Itchy, and the water will cure dogs of mange and people of skin irritations.

First Saturday in August
SCOTLAND

✺ Summer Festival, Town Yetholm and Kirk Yetholm   Border
The Yetholms were frequently raided and looted in the past, being close to the English border. The last Gypsy King, Charles Faa Blythe, was crowned on Kirk Yetholm village green on 30th May 1898, to die in 1902. Records of the Summer Festival of 1959 show that a Gypsy King and Queen were elected, with the ceremony conducted in both English and Romany. Since then much gypsy ceremonial has lapsed, except for nominal appointments of Bari Gadgi (Braw Lad) and Bari Manushi (Bonnie Lass), and the Yetholm Festival Queen is crowned instead. The song 'The Wraggle-Taggle Gypsies O!' relates how Johnny Faa, a Yetholm gypsy, runs off with the wife of the Earl of Cassilis, head of the Kennedys in Ayrshire. The annual Ba' game is played the next Monday.
THESE NEIGHBOURING VILLAGES ARE ON THE B6401. TAKE THE A698 SOUTH FROM KELSO, THEN LEFT ON THE B6401.

BRITTANY

✺ Mussel Festival, Lannilis   Finistère
LANNILIS IS ON AN UNCLASSIFIED ROAD WEST OF LESNEVEN.

CELTIC Lammas customs were largely transferred here so as not to lose a working day in the fields.

IRELAND This was called Garlick Sunday, or Garland Sunday, the latter from the old custom of making corn garlands for the worship of the corn goddess.

ISLE OF MAN This was one of the most important days for visiting wells, particularly St Catherine's Well, Port Erin; Çhibbyr Parick or Pherick (St Patrick's Well) on the west end of the hill of Lhargey-grave; Çhibbyr Pherick south of Peel; the well at Maughold Head; Lord Henry's Well on the south beach at Laxey; and the Nunnery Well in Braddan parish.

SCOTLAND This was one of the four days to take the curative waters of Loch Mochrum, near Wigtown, Dumfries and Galloway. The others are the first Sundays in February, May and November. It is said that the loch never freezes properly and ice-skaters still avoid it. Nearby is St Medana's Well, a healing well.

WALES Today families traditionally climbed to hilltops in the Brecon Beacons, to have picnics and enjoy the spectacular views.

BRITTANY

Fête des Ajoncs d'Or (Golden Gorse Festival), Pont-Aven   *Finistère*

This festival was started in 1905 by the Breton poet Théodore Botrel, who also wrote the song 'La Paimpolaise'.

PONT-AVEN IS ON THE D783 EAST OF CONCARNEAU.

Pardon de la Mer, Douarnenez   *Finistère*

DOUARNENEZ IS ON THE D765 NORTH-WEST OF QUIMPER.

Pardon de Notre-Dame-de-Pénéty, Persquen   *Morbihan*

PERSQUEN IS ON AN UNCLASSIFIED ROAD SOUTH OF GUÉMENÉ-SUR-SCORFF.

Fête de la Mer, Erquy   *Côtes d'Armor*

ERQUY IS ON THE COAST, ON THE D786 WEST OF MATIGNON.

Pardon, Huelgoat   *Finistère*

HUELGOAT IS ON AN UNCLASSIFIED ROAD NORTH OF THE D764, NORTH-WEST FROM CARHAIX-PLOUGUER.

SCOTLAND

Lammas Fair, St Andrews   *Fife*

This is one of two surviving Lammas fairs in Fife. The charter was granted by James VI of Scotland (James I of England), including a monopoly on sales of ironmongery, which ceased in 1800.

TAKE THE A91 EAST FROM CUPAR.

Lammas Fair and Hat and Ribbon Race, Inverkeithing   *Fife*

This is the second surviving Lammas Fair in Fife. At the opening of the three-day fair there is a foot-race, called The Hat and Ribbon Race. This race was originally run between the herd-laddies who were there to hire themselves out to farmers, for a prize of a beribboned lum hat (for the herd-laddie) and ribbons (for his lass). The race dates from the 16th century. The 760-yard course runs from the old Roman road to Hope Street and back. The prizes are carried on a halberd by the Burgh Officer in a procession to the finishing line, and are then presented to the winner by the Provost.

INVERKEITHING IS ON THE A90 SOUTH OF DUNFERMLINE.

Coldstream Common Riding, Coldstream   *Border*

TAKE THE A698 NORTH-EAST FROM KELSO.

WALES

Royal National Eisteddfod

This is held at a different venue each year, alternating between north and south Wales. Records of this gathering of singers, musicians, poets and specialists in folk crafts date from AD 1176. In the 6th century bards were harpers, genealogists, poets, soothsayers and story-tellers, and by the 10th century they had legal recognition. In 1176 at Card gan the Lord Rhys presented chairs for poetry, harp-, pipe- and crwth- (Welsh fiddle) playing. It has been held on a regular basis since the 15th century, among the aims of the early gatherings was the maintenance of poetic standards by professional bards. There was a decline after the 16th century, during the period of strong English influence, to local village events, but 1792 saw a revival and once more Welsh poets and musicians competed for an eisteddfa or bardic chair. In this year Iolo Morganwg (Glamorgan Ned) or Edward Williams (1747–1826) invented the so-called Druidic rituals used ever since at the Eisteddfford and organised a Gorsedd (enthronement) of a 'Druidic Bard' at Primrose Hill, London. Since the late 17th century amateurs have dominated the competition, and in 1819 the first crowning of the best bard of the year was done, using the invented 'Druidic' façade

The Eisteddfod is proclaimed a year and a day in advance, as in 1176, and the proceedings are in Welsh. The Arch Druid of the Gorsedd, in oak-leaf coronet and copper breastplate, partly draws his sword and says 'A oes Heddwch?' ('Is there peace?'), to which the assembly answers 'Heddwch'. Poetry is still the principal art; competitors compose verses on set subjects, in Welsh metres.

Regional Eisteddfodau take place in Welsh-speaking areas each year, Cardigan in early July, Lampeter in early August, and also in Caernavonshire and Merionethshire.

First fortnight in August
BRITTANY

Festival Interceltique (International Celtic Arts Festival), Lorient   Morbihan

This huge festival attracts Celts from all over the world. It presents a good opportunity to see Breton sports. Among those which may be seen are Breton wrestling (Ar Gouren), trials of strength such as tossing the caber, tug-of-war, discus-throwing and Tire-Bâton where the contestants try to lift each other using a pole. There are also stalls, shows and much live music.
LORIENT IS ON THE SOUTH COAST, ON THE N165 BETWEEN QUIMPER AND VANNES.

✸ Festival Folklorique Ménez-Hom, Plomodiern   Finistère
PLOMODIERN IS ON THE D63 WEST OF CHÂTEAULIN.

✸ Fête de la Brière et Course de Chalands, Île de Fédrun   Loire-Atlantique
This takes place in the Parc Naturel Régional de Brière around mid-August, in the marshland of
La Grande Brière. The Parc can only effectively be explored by chaland, a flat-bottomed punt
propelled by a long pole. The inhabitants traditionally depend on fishing and hunting, peat-cut-
ting and, for weaving and basket-making, reed-cutting. Local foods sold include cider and eel
sandwiches. There is a lottery for people to try to win live geese, and water games such as a barrel
race and egg-throwing. The latter is a piggy-in-the-middle game played by three men in chalands,
between Fédrun and the rest of the world. The man in the centre chaland tries to hit (with his pad-
dle) eggs thrown between the two men in the outside chalands. If he misses an egg, and it is
caught, it is broken over his head.
THE PARC IS NORTH-WEST OF ST NAZAIRE.

✸ Peat Festival, St-Lyphard-en-Brière   Loire-Atlantique
ST-LYPHARD-EN-BRIÈRE IS ON THE WEST SIDE OF THE PARC.

4th August
SCOTLAND This was the traditional date for the Ferry Fair, South Queensferry, Midlothian. Established in 1687 the Ferry Fair had stalls and booths along the High Street and numerous activities,
but the only significant survival was the Burgh Race, for a prize of a pair of boots. There was also a
crowning of the Ferry Queen.

5th August Old St James' Day
CELTIC Oysters (for Old St James' Day) are eaten on this day as it marks the opening of the oyster
season. Oysters used to be eaten in large numbers by the poor.
ISLE OF MAN Laxey Fair was held. Originally it was on 2nd August, and called St Lonan's Fair
because it was in Kirk Lonan parish.
BRITTANY Today is Notre-Dame des Neiges (Our Lady of the Snows), and if there are no clouds
seen in the sky then there will not be snow falling in the coming winter. However, if the wind
blows up then the price of grain will rise in proportion to the extent of the cloud cover or
wind strength.
CORNWALL A cattle fair was held at Goldsithney in the parish of Perran-Uthnoe. This was a glove
fair, but it was said that the glove and pole were stolen from the Sithney Fair near Helston. As an
acknowledgement the Lord of the Manor of Goldsithney paid one shilling per annum to the
churchwardens of Sithney.

6th August Old St Anne's Day
BRITTANY Today is the Transfiguration, and if the wind is harsh today grain will be dear, but a
gentle breeze foretells reasonable prices.

8th August St Lide's Day
CELTIC St Lide was an 11th-century hermit on the Isles of Scilly. St Helens island was once named
after him. His chapel was formerly a place of pilgrimage.

Second Sunday in August
BRITTANY

✸ Fête du Cheval, Loudéac   Côtes d'Armor
LOUDÉAC IS ON THE N164.

✸ Fêtes de la Cité des Hortensias (Hydrangeas), Perros-Guirec   Côtes-d'Armor
PERROS-GUIREC IS ON THE D788, ON THE NORTH COAST, NORTH OF LANNION.

Second Friday in August
SCOTLAND

The Burry Man and Ferry Fair, South Queensferry   Lothian

Formerly done on 3rd August, The Burry Man now walks the 7 miles of the Queensferry boundaries. He must be born in the town, and is elected by the Ferry Fair Committee. He has a wreath of roses and one red dahlia stuck into netting covering the bowler hat on his head, and holds a stave decorated with flowers in each hand. His body is covered in a flannel material covered in burrs from the burdock. He starts at 9 am and ends after 9 miles and about 9 hours. At about 6 pm he opens the Ferry Fair, formerly a Lammas fair, from outside the Hawes Inn.

This is an unusual time of year for a custom involving disguise, perambulation and collection of money. The Burry Man resembles the Green Man elsewhere, and may be a surviving scapegoat figure as well as a symbol of the renewal of greenery in spring. A scapegoat going through the town absorbs the sins of the population. Another theory connects him with an old ceremony to ensure good herring catches, as a similar figure existed in the north-eastern Scottish ports of Buckie and Fraserburgh. As the burrs stick to the netting, so may the fish, and he may have been called upon to remove the ill luck following poor catches.

TAKE THE A90 WEST FROM EDINBURGH.

10th August St Lawrence's Day
IRELAND

Fair of Puck, Killorglin   Co. Kerry

This surviving Lúnasa fair and pattern, at the head of Dingle Bay, runs until 12th August (formerly from the 1st August). 10th August is Gathering Day, when a procession headed by a beribboned billy-goat, who presides over the fair, goes from the bridge to Central Square. The goat (or puck) symbolises fertility and good fortune. Tinkers gather at the fair, but its main business is livestock. The 11th August is Fair Day, and on the 12th August, Scattering Day, the puck (goat) is taken triumphantly back to the bridge. Mutton pies are a speciality.

At other puck fairs in the past a white horse presided.

KILLORGLIN IS NORTH-WEST OF KILLARNEY, AT THE JUNCTION OF THE N70 AND N72.

The Burry Man, South Queensferry, Lothian, Scotland

BRITTANY

International Festival of Folk Dancing and Traditions, Châteauneuf-du-Faou Finistère
This festival lasts until the 15th August.
CHÂTEAUNEUF-DU-FAOU IS JUST SOUTH OF THE N164, BETWEEN CHÂTEAULIN AND CARHAIX-PLOUGUER.

11th August Old Lammas Eve

CELTIC Sheep fairs were traditionally held on or near this day.
SCOTLAND Protective measures as at Beltane were taken.

12th August Old Lammas

CELTIC The game season opens on this day, the so-called Glorious Twelfth, until 10th December.
ISLE OF MAN Ballasalla Fair (or Lammas Fair) was held until the end of the 19th century.

First Sunday after Old Lammas

ISLE OF MAN This was Lhuany's Day, the day of a festival dedicated to the god Lugh. An orgy was held at the top of Snaefell.

The water in healing wells is said to be particularly potent today, and in the past they were much visited. St Maughold's Well, near Ramsey, is said to cure sterility; either by immersion in it or by dropping a pin into it.

Sunday and Monday after 12th August

Revel, Marhamchurch, near Bude Cornwall
Revel Sunday is a church festival in honour of St Morwenne, patron saint of the village.

The revel originally started as a celebration of the founding of the village by St Morwenne, whose feast day is on 5th July, but was formerly the 12th August. After a procession headed by the Queen of the Revel, Cornish wrestling, gymnastics, trials of strength, a pram race and other games are featured, as well as country dancing and a fancy dress competition. Cornish teas are served.
MARHAMCHURCH IS ON AN UNCLASSIFIED ROAD SOUTH–EAST OF BUDE.

Fair of Puck, Killorglin, Co Kerry

Friday of the second week in August
SCOTLAND

🏰 **Ridings Festival, Sanquhar**   Dumfries and Galloway

This is the last of the Scottish Ridings in the calendar, reinstated as a week-long annual event in 1947. On the Saturday morning the Court of the Marches is convened, and the Fencing of the Court ceremony held, at which the Cornet receives the burgh flag and the Ensign a spear with golden thistles attached, with which to defend the Cornet. The Riding takes in the 'dumping' of the two most recently elected councillors on the dumping stone. Afterwards the Sanquhar Queen is crowned.

TAKE THE A76 EAST FROM NEW CUMNOCK.

14th August
BRITTANY

✳ **Fête des Artisans (Festival of Working Folk), Lizio**   Morbihan

LIZIO IS ON AN UNCLASSIFIED ROAD WEST OF THE N166.

Second Sunday in August
BRITTANY

✳ **Fête des Bruyères, Buezec-Cap-Sizun, near the Pointe du Raz**   Finistère

Bruyères means heather. It is sometimes held on 14th August.

BUEZEC-CAP-SIZUN IS ON AN UNCLASSIFIED ROAD DUE WEST OF DUARNENEZ.

✳ **Fêtes des Mouettes (Seagulls), St Briac-sur-Mer**   Ille-et-Vilaine

This features a procession of Breton dancers and pipe bands and a Fest-Noz (Night Festival). It is sometimes held on 14th August.

ST BRIAC-SUR-MER IS ON THE D786, WEST OF ST MALO.

✋ **Festival of Breton Dancing, Douarnenez**   Finistère

DOUARNENEZ IS ON THE D765 NORTH-WEST OF QUIMPER.

❁ **Festival de la Mer, Plougasnou** — Finistère

PLOUGASNOU IS ON AN UNCLASSIFIED ROAD NORTH OF MORLAIX.

💃 **Festival Folklorique des Genets d'Or (Golden Broom), Bannalec** — Finistère

BANNALEC IS ON AN UNCLASSIFIED ROAD NORTH-WEST OF QUIMPERLÉ.

15th August Feast of the Assumption of the Virgin Mary Marymass

IRELAND This day provided a welcome holiday during harvest, and trips to the coast were popular for the therapeutic value of sea water.

At shrines dedicated to the Virgin Mary patterns were held. They had both a religious and a festive component.

In the north of Ireland, the Ancient Order of Hibernians, on organisation opposed to the Orangemen, held marches on this day.

SCOTLAND Marymass or Murmass was a first-fruits festival in the Highlands. Lammas Bannocks called Moilean Moire (Mary's fatling) were made from hand-picked corn, dried in the sun, ground in a quern and kneaded in a sheep-skin. Moilean baked over a rowan fire was broken by the man of the house and he handed a piece to his wife, then to the children in order of age. Songs would be sung in praise of Mary, and the family would walk or dance sunwise round the fire. When it burned low they would dance round the house carrying the embers and bits of iron in a pot. This custom is clearly a mixture of Christian and pagan elements.

There are two surviving Marymass Fairs, at Inverness, Highland, and at Irvine, Strathclyde, but they are not now held on this day. Horse-races were a feature of Marymass Fairs.

BRITTANY Today is a public holiday. Many pardons and processions also hold events on the 14th.

✚ **Pardon de Notre-Dame de la Clarté, Perros-Guirec** — Côtes-d'Armor

PERROS-GUIREC IS ON THE D788 DUE NORTH OF LANNION.

❁ **Fête Folklorique du Ménéz-Hom, Plomodiern** — Finistère

This is named after the mountain that overlooks the village. There is a procession and pageant.

PLOMODIERN IS ON THE D63, WEST OF CHÂTEAULIN.

✚ **Pardon, Moncontour** — Côtes d'Armor

MONCONTOUR IS ON AN UNCLASSIFIED ROAD SOUTH-WEST OF LAMBALLE.

✚ **Pardon de Notre-Dame de Roscudon, Pont-Croix** — Finistère

PONT-CROIX IS ON THE D765 NORTH-EAST OF AUDIERNE.

✚ **Pardon, Plougastel-Doulas** — Finistère

PLOUGASTEL-DOULAS IS TO THE EAST OF BREST, ACROSS THE RADE DE BREST.

✚ **Pardon de Notre-Dame de la Joie, St Guénolé-Penmarc'h** — Finistère

ST GUÉNOLÉ-PENMARC'H IS ON THE D785 SOUTH-WEST OF PONT L'ABBÉ.

❁ **Grandes Fête d'Arvor, Vannes** — Morbihan

VANNES IS ON THE SOUTH COAST, ON THE N165.

❁ **Fête de l'Aven, Port Manech** — Finistère

PORT MANECH IS ON THE COAST ROAD FROM PONT-AVEN TO CONCARNEAU.

❁ **Fête d'Armor, Audierne** — Finistère

AUDIERNE IS ON THE D765 SOUTH-WEST OF DOUARNENEZ.

✚ **Pardon de Notre-Dame, Quelven** — Morbihan

QUELVEN IS ON AN UNCLASSIFIED ROAD SOUTH WEST OF PONTIVY.

✠ Pardon de Notre-Dame de Rumengol, Rumengol   Finistère
RUMENGOL IS ON AN UNCLASSIFIED ROAD NORTH-EAST OF LE FAOU.

✠ Pardon of the 'Madone des Motards' (Our Lady of Bikers), Porcaro   Morbihan
PORCARO IS ON AN UNCLASSIFIED ROAD EAST OF PLOËRMEL.

✠ Haute-Bretagne Troménie, Bécherel   Ille-et-Vilaine
BÉCHEREL IS ON THE D27 NORTH-WEST OF RENNES.

Thursday nearest 15th August (or the third or fourth Monday in August, or the third Saturday in August)
SCOTLAND

✠ Marymass Fair, Irvine, near Kilmarnock   Strathclyde
Originally the Great Feast of Mary, coinciding with Old Lammas, was celebrated round hilltop fires. Then it became part of the fair, which now lasts for 12 days. Horse-races are held (dray parades were once a traditional Marymass feature) and there is a live music festival. The fair is known from as early as the 12th century, when it was run by the Carters' Society and featured a parade with a Marymass Queen. Until the 19th century it was still accompanied by Lammas fires lit on the hills around the town. Since 1563, in which year Mary Queen of Scots visited the Fair, the elected Queen has dressed up as her rather than as the Virgin Mary, to whom the fair was originally dedicated. She is crowned after the Carters' Common Riding in the afternoon, which in turn is followed by amateur horse-racing and carthorse races.
IRVINE IS ON THE A71 WEST OF KILMARNOCK.

Saturday nearest 15th August
SCOTLAND

✠ Inverness Marymass Fair   Highland
This dates from 1591, but was revived in 1986. There are various processions, an election of the Marymass Queen, and general fairground entertainment is enjoyed. Since 1562, after a visit by Mary Queen of Scots, the elected Marymass Queen has dressed up as her, not as the Virgin Mary.
INVERNESS IS AT THE JUNCTION OF THE A9 AND A96.

16th August St Roch's Day
CELTIC St Roch was a 14th-century saint said to be able to cure sufferers of the plague and dysentery.
BRITTANY Dysentery sufferers invoke St Roch, and pilgrims to one of his shrines say Mass and make offerings.

Third week in August
SCOTLAND

✠ March Riding, Musselburgh   Lothian
Founded in 1682, the Riding is now done every 21 years from 1935 (due in 2016). Beforehand the Turf-Cutter cuts turfs at the 12 boundary points, with the Champion on hand, in armour and with spear, to deal with challenges to his judgement. The Notary Public defends the claim on behalf of the town. On the Tuesday burgesses are sworn in and given baps inside which are pressed three mussel shells. One of the guests at the Riding on Wednesday is the winner of the Musselburgh Silver Arrow, a trophy competed for by the members of the Royal Company of Archers since 1676. The trophy dates from 1603 and is the oldest archery trophy in the world. On the Thursday there a trade procession takes place.
MUSSELBURGH IS ON THE A199 EAST OUT OF EDINBURGH.

BRITTANY

✸ **Fêtes Folkloriques, Vannes** (due in 2016).   Morbihan
VANNES IS ON THE N165.

🖐 **Festival de la Danse Bretonne et Fête de la St-Loup, Guingamp**   Côtes-d'Armor
The festival sometimes takes place during the first fortnight in August.
GUINGAMP IS ON THE N12 WEST OF ST BRIEUC.

Third Saturday in August (formerly on a Wednesday in August)
SCOTLAND

🎏 **Festival of Boys and Horses Ploughing Match,**
St Margaret's Hope, South Ronaldsay   Orkney
This Easter custom has its origins in a Viking gathering and was done at Easter, which may
indicate its origin as a spring ploughing rite. There was also such a custom on Burray. The 'horses'
are girls and the 'ploughmen' are boys, both elaborately costumed, in treasured family heirlooms –
a Norse custom, Orkney having been under Danish rule until the late Middle Ages. The girls wear
horse collars, pointed head-dresses, jackets with ribbons and shiny attachments, and fringed
shorts. Their shoes are painted to look like hooves, and hair fringes are worn round the ankles to
resemble a horse's feathering. Before the match both boys and girls are judged on their costumes in
Cromarty Hall, St Margaret's Hope, and the 'horses' for the best grooming (teeth, nails and
hooves). Then, the contest begins on Sand O'Right beach, with the boys (who are under 15) using
their own ploughs, often miniatures handed down in families. Judges look for the best unbroken
furrow in the sand and make an award for the best kept plough. Beach ploughing is an ancient ritual to honour the sea god and ensure good catches. In former times the ploughs' potency was
enhanced by urinating on them.
ST MARGARET'S HOPE IS ON THE A961 SOUTH OF KIRKWALL.

Festival of Boys and Horses Ploughing Match, Orkney

First Sunday after 15th August

IRELAND This was Gleaning Sunday in Co. Kildare and Co. Meath, when farm labourers and their wives did the gleaning and picnicked in the fields. Gleaning is the gathering of stalks of stray corn that remain after the harvest.

Third Sunday in August

BRITTANY

Grande Fête des Menhirs, Carnac   Morbihan

The Carnac standing-stones (menhirs) are Neolithic, and number 2792 in parallel alignments stretching for 2 miles (3.8 km). They are the three great alignments, of Ménec, Kermario and Kerlescan. They pre-date the Celts, but their precise date and function are uncertain, although they were probably erected between 4000 and 1800 BC.

CARNAC IS ON THE D781 SOUTH-EAST OF LORIENT.

Pardon de la Mer, Dinard   Ille-et-Vilaine

This sometimes takes place on 21st August.

DINARD IS ON THE D786, WEST OF ST MALO.

Pardon de Notre-Dame de la Tronchaye, Rochefort-en-Terre   Morbihan

This sometimes takes place on 21st August or the Sunday after 15th August.

ROCHEFORT-EN-TERRE IS ON AN UNCLASSIFIED ROAD WEST OF REDON.

Pardon de Notre-Dame-de-Callot, Carantec   Finistère

This sometimes takes place on the first Sunday after 15th August.

CARANTEC IS ON AN UNCLASSIFIED ROAD NORTH OF THE D58, NORTH-WEST OF MORLAIX.

⊕ Pardon de Notre-Dame-de-Crénenan, Plöerdut   Morbihan
    PLÖERDUT IS ON AN UNCLASSIFIED ROAD WEST OF GUEMENÉ-SUR-SCORFF.

✸ Fête des Filets Bleus (Festival of the Blue Nets), Concarneau   Finistère
    This festival, which sometimes takes place on 21st August, takes its name from the blue fishing
    nets hung along the approaches to the Ville Close, the walled town over the harbour. The main
    action is in the narrow main street of the Ville Close. It started as a blessing of the nets to ensure a
    good catch, but is now a week-long folk festival.
    CONCARNEAU IS ON THE D44 EAST OF FOUESNANT.

Saturday after the 19th August
WALES

◉ Cilgerran Coracle Races, River Teifi, Cilgerran, near Cardigan   Dyfed
    These come at the end of the village's Festive Week. A coracle (Welsh cwrwgl) is traditionally made
    by constructing a framework of hazel or willow withies around which is stretched tarred, untanned
    animal hide. Nowadays calico waterproofed with pitch is used. They have a circular shape, and
    were used for transport as well as fishing as long ago as the Bronze Age. They are light enough to be
    carried on the back, bottom outwards. Although coracles were never intended for racing, the
    occasion is interesting to watch because of the skill required to negotiate such a fast-flowing and
    rocky river as the Teifi. The most keenly contested race is between the fishermen who come from the
    Teifi and Tywi rivers.
        From March to August sewin, or Welsh sea trout, are caught by coracle fishermen in the Teifi
    and in the Tywi. Two coracles are used, a weighted net being stretched between them. Salmon is
    caught the same way. Traditional recipes eaten at this time include Trout with Bacon *(see p.201 for
    recipe)* and **Salmon with Lemon Butter** *(see p.201 for recipe).*
    TAKE THE A478 SOUTH FROM CARDIGAN THEN LEFT ON AN UNCLASSIFIED ROAD.

20th August St Philibert's Day
    CELTIC St Philibert lived in the 7th century. The filbert nut harvest traditionally started today.
    Filberts are the nuts of the cultivated hazel.

22nd August St Symphorien's Day
    BRITTANY St Symphorien is invoked by sufferers of diarrhoea. The fountain dedicated to him at
    Gael was thought to be able to cure rabies.

Saturday nearest 23rd August
SCOTLAND

✸ Wallace Day, Elderslie   Strathclyde
    This commemorates the execution, on 23rd August 1305, of William Wallace by order of Edward I.
    TAKE THE A737 WEST FROM PAISLEY.

24th August St Bartholomew's Day
    CELTIC St Bartholomew lived in 1st-century Palestine. He was flayed alive so he was made the
    patron saint of butchers and tanners. He was also the patron saint of beekeepers and honeymakers.
    IRELAND It was the day when the corn was threshed, so it provided a target day for the reapers.
    CORNWALL

⊕ The Blessing of the Mead, Mead House, Gulval   Mount's Bay
    As St Bartholomew is the patron saint of beekeepers and honeymakers, this is the day when the
    monks of Gulval bless their Cornish mead. The blessing is given by the Almoner of the Fraternity
    of St Bartholomew of the Craft or Mystery of Free Meadmakers of Great Britain and Ireland.
    GULVAL IS AT THE JUNCTION OF THE A30 AND A394.

BRITTANY If the buckwheat is in flower on St Barthelemy's Day the bees will make excellent honey.

26th August St Ninian's Day
CELTIC The 4th-century St Ninian was one of the first Christian missionaries to the Picts in Scotland. He was a Briton, sent by the Pope, and set up the first Christian church in Pictish territory at Whithorn, near Burrow Head, Dumfries and Galloway. Later a priory was built. St Ninian's Cave is on the coast nearby. St Ninian's Isle, off Mainland, Shetland, was probably named by followers who established the first Christian chapel on Shetland, near what became St Ninian's Well.

27th August St Maelrubba's Day
CELTIC St Maelrubba (or Malrubius), a 7th-century Irish missionary, may actually have been (or been confused with, it is not clear) the pagan God Mourie, to whom bulls were sacrificed. His chapel is on Eilean Maree island in Loch Maree in the north-west Highlands, and this site is known as a site of bull sacrifice, tree worship and worship at what is now known as St Mourie's Well. The mentally ill were also brought here by relatives hoping for a cure by drinking its waters at the altar and walking wunwise (anticlockwise) round the island, stopping three times to be immersed in the loch. This ritual would be repeated many times if it failed to work, often for a number of days.

28th August
BRITTANY

✠ Pardon de Kerbader, Fouesnant   Finistère
FOUESNANT IS ON THE D44 WEST OF CONCARNEAU.

✠ Pardon de St Philibert, Trégunc   Finistère
TRÉGUNC IS ON THE D783 WEST OF PONT-AVON.

29th August Feast of the Decollation (Beheading) of St John the Baptist
SCOTLAND Daisies (gowans) were taken to church today, their red-tipped petals symbolising the beheading of St John.

Fourth Saturday in August
SCOTLAND

◉ Lonach Highland Gathering and Games, Strathdon   Grampian
STRATHDON IS ON THE A944.

Last Tuesday in August
IRELAND This is the date of the 350-year old Lammas Fair at Ballycastle. Sheep and ponies are sold, and traditional fairings available include Dulse (edible seaweed) and **Yellowman** *(see p.201 for recipe)*, a brittle yellow toffee.

Last Friday in August
CORNWALL

🌾 Crying the Neck, Helston   Cornwall
See Harvest Customs for details of this ceremony, which starts at 7.30 pm. The dolly is decorated with cornflowers.
HELSTON IS ON THE A394 BETWEEN FALMOUTH AND PENZANCE.

Last Sunday in August
IRELAND This was the traditional date for the Harvest Festival and supper, the latter including a main course of new potatoes, bacon and cabbage.

BRITTANY

✠ **Grand Pardon de Sainte Anne La Palud, Plonévez-Porzay, near Locronan**　Finistère

St Anne is the subject of a famous poem by Tristan Corbière and of a painting by Charles Cottet in the Musée des Beaux-Arts, Rennes. There are associated events on the eve and on the following Tuesday. This event sometimes takes place on 28th August.

PLONÉVEZ-PORZAY IS ON THE D107 SOUTH-WEST OF CHÂTEAULIN.

✠ **Pardon, Châteauneuf-de-Faou**　Finistère

CHÂTEAUNEUF-DE-FAOU IS ON THE D72 SOUTH-WEST OF CARHAIX-PLOUGUER.

✠ **Pardon de St Fiacre, Le Faouët**　Morbihan

There are associated events on the eve and on the following Tuesday.

ST FIACRE CHURCH IS TO THE SOUTH OF LE FAOUËT.

Nearest Sunday to the last Sunday in August

CORNWALL Lanivet Feast was held, whose patron saint is unknown. Wrestling was featured.

30th August

BRITTANY Gardeners make an offering of carrots, cabbages, onions and other vegetables to St Fiacre today. At Guenroc St Fiacre is invoked by those seeking a cure for stomach-ache.

31st August St Aidan's Day

CELTIC St Aidan was an Irish missionary who travelled via Iona to become the first Bishop of Lindisfarne, Northumberland, dying in AD 641. He converted King Oswald of Northumbria to Christianity, after the king showed much admiration for his humility, and he became a pious and charitable monarch, meeting his end at the bloody hands of King Penda of Mercia, one of Aidan's more unsuccessful subjects for conversion.

Crying the Neck, Helston, Cornwall

Harvest customs

For the rural Celts harvest was the most critical time of the year, and there were many superstitions and protective practices. The successful completion was a cause for great celebration. Special ceremonies accompanied the cutting of the first and last corn, a number of ways being employed to select the person honoured to do it. Although there were local variations in harvest customs where was a great deal of similarity in what was a crucially important task, and even though that task is now done by efficient mechanisation the similarity remains. Gone is the ritual, born of the fear that if it was not properly conducted then the family would starve or be short of funds and supplies to see them through the winter. It was a communal task, in which no-one dared to depart from long-established custom, for too much depended on it.

CELTIC The last sheaf would be cut by a young girl, or the oldest reaper, or the reaper whose sickle, when thrown, cut the last stalks. After plaiting and decorating the last sheaf it was taken in procession to the farmer's house and hung up where the harvest supper was to be served. Sometimes a barring-out custom was observed before the reapers could enter. The corn spirit was thought to reside in the last sheaf, so it could not be allowed to touch the ground. The cutter of the last sheaf had the place of honour at the table, and after the meal there would be music and dancing. Another variation was to throw the last sheaf into a neighbouring farmer's field who had not finished harvesting. This would bring him bad luck next season. In the following spring some of the corn from the last sheaf was added to the first seed corn to be sown and to the animals' first feed. Thus the spirit returned to the soil.

In 1843 the Reverend R S Hawker of Morwenstow, Cornwall, revived the Lammas Thanksgiving Service, for the harvest, and this became a civilised alternative to the sometimes rowdy harvest suppers. The Church also took the opportunity to distribute some of the produce to the needy.

The first full moon after 21st September is called the harvest moon. Couples desiring a child would sleep outside under its fertile light.

IRELAND The last sheaf (Cailleach or hag) was surrounded by the reapers, who shouted 'Put the hare (or any other animal that might have taken refuge) out of the corn!' The bearer was sprinkled with water. In Protestant areas it was used as part of the church decorations for the Harvest service. Typical fare would be beef, bacon, potatoes, cabbage and beer. Music, dancing and a punch bowl would follow. In areas of English influence labourers made 'harvest knots', from plaited straw, to wear at the feast.

In addition to the festivities following the corn harvest, there were celebrations to mark the end of the potato and flax harvests. In south-west Ireland potato harvesters held a Stampy Party, at which stampy, a type of bread made from grated potato and flour, was eaten.

ISLE OF MAN A young woman reaper would ceremonially cut the last corn and bind it with wild flowers and ribbon into a 'babban ny mheillea' or harvest baby, which was thought to contain the corn spirit. This tradition may have come from England, adopted principally in the wheat areas of Castletown and beyond Ramsey. Crofters, cutting their oats and barley, are not known to have done it. After supper a fiddler played for dancing. The prettiest girl was given a bouquet of wild flowers and called the Queen of the Mheillea. The mheillea, or a smaller sheaf called the 'harvest doll', was kept all year on the chimney-piece in the kitchen. Another variation was the taking of the Mheillea by the women reapers to the top of a hill where the celebrations and feast were held in the open. A traditional harvest dish was **Manx Herring Pie** *(see p.202 for recipe)*.

On the first Sunday after the harvest a Harvest Thanksgiving service would be held.

One of the crafts which was done after the harvest, when there was a little time to relax, was rush-plaiting, used to make toys for children.

SCOTLAND In Buchan, until the 19th century, they preserved the rite of Streeking the Plough on the first day of ploughing. The farmer's wife greeted the ploughman with 'Guid speed the work!' and handed him bannocks, cheese and ale or whisky, which he consumed there and then, putting a little in a furrow or on the plough. In the evening the Pleuch Feast of milk porridge, bread and cheese was held.

On the first day of reaping everyone turned up in their best clothes to watch the farmer, facing the sun, cut a handful of corn with his sickle and swirl it round his head sunwise three times, uttering an invocation. The whole family then sang a reaping song.

The last sheaf had many names depending on the region and whether it was cut before or after Hallowmas, names such as Cailleach, Carline or Auld Wife (all after Hallowmas), or Bride, or the Maiden (before Hallowmas). Sometimes the Auld Wife was made out of the first stalks cut and the Corn Maiden out of the last. In Galloway a hare was woven. There was much celebration as it fell (Crying the Kirn). It was woven and dressed as a doll in either form, and as it was bound it was not allowed to touch the ground lest the corn spirit return to it. As it was carried back to the farmer's house in triumph, water was sprinkled on it.

The first sheaf in Orkney was made into a kind of porridge and ritually eaten. The bringer of the last sheaf was given a sweet bannock, called a drilty, and was then chased. He ran to try and hold on to it. In Orkney and Shetland the last to finish harvesting was presented with a Strae Bikko or Straw Bitch, a dog made of woven straw.

At the end of reaping divination games were played with sickles. They were thrown into the ground, predictions being made from the way they stuck in.

The corn dolly made from the last sheaf was called a carlin, and might be fed to the plough horses on the first day of ploughing (through which it would find its way to the soil), or given to someone due to be married that year, as a fertility token, or to the prettiest girl. In the Highlands, the left-over pieces of the last sheaf, after making the dolly, were woven into corn-brooches for good-luck tokens.

The Harvest Home feast after the oats harvest had many names, commonly the Kirn. That after the earlier barley (bere) harvest was known as the Bere-barrel, after the barrel of whisky drunk at it. The Burns ballad 'The Life and Death of John Barleycorn' would often be recited. At the Kirn the Corn Maiden was placed at the head of the table in front of the girl or reaper given pride of place. Lamb was usually the main dish, with a selection also from beef, chicken, haggis, potatoes, vegetables, oatcakes, plum pudding and cheese. Whisky or ale was drunk. Two dishes were made out of the first grain. Ale-Crowdie (or Meal-and-Ale) was made by pouring ale on meal in a bowl, then adding honey or treacle to sweeten, and finally whisky. **Cranachan or Cream Crowdie** *(see p.202 for recipe)* was a mixture of toasted oatmeal and whipped cream, containing a ring. The lucky finder was sure to be first to marry. A popular dance after the feast was Babbity Bowster.

The Corn Maiden would be taken down on the morning of St Bride's Day or Candlemas (or in Buchan on Old Yule Eve) to be fed to plough horses and used to make Bride's Bed, or on New Year's Day in some areas to be fed to pregnant cows or mares.

Sadly, most of these harvest customs died with the introduction of mechanised harvesting in the 19th century. A supper and dance is all that is left in most areas.

This takes place on the Sunday after the conclusion of the harvest. As the fish market and most of the fishing boats have gone this is only a small vestige of the celebration it was, but the pulpit is still decorated with nets and other fishing paraphernalia for the service. A model sailing ship can still be seen in the kirk.

TAKE THE A917 SOUTH-EAST FROM ST ANDREWS ALONG THE COAST TO ST MONAN'S.

WALES A Corn Maiden (y gaseg fedi (literally, harvest mare), hag, wrach or corn dolly) was made or plaited in situ from the last stand of corn and then cut. In the latter case it was called the tuft (y gaseg ben fedi – 'the end-of-the-reaping mare'). On returning to the farmhouse, the men were subject to a barring-out custom and had to try subterfuges to gain entry. The women tried to throw water over the mare, which had to be kept dry if at all possible. The mare was generally not made if reaping continued after mid-September. These customs died out about 1889.

Throughout Wales there was a tradition of helping one's neighbour with farming tasks like harvesting, and farmers in an area would co-ordinate their schedules so that a combined labour force was available to all, such as the wheat reaping-party, y fedel wenith. Collaborating families exchanged gifts, and cottagers and smallholders who helped would be allowed to grow potatoes on the farmer's land. Harvest supper might include beef, mutton, potatoes, mashed turnips, a wheaten flour pudding, oatcake, **Flummery** *(see p.202 for recipe)*, whey, whipod, a dish of rice, currants, raisins, white bread and treacle, and a tart called **Teisen Blat (Harvest Cake)** *(see p.202 for recipe)*.

This was followed by dancing to a fiddler and games. There may also have been harp playing and the singing of penillion stanzas. Dai Siôn Goch was a broom dance performed by two dressed in rags. A popular game was Rhibo, which has the look of a vestigial fertility rite.

Rhibo *Six men stand in two rows of three, facing each other. Opposite pairs hold hands. A man and a woman are laid side by side across the arms and thrown up and down.*

Some farmers provided a whole day of festivities for their reapers, including a breakfast of bread, cheese, buttermilk and whey.

Sometimes the harvest feast was delayed until Winter's Eve (Nos galan gaeaf) – All Hallows' Eve, when the potatoes would have all been lifted. Llandysul Harvest Pie *(see p.202 for recipe)* was eaten at this time.

CORNWALL Harvest Supper and Harvest Home customs were found, including binding the last sheaf – called 'the neck'. In West Cornwall this was always cut by the oldest reaper, with much celebration. The old reaper shouts 'I hav'et!' three times. Each time the others reply 'What hav'ee?' and the old reaper rejoins 'A neck!' This exchange is called 'Crying the Neck'. The sheaf was decorated with ribbons and flowers before hanging it up on a beam in his kitchen. A girl with a pail of water stood ready for a barring-out custom, to soak whoever tries to enter with the sheaf.

The last sheaf of the barley harvest was called the 'crow-sheaf' or 'crow'. In East Cornwall the neck was made a different shape and first carried to the mowhay – an enclosure for ricks of corn or hay – for Crying the Crow. Then it was hung up until Christmas Day, when it was given to the best ox in the stalls.

In Scilly a sheep was killed and every scrap eaten.

The Old Cornwall Society has revived the Crying the Neck ceremony in Helston, on the last Friday in August.

BRITTANY Many workers hired themselves for the harvest period, wearing an ear of corn in their hat or belt at hiring fairs. Small tenant farmers joined forces and harvested each other's fields with a larger labour force. Before the harvesting started the food was made for their midday break. At Plouër hard rolls were made with egg in the dough, and they were soaked in milk in the morning to soften them for eating. A similar recipe using sugar was made into a cake. The first two handfuls of corn cut were made into a cross for luck and protection from eddies. The last sheaf was decorated with flowers and oak branches, made to look like a person. If the farmer was married then two were made, a small one within a larger one, the whole being called La Mère Gerbe (Mother Sheaf). It was presented to the farmer's wife, and she then served the cider and food, first to the reaper who cut the last sheaf. The procession back from the fields was led by the cutter of the last sheaf, who held it aloft on a pitchfork, while the others held their tools aloft like flagpoles. The sheaves were in wagons. Sometimes the farmer and his wife were taken triumphantly round their fields in a barrow, sitting on the last sheaf, handing out apples. The reapers put flowers in their hats. The farmer's wife served the harvest meal (pleurzorn) with wine.

Before threshing, the children unbound the sheaves. When threshing machines replaced flails in the 1920s they too were adorned at the end of their work. Afterwards came the winnowing, to separate the chaff from the grain by using a sifter and the breeze. The chaff was collected on a cloth and used to stuff mattresses and pillows. Vanning machines replaced this job.

The grain was stored in a loft to dry before being taken to the miller to produce flour and bran in watermill and windmill.

The oats harvesters had a custom of concealing the last sheaf under the straw and the other workers had to find it. The one who did had the honour of leading the farmer in the procession round the fields, his wife being carried on a chair. After a drink of cider the last sheaf was then beaten to pieces. Oat bales were used to make straw beds to sleep on, whereas animal bedding was of wheat straw.

The buckwheat harvest was normally in September, and sickles were preferred to a reaping machine because there was so much grain loss in the latter. The sheaves were made into a conical shape and stood unbound. Also, flails were preferred for threshing, then the pellicules were removed by stamping the feet in a circular movement before winnowing. Buckwheat was used for crêpes and 'black bread', and the honey was thought superior to heather or white-clover honey.

Cider apples were also harvested in September and pressed with buckwheat awn, in alternate layers, which flavoured the cider.

The potato harvest was also during the month of September, using hoes and osier basket sieves. The remains of the plants were called haulins, and were burned in the evening, roasting misshapen potatoes on the embers.

September saw the seaweed harvest, by women at low tide. They took it to ovens built and operated by the men. They lined ditches with stones, using more stones to create compartments. The ash, rich in sodium, was either used on the fields as fertilizer or sold to manufacturers of pharmaceuticals.

After the harvest farmers washed their horses for luck and good health as well as cleanliness, and paid a tithe to the Roman Catholic Church.

Threshing corn for Harvest, Brittany, 1925

September customs

The corn harvest finished this month, and what was not kept was sold. Hazelnuts were picked early in the month, then blackberries and later crab apples for roasting or making into preserves. Eating and cooking apples were picked, and cider-making started at the end of the month.Gorse was cut for fuel for ovens and bracken was cut to make bedding. The whitebait season began for fishermen.

Then the hired hands were paid off, packed their belongings and left for hiring fairs to look for other work. Geese were sold at these Michaelmas fairs, and were the main course at Michaelmas feasts.

In Brittany this was the second of the two months when washing was done. It was called the month of the 'White Straw' because harvesting had finished. The buckwheat, cider-apple, potato and seaweed harvesting was this month.

Variable Dates

IRELAND

Galway Oyster Festival, Galway Co. Galway

The Galway Bay oysters are highly prized in Ireland. Nowadays they are served with brown bread and butter, cayenne pepper and lemon wedges, but in the past, when much cheaper, they were fried in batter and put in soups and soufflés.

GALWAY IS THE PRINCIPAL TOWN OF THE COUNTY.

SCOTLAND

Highland Games, Blairgowrie Tayside

A characteristic local event is a tug-of-war using a 736 ft rope and 300 pullers, which takes place in early September.

BLAIRGOWRIE IS ON THE A923, NORTH-EAST OF DUNDEE.

Highland Games, Oban Strathclyde

OBAN IS AT THE JUNCTION OF THE A85 AND A816.

Highland Games, Aboyne

ABOYNE IS ON THE A93 WEST OF ABERDEEN.

The Arbroath Pageant, Arbroath

This occasional event dates from 1947 and re-enacts a number of episodes connected with the Declaration of Independence at Arbroath on 6th April 1320. The declaration was sent as a letter to Pope John XXII, who favoured the English, but he was so moved by its plea for freedom and justice that he beseeched Edward II to be reasonable. Unfortunately, the pageant has not been held since fire destroyed the props and costumes in 1981, but interest in reviving it remains.

ARBROATH IS ON THE A92 NORTH-EAST OF DUNDEE.

CORNWALL When the hazelnuts were ripe and nutting day was held, Penryn, near Falmouth, chose a Mock Mayor. The journeymen tailors went to Mylor parish, on the opposite side of the Fal, and chose the wittiest candidate as the Mayor of Mylor. He was then borne on the shoulders of four men back to Penryn, preceded by torch-bearers, two town-serjeants in gowns and cocked hats with cabbages instead of maces, and surrounded by a guard armed with staves. A band met them on the edge of Penryn and played them into the Town Hall, where the 'Mayor' made an amusing speech. Then feasting, bonfire and fireworks closed the day.

Crying the Neck, St Ives

See Harvest Customs for details of this custom, which takes place in early September.

TAKE THE A3074 NORTH FROM LELANT OR THE B3311 NORTH FROM PENZANCE.

The Gorsedd of Cornish Bards, Nine Maidens standing stones, Boscawen Un

This takes place in early September. The stones at this ancient earthwork are said to be petrified maidens, turned to stone for dancing on a Sunday. The proceedings at the Gorsedd, instituted in 1928, are held in Cornish, and representatives from the other Celtic nations are invited.

TAKE THE A39 SOUTH-WEST FROM WADEBRIDGE AND THE NINE MAIDENS ARE ON THE LEFT BEFORE ROSENANNON.

Crying the Neck, St Keverne

This takes place at the end of September.

TAKE THE A3083 SOUTH FROM HELSTON, THEN LEFT ON THE B3293, THEN LEFT TO ST KEVERNE.

At some time this month the Cornish wrestling championships are held in one of the villages where the sport has been preserved. One of these is St Wenn, in the kaolin-producing district of mid-Cornwall, the home of the Chapman family of wrestlers. Devonian wrestling is similar to Cornish wrestling but the former allows kicking.

BRITTANY

✿ Buckwheat Festival, Dol-de-Bretagne   Ille-et-Vilaine
DOL-DE-BRETAGNE IS ON THE N176 EAST OF CHÂTEAUNEUF D'ILLE-ET-VILAINE.

♪ Festival de la Chanson Québécoise, St-Malo   Ille-et-Vilaine
This takes place in early September.
ST-MALO IS ON THE N137, ON THE NORTH COAST.

✿ Les Paradis de Christoph Colomb, Fougères   Ille-et-Vilaine
This takes place in early September.
FOUGÈRES IS ON THE N12 NORTH-EAST OF RENNES.

✚ Pardon Notre-Dame, Bulat-Pestivien   Côtes d'Armor
This takes place in the first half of September.
BULAT-PESTIVIEN IS ON AN UNCLASSIFIED ROAD EAST OF RENNES.

✚ Pardon de la Peinière, Saint-Didier   Ille-et-Vilaine
This takes place in the second half of September.

Fixed Dates

1st September St Giles' Day
CELTIC St Giles lived in the 8th century. He was crippled by a wound and became the patron saint of cripples and beggars. Many feasts and fairs were held on this day.
SCOTLAND St Giles was patron saint of Edinburgh, and today, before the Reformation, a procession of guild craftsmen, with the relics of the saint, was held.

3rd September Nutting Day
CELTIC On the old calendar this was the day when hazelnuts were collected, but now they are unlikely to be ready.
   Lacemakers were allowed to light candles on this day to work by, and could so do until Shrove Tuesday.

First Friday in September
CORNWALL

⚑ Crying the Neck, Madron, near Penzance   Cornwall
See Harvest Customs for details of this ceremony, which starts at 6.30 pm.
MADRON IS ON AN UNCLASSIFIED ROAD NORTH-WEST FROM PENZANCE THROUGH HEAMOOR.

First Saturday in September
SCOTLAND

✿ The Fishermen's Walk, Musselburgh   Lothian
The town is decorated with nets and other fishing paraphernalia for this procession led by the Fish Callant and Fishwife. There are various games, such as loading the needle, for ladies; a shawl race and rope-throwing.
MUSSELBURGH IS ON THE A199 EAST OUT OF EDINBURGH.

◉ Braemar Highland Gathering and Games,
Princess Royal and Duke of Fife Memorial Park, Braemar   Grampian
The games sometimes take place in the second week of September.
TAKE THE A93 WEST FROM ABERDEEN.

First Sunday in September
BRITTANY

✙ **Grand Pardon de Notre-Dame, Le Folgoët**   Finistère

This sometimes takes place on 8th September, or 2nd September if the 8th is a Sunday. The venue is the famous shrine of the 'Fool in the Wood', and is a very large pardon. The shrine is at the site of a simpleton's grave, above which a miraculous lily with the words 'Ave Maria' was found in flower. It has been a place of pilgrimage since the 15th century.

LE FOLGOËT IS JUST SOUTH OF LESNEVEN.

✙ **Pardon Notre-Dame de Rocamadour, Camaret-sur-Mer**   Finistère

This includes a blessing of the sea.

CAMARET-SUR-MER IS ON THE D8 WEST OF CROZON.

✙ **Grand Pardon de Penhors, Pouldreuzic (Penhors)**   Finistère

POULDREUZIC IS ON AN UNCLASSIFIED ROAD SOUTH-EAST OF PLOZÉVET.

✙ **Pardon St-Antoine, Ploudiry**   Finistère

PLOUDIRY IS ON AN UNCLASSIFIED ROAD NORTH-EAST OF BREST.

✙ **Pardon de Notre-Dame-de-la-Grande-Puissance**   Lamballe

LAMBALLE IS ON THE N12 EAST OF ST BRIEUC.

7th September
SCOTLAND The Riding of the Landimyrs took place in Aberdeen today in 1840, and was held for the last time in 1889.

8th September Our Lady's Birthday, Feast of the Nativity of the Blessed Virgin Mary
BRITTANY

✙ **Pardon de Notre-Dame-de-Bulat, Bulat-Pestivien**   Côtes-d'Armor

BULAT-PESTIVIEN IS ON AN UNCLASSIFIED ROAD SOUTH-WEST OF GUINGAMP.

✙ **Pardon de Notre-Dame-du-Roncier, Josselin**   Morbihan

This is also known as the 'Barker's Pardon' after three local children were cured of epilepsy at a festival in 1728.

JOSSELIN IS ON THE N24 WEST OF PLOËRMEL.

✞ **Pardon de St Carnély and St Carnély (Cornély, Cornelius) Cattle Festival, Carnac**   Morbihan
St Carnély is the patron saint of Carnac, and the festival used to be a full pardon with fair and animal market. Pilgrims went round the church on their knees. As the date is near the autumnal equinox the ceremony may have a pagan origin. Cattle used to be driven through the smoke of Midsummer Eve bonfires to keep diseases at bay, the biggest such bonfire being lit on Mont Saint-Michel, outside Carnac. Farmers drove cured cattle in silence to the church and on to St Cornély's Fountain, where water was poured over them. They returned in silence, via the church.
CARNAC IS ON THE D781 SOUTH-EAST OF LORIENT.

Second Thursday and Friday in September
SCOTLAND

🎵 **The Piping Championships, Inverness**   Highland
INVERNESS IS AT THE JUNCTION OF THE A9, A96 AND A82.

14th September Holy-Cross Day, Finding of the Cross, Holy-Rood Day
CELTIC It is said that 'The Devil goes a-nutting' on this day; young people gather nuts, but some avoid them lest the Devil abduct them. Nuts were thought to improve fertility, and girls also tended to avoid collecting them because they feared they would fall pregnant.
SCOTLAND The Devil ends the blackberry-picking season today; see 10th October for details.
BRITTANY Today a gathering took place at Médréac called Little Summer, as the weather was guaranteed to be fine today. A similar event called L'Ocraquelin took place at Saint-Cast.

17th September
CORNWALL Probus and Grace Fair, Probus, East Cornwall, was held. The charter was granted by Charles II after the Restoration to a Mr Williams, with whom he had stayed for a time during the Civil War. It is said that St Probus built the church but his funds ran out before the tower could be built. He had to ask St Grace for help, so giving the village two patron saints.

20th September
BRITTANY This is St Eustache's Day, and he was credited with being able to cure all illnesses. At his chapel in Taillay gatherings of pilgrims occurred today, at the Feast of Saint Jean and at Pentecost.

21st September The Autumnal Equinox, St Matthew's Day
CELTIC This is the Devil's principal Nutting Day; see 14th September for details.
BRITTANY

✞ **Pardon de Notre-Dame Tronoën, St Jean-Trolimon**   Finistère
ST JEAN-TROLIMON IS ON AN UNCLASSIFIED ROAD, WEST OF PONT L'ABBÉ.

Third Sunday in September
BRITTANY

✞ **Pardon of St Cado, Belz**   Morbihan
St Cado came originally from Wales. The event sometimes takes place on 21st September.
BELZ IS ON THE D22 WEST OF AURAY.

✞ **Pardon de Kermaria-en-Isquit, Plouha**   Côtes-d'Armor
The event sometimes takes place on 21st September.
PLOUHA IS ON THE D786 NORTH-WEST OF ST BRIEUC.

Pardon de Notre-Dame de la Joie, Pontivy — Morbihan

PONTIVY IS ON THE D764 NORTH-WEST OF JOSSELIN.

Pardon, Notre-Dame-de-Tronoën — Finistère

NOTRE-DAME-DE-TRONOËN IS ON AN UNCLASSIFIED ROAD WEST OF PONT L'ABBÉ.

Third Friday in September

SCOTLAND

The Fishermen's Walk, Cockenzie — Fisherrow and Port Seton

This is now commemorated just by a dinner-dance in the burgh hall.

TAKE THE B1348 EAST OUT OF EDINBURGH.

23rd September St Tegla's Day

CELTIC St Tegla (or St Thecla) lived in the 1st century and she was a hermit, persecuted by the Romans. It may be that she is the same Tegla after whom Llandegla in Clwyd and Llandegley in Powys are named. St Tegla's Well in the former was visited by epileptics at sunset. Men brought a cockerel and women a hen, and proceeded to put the birds through a series of rituals in order to transfer the condition to the birds.

25th September Old Holy Rood Day, Old Holy Cross Day

SCOTLAND This is St Barr's Day. On Barra the Ridings described under Michaelmas were held at Traigh-cille-Barra.

The Riding of the Marches at Haddington took place today in 1430, and was last done in 1820.

CORNWALL

Old Fair, Summercourt — Cornwall

This is Cornwall's largest fair, and was formerly a trading fair, with travelling theatre, waxworks and puppet shows.

SUMMERCOURT IS SOUTH-EAST OF NEWQUAY, AT THE JUNCTION OF THE A30 AND A3058.

Old Fair, Summercourt, Cornwall, 1912

Last week in September
SCOTLAND

⬤ Walking the Marches, Stirling   Central

This is an official, rather than a public, occasion, which takes place every seven years (revived 1962).
STIRLING IS TO THE EAST OF JUNCTION 10 OF THE M9.

Fourth Sunday in September
BRITTANY

🖐 Pardon Biniou-Bombarde (Musicians' or Bellringers' Pardon), Gourin   Morbihan

This sometimes takes place on the Sunday nearest 29th September.
GOURIN IS ON THE D1 WEST OF GUEMENÉ-SUR-SCORFF.

✠ Feast of the Archangel St Michael, Mont-St-Michel   Ille-et-Vilaine

This sometimes takes place on the Sunday nearest 29th September.
MONT-ST-MICHEL IS ON THE D976 NORTH OF PONTORSON.

✠ Butter Festival Pardon, St Herbot Church   Finistère

St Herbot was the patron saint of horned animals, and his statue shows him with a dish of butter.
ST HERBOT CHURCH IS SOUTH-WEST OF HUELGOAT.

Last Sunday in September
BRITTANY

✠ Pardon de Notre-Dame-du-Voeux (Vows), Hennebont   Morbihan

HENNEBONT IS NORTH-EAST OF LORIENT.

✠ Pardon, Pont l'Abbé   Finistère

PONT L'ABBÉ IS ON AN UNCLASSIFIED ROAD SOUTH-WEST OF QUIMPER.

✠ Pardon de St-Michel, Plouguerneau   Finistère

PLOUGUERNEAU IS ON AN UNCLASSIFIED ROAD NORTH OF LANNILIS.

Sunday before St Michael's Day
SCOTLAND This was Carrot Sunday, when that vegetable was traditionally lifted. Some were saved for the horses at the Michaelmas Ridings.

27th September St Barry's Day
CELTIC St Barry lived on Glamorgan Island, South Glamorgan, now renamed Barry Island. It became a place of pilgrimage.

28th September Michaelmas Eve
CELTIC Bonfires were lit on Michaelmas Eve in some locations and a traditional evening meal was roast lamb.

SCOTLAND St Michael was the patron saint of fishermen and horsemen, and in the Hebrides the cult of an ancient sea god was transferred to him. In addition to the feasting and dancing this evening there was a mumming play performed in which, unusually, a heroine is slain and revived. The main dish was roast unmated lamb, followed by Struan Micheil, a cake made from sheep's milk, eggs, butter and cereals. It was cooked in a lamb's skin over a fire of burning rowan, oak and bramble. A cross was marked on each cake, and a piece was thrown on the fire to placate the Devil. Each region had its own traditional recipe and shape for the cake.

    Horses were guarded lest they be taken for the rides tomorrow.

    On St Kilda animals were sained with salt, fire and water.

29th September Michaelmas Day, St Michael's Day, Feast of St Michael and All Angels

CELTIC Today marked the end of harvesting, and farmers could calculate how many animals they could feed during the winter and how many would have to be sold, slaughtered or salted down. As a quarter day it was a time to pay rents and settle other financial transactions. In addition to fairs for animal sales there were many hiring fairs for domestic servants and for farm labourers to try and get winter employment after the harvest.

Curfew ('cover fire') bells were often rung from Michaelmas to Lady Day.

Roast goose stuffed with apples is traditionally eaten, with fresh produce and freshly baked bread. Goose is less fatty at this time of year than at Christmas, but it is still stuffed with apple when cooked to absorb the fat. There were many Goose Fairs held on this day, to which geese were often walked many miles. Tenants used to include a goose in the payment of their Michaelmas rent.

IRELAND The English introduced this feast day into Ireland, and on it were done many transactions in areas of English influence which were characteristic of a Celtic quarter day.

Farmers gave geese as gifts, even to the poor, and sold the down for the filling of pillows and mattresses. The killing of a goose or cock may have originally been a sacrifice to St Michael. **Roast goose** *(see p.202 for recipe)* was traditionally served with **Gooseberry and Fennel Sauce** *(see p.202 for recipe)*, **Onion Sauce** *(see p.202 for recipe)* or **Apple Sauce** *(see p.202 for recipe)*.

In various parts of Ireland Michaelmas marked the beginning of apple-picking and cider-making, and of the hunting season, and the end of the fishing season.

The people concerned with the holiday trade in the Co. Waterford resort of Tramore used to hold a procession to the beach and throw an effigy of St Michael, called 'Micil', into the sea. This was a ceremonial act of retaliation for their loss of earnings at the end of the tourist season.

ISLE OF MAN Kirk Michael village and parish was named after this saint. There used to be a great market today in Douglas, and a fair at Ballasalla. A roast goose dish such as **Manx Michaelmas Goose with Apple Sauce** *(see p.202 for recipe)* was eaten.

SCOTLAND St Michael was patron saint of horses and riders, of the sea and maritime lands, and of boats and sailors. This was an important day in the Hebrides and the west-coast towns. Wild carrots were dug up and given as presents, cakes were baked of mixed flour, and a lamb was killed for the evening feast. Before this, there was a thanksgiving service for the fruits of the fields and flocks, at which the lamb and struan were blessed. Then, pieces of lamb and struan were put in a basket and taken round to the poor. Families would then visit graves of deceased relatives, often on horseback – called circuiting. Circuiters used to exchange gifts, especially carrots. Horses were raced along the beaches, ridden bareback with woven straw harnesses, as part of a surviving sea god ceremony. Men had their sweethearts up behind, and they gave each other gifts afterwards. Sometimes horses were 'borrowed' from neighbours, but were always returned the next day. These Michaelmas Ridings (called Oda) have been recorded from Coll, Harris, Lewis, Skye and Tiree. There were also athletics events. In the evening a dance was held, at which young men and women exchanged gifts. Those not attending exchanged struans and carrots with their neighbours. Although the Michaelmas struan is still baked in the Western Isles, the other customs died out in the mid-19th century.

Galashiels had a Michaelmas Fair, which is commemorated today by a Michaelmas Dinner.

BRITTANY St Michel's Day was a house and share rent day for many farms, particularly in Côtes-du-Nord ('All out, St Michel has come!'). This saying was used to get reluctant children to leave the house, or to men to tell them it is time to go to work.

At Matignon today corn seeds were blessed and mingled with the first sowing, while at Renac in Morbihan it was done on St Julien's Day.

✹ Michaelmas Fair, St Brieuc　　　　　　　　　　　　　　　　　　Côtes d'Armor
ST BRIEUC IS ON THE NORTH COAST, ON THE N12.

30th September

BRITTANY This was Saint Jérôme's Day. Yesterday, before paying the rent, people would say, 'Tomorrow is Saint-Jérôme, give the money to the man.' At Planguenoual, at the chapel dedicated to St Michel, corn seeds were blessed and mingled with the first sowing.

October
customs

As the last month of the Old Celtic Year October signalled the close of autumn and the beginning of winter after Samhuin on the 31st. People began to stockpile fuel, dry and preserve produce, and sort out warm clothing, and then prepared for the quarter day rituals, devotions and divinations which would see them through Samhuin, the most feared day of the year.

The blackberry, nut and oyster seasons closed and most harvesting activity ended. In the Isle of Man shares were paid to herring fishermen as the season ended in October, and new hiring contracts were made. Sometimes a Boat Supper would be held in celebration. In Brittany the chestnuts were gathered. Those livestock which were not to be kept over winter, and yearlings born early, were sold, and, as hiring fairs continued, domestic workers and labourers for the winter would be taken on.

Variable Dates

SCOTLAND In the new term at St Andrews University bejants (first-year undergraduates) are assigned to a mentor, a senior undergraduate, to help them settle in. After four weeks it is customary for them to give a gift of raisins (nowadays wine) for which a receipt in Latin must be written. The receipt must be carried by the bejant for the whole day, including into lectures. This has given rise to the prank by seniors of writing the receipt on an unwieldy object such as a wrecked car or cow.

Fixed Dates

1st October
ISLE OF MAN All peat stacked in public turbaries had to be removed by this date.

First Sunday in October
CELTIC This was Harvest Festival in English areas. In 1532 Henry VIII decreed that this day be used for wakes, dedication feasts to church saints. The association with saints and the over-indulgence brought opposition from Protestants after the Reformation, and, like Ales, the wakes declined. Cornish revels continued into the 20th century, with one surviving at Marhamchurch, now on the Sunday and Monday after 12th August.

3rd October St Blanche's Day

BRITTANY St Blanche's chapel at St-Cast was visited by those seeking a cure for a whitlow.

First week in October
SCOTLAND

✿ National Gaelic Mod

This gathering is held on a different site each year.

5th October St Faith's Eve

CELTIC Unmarried women would engage in divination to learn the name of her future husband.
IRELAND This was the start of Ballinasloe Fair in Co. Galway, whose site was on an ancient drove road. Sheep and cattle sales featured in this fair, which lasted until 9th October.

8th October St Keyne's Day

CELTIC The daughter of the 6th-century Welsh King Brychan, St Keyne became a missionary in South Wales and West Wales (now called Cornwall).

Second week in October
SCOTLAND

⚜ Riding of the Marches, Elgin

Grampian

This is held every second year.

TAKE THE A96 EAST FROM NAIRN.

9th October

BRITTANY Today and on Saint Simon's Day husbandmen had fairs which were used to find a business partner and for exhibiting items for sale.

Crowning the Bard at the Rothesay Mod, 1952

10th October Old Michaelmas Day

CELTIC When St Michael, the chief of the archangels, ejected the Devil from heaven the incident led to the tradition of ceasing the picking and preserving of blackberries, or regarding it as unlucky, on this day, as the Devil, according to legend, landed on a bramble bush. So, he got his just desserts and we lost ours. The mildew that begins to grow on late blackberries is said to be the Devil's spit. The tradition on this day was strongest in Wales and Cornwall.

ISLE OF MAN Kirk Michael Fair was held, originally at Michaelmas, and was still in existence in 1941. It was a hiring fair for farm labourers. A traditional way to preserve the last of the blackberries was to make **Blackberry Wine** *(see p.203 for recipe)*.

CORNWALL A Mock Mayor was elected at Lostwithiel by torchlight. A similar ceremony took place at St John's, Helston and Buryan, while at Penzance there was an election for the Mayor of the Quay.

Sunday nearest 10th October

CORNWALL This is the Feast of St Pol-de-Lion, Paul, near Penzance, which is still celebrated. There was an annual bowling match between the men of Paul and Mousehole on the Feasten Monday.

11th October St Canice's Day

CELTIC St Canice was a 6th-century Irish abbot who worked at Inchkenneth on Mull.

12th October

CORNWALL Roast Goose Fair was held at Redruth. Goose was served to visitors, and free to the poor. However, as farm labourers had to give a goose to their employer at Michaelmas this was probably the same one they were eating.

14th October St Selevan's Day

CELTIC St Selevan was a Cornish saint of uncertain provenance, but may have given his name to St Levan near Land's End.

18th October St Luke's Day

SCOTLAND Rutherglen in Glasgow used to have a St Luke's Fair, at which were sold sour cakes made from fermented oat dough.

Third Sunday in October

SCOTLAND This was Winter Sunday in Shetland, when cattle were brought into their byres for the winter and people held their last feast before its onset.

25th October St Crispin's Day, St Crispinian's Day

CELTIC St Crispin and his brother St Crispinian were French, martyred in the 3rd century. St Crispin was the patron saint of shoemakers, and many in the trade took a holiday today. Some also took every Monday as a holiday. On this day also people gave their old shoes to the poor and bought new ones.

SCOTLAND The Cordiners' (Shoemakers') Procession was held before the Reformation.

BRITTANY On Saint Crépin's Day today shoemakers, whose patron he is, in the villages said Mass and this was followed by a feast paid for with money that they had saved during the year.

27th October St Odran's Day

CELTIC St Odran was a contemporary of St Columba on Iona. The story that St Odran was sacrificed and buried in the foundations of St Columba's new church on Iona to protect it is scarcely credible, though it would be perfectly believable had the construction been pagan.

Saturday nearest Hallowe'en

CORNWALL Fruiterers in Penzance and St Ives sold large 'Allan' apples, which everybody in a household ate for luck. Girls put them under their pillows, to dream of their future sweethearts, before eating them.

Sunday nearest Hallowe'en

CORNWALL This day was called Allantide, or Allan's Eve. St Just-in-Penwith held its feast day today. In St Just, St Ives and elsewhere children took apples to bed, ready to eat next morning for luck. Unmarried girls did likewise, hoping to dream of their future partners.

31st October Hallowe'en, All Hallows' Eve, All Saints' Eve, Hollantide Eve

CELTIC After sunset today began the ancient Celtic festival of Samhain, *summer's end* or *the feast to the dying sun*, and the last day of the Celtic Year. This quarter day also combined the functions of Harvest Festival and the Festival of the Dead. It was a Druidic belief that Saman, the Lord of Death, summoned together the souls of the evil people condemned to inhabit the bodies of animals, hence the Irish name for Hallowe'en Oiche Shamhna (The Vigil of Saman). As the leaves fell, annual growth decayed, the sun's strength waned and the nights drew in, the Celts prepared for winter and for the sun to rise next morning. Bonfires were lit. House fires were extinguished, to be rekindled later to welcome the returning souls of the dead, along with offerings of food. At Beltane in the spring the cycle of life would begin again.

The end of year feasting was tempered by fears of, and preparations for, incursions by evil spirits, witches and faeries. Rowan wood was thought to give protection from witches. The harvested crops were already under cover, but animals too were brought in and saining of the farm was done by fire. Anyone going out would hide their face so as not to be recognised by faeries, and they would preferably travel in company. Children were kept indoors. It was the main divination night of the year, for future success, occupations and partners, and also to see who would die in the coming year. Several games played had their origins in Druidic ritual, such as Apple-Ducking and Snap Apple, the use of apples and nuts being very common. Patterns of weather revealed the winter climate to be expected.

Mischief was played, as Trick or Treat or unannounced. Children dressed in masks, carried pumpkin or turnip lanterns, and went from door to door asking for apples, nuts or money. In some areas guisers entertained each household, the disguises being originally to prevent spirits recognising and snatching you.

In an effort to Christianise the festival, the Church substituted the Festival of All Saints (in honour of the blessed dead who had been canonised), or Hallowmas, for Samhuinn, which was originally on 21st February (the date of the Roman Feralia) until moved by Pope Gregory to 1st November. The result is a day of very mixed ritual and celebratory elements.

IRELAND Faeries spat on blackberries so they could not be eaten, and generally it was thought that all unpicked fruit was befouled. Offerings of food and water were left outside for them, and holy water sprinkled on the children, doors and animals. Milking cows were put into the byre and other

Right: Hallowe'en guisers Left: Hallowe'en bonfire

animals brought near the farm. Iron, or a cold ember, was put in cradles. Crosses were put up to protect family and livestock from all malevolence for a year. These might have been of wood or straw woven around two cross-sticks, the latter called Parshells. An additional protection was afforded to travellers by carrying a black-handled knife or by putting a steel needle through the collar or sleeve. Straw dresses were worn, with plaited straw or rush caps. Pots were broken.

The Feast of All Saints tomorrow was a day of abstinence, so meat would not have been on the table tonight as feasting may well have gone on past midnight. Typical fare would include stampy, apple cake, **Potato Apple Cake** *(see p.203 for recipe)*, bairín breac or barm brack, **Champ** *(see p.203 for recipe)* and Colcannon (the last four with divination tokens inside). There are several types of brack (breac), which refers to the fruit in the dough, some cakes, some breads. Bairín just means yeast. **Tea Brack** *(see p.203 for recipe)* is a typical cake and **Currant Soda** *(see p.203 for recipe)* a typical bread. Nuts, **Nut Biscuits** *(see p.203 for recipe)*, cream pancakes, boxty, **Irish Oatcakes** *(see p.203 for recipe)*, **Apple Dumplings** *(see p.203 for recipe)*, blackberry pie, **Brown Cake** *(see p.204 for recipe)* and various puddings such as one similar to the Scottish cloutie dumpling would also have been served.

Last century in Co. Cork there was a Mari Lwyd-type character, called the White Mare (Láir Bhán), but this is no longer seen. It was a horse's head covered by a white sheet, as in Wales, and youths accompanied it, blowing cowhorns, to collect money from householders in the name of Muck Olla, a huge mythical pig that had been slain. Dublin children still dress up in masks and other disguises and go from door to door asking for apples and nuts for a Hallowe'en party. Trick or Treat is still done and was also common in Belfast.

In Co. Galway, similar crosses to St Brighid's Crosses, of wood or straw, were put up in the byre. **ISLE OF MAN** Effectively, winter and Savin, the start of the Celtic New Year, began this evening. Savin was also called Hop Tu Naa ('This is the Night'), the same as the New Year Feast. Hollantide Eve was also called Hogmanaye Night. Animals that could not be kept through the winter would be slaughtered and salted down. It was customary for children to go round with turnip lanterns, singing 'Oie Houney' and collecting money. There was much prophesying, weather prediction and fortune-telling, customs that gradually were transferred to Christmas and the New Year in January.

The traditional supper this evening is potatoes, parsnips and fish pounded together with butter. Children carried turnip lanterns from house to house, asking for bonnags (oatcakes).
SCOTLAND The goddess of winter, Cailleach Bheur, wakes up and begins her reign tonight. Families lit bonfires on hilltops at dusk to combat the powers of darkness, and guarded them well lest others should steal material from them, and with it their luck. This custom was still observed in the early 1900s in Balquhidder, Central Region. Generally household fires were put out tonight and rekindled from the Hallowe'en fire. The flames were thought to consume invisible spirits, and the smoke and ashes also had purifying powers. Up to the mid-19th century blazing torches were carried sunwise round fields to purify them, or in some places blazing faggots on poles, which is still done for commemorative purposes at Braemar. Young people ran through the fire. Other fire customs existed in Scotland. At Balmoral, Grampian, an effigy called Shandy Dann was burned, and on the White Cart River at Paisley, Strathclyde, platforms were built on which to light fires. When fires died in Callander, Tayside, an ash circle was made and a stone placed on it for every person present. If any were removed or damaged in the night that person was 'fey' and would die within the year. Hallowe'en fires are still lit, but most accompanying customs have lapsed.

As on all quarter days bannocks were baked, except in Hebrides where this was carried out at Michaelmas. The shapes varied, with that on St Kilda being large, triangular and furrowed. At Rutherglen, Strathclyde, sour cakes were ceremonially baked in preparation for St Luke's Fair the following day. Whoever made them was referred to as 'Bride', after the goddess whose reign ended at Hallowe'en. The other women sat round the fire in a circle, as in the trench around the Beltane fire.

Hallowe'en is Mischief Night in Sutherland and Caithness, with pranks such as removing gates and switching property, including animals, between owners. Pranksters disguise themselves for obvious reasons, but this is a custom designed to prevent evil spirits recognising anyone abroad tonight. In earlier times mischief was more widespread, but even today if anyone complains they are remembered, and given more severe treatment next year.

Bannocks, cream-crowdie: a Hallowe'en variant was **Fortune-telling Crowdie** *(see p.204 for recipe)* champit tatties, buttered sowans and **Cloutie Dumpling** *(see p.204 for recipe)* were all eaten today.

Prior to Hallowe'en in Bragar, Lewis in the Hebrides, local people brewed ale in St Mulray Church from their own malt for offering to the sea god Shony (or Spony) for a bountiful crop of seaweed for fertilising the land.

Guisers went from house to house entertaining as at Hogmanay and Yule, but unlike the latter two this was never Christianised. Hogmanay and Yule guisers appeared in their play The Goloshan as the Twelve Apostles, but the Hallowe'en guisers hid their faces, from evil spirits, with masks and dressed as ghouls. Some groups blackened their faces instead, a relic of the Druidic custom to give protection and good luck. Shetland guisers were called Grülacks, and they collected food for their feast The Hallowmas Foy. Nowadays children do the guising, in masks and fancy dress, and are given coins, apples and nuts. They light a bonfire afterwards and jump through the flames, then blacken their faces with the ash.

In more recent times decorated Hallowe'en cakes have been made, often in orange and black, and eaten at fancy-dress parties, with games played and dancing. **Ginger Biscuits** *(see p.204 for recipe)* are popular.

✪ Hallowmas Fair, Grassmarket, Edinburgh   Lothian
This was originally held on the fairy hill Calton Hill. Gingerbread is traditionally sold.
EDINBURGH IS THE PRINCIPAL CITY OF SCOTLAND.

🎭 Hallowe'en Guisers, Brechin   Tayside
These are all that remains of what was a large parade of costumed characters and decorated vehicles, with accompanying festivities, followed by a ball.
BRECHIN IS ON THE A90 NORTH OF DUNDEE.

WALES This was Winter's Eve, Nos Galan Gaeaf, also called Apple and Candle Night.

Bonfires, often of furze and faggots, were lit on hilltops, and youngsters would scare away spirits by blowing horns, roast apples and potatoes, dance and sing, and jump through the flames. An older custom was to run sunwise round the fire, spiralling nearer each time until it was too hot to venture further. The bravest had the most luck to look forward to in the new year. Stones were individually marked and put in the fire, to be searched for next morning. Finding your own was a good omen for the year, your luck depending on how clean it had been burned, but failure to find it was an omen of death.

On retiring from the hills a feast was had, which in north Powys may have included the meal **Mash o' Nine Sorts** *(see p.204 for recipe)*. This dish contained potatoes, carrots, turnips, peas, parsnips, leeks, pepper, salt and milk made into a mash, with a ring buried in it. Everyone dipped in, and whoever found the ring would be first to marry.

Another dish used was punch nep, which is a buttered mixture of mashed potato and mashed turnip. A wassail bowl is recorded from south-east Dyfed. Apples were hung over a fire to roast, then added to hot ale, followed by buns, biscuits, sugar, raisins and spices. Sometimes it would be drunk from a puzzle-jug, several of whose many openings must be stoppered to avoid pouring ale over yourself. In north-west Gwynedd white cheese and oatmeal bread were eaten, and a piece of bread placed on an outside window sill in the hope of reciprocal kindness for those inside.

The harvest feast was sometimes held today, and the participants invited to a feast on New Year's Day (or Old New Year's Day). Animals were often slaughtered today for winter, and some farmers gave poor neighbours a little meat.

Guisers, called gwrachod (hags), men dressed in women's clothes and women dressed in men's clothes, went from door to door singing and soliciting nuts and apples. This tradition is recorded from Llansanffraid-ym-Mechain, Powys, until the end of the 19th century, and today children go round asking for fruit. Masks or animal skins, particularly sheep, were often worn. A prank played tonight was to leave a turnip lantern in a place where someone would suddenly come across it.

BRITTANY Food is still left out in case the souls of the dead return home. By today graves had fresh flowers put on in preparation for All Saints' Day tomorrow.

Children hollowed out beets, cut eyes, a nose and a mouth, put a candle inside, then left them partly concealed to frighten people after dark, or put them on window sills and tapped the window.

November
customs

The darkness and foreboding of Samhuin safely over, the first month of the Old Celtic Year began with a remembrance of the family dead, and then final preparations for the winter sojourn made. The last of the hiring and other fairs dispersed after Martinmas. St Martin's Fair, Trevine, Dyfed, lasted into the 20th century. In Cornwall the pilchard fishing season ended this month. In Brittany November was called the Black Month because of the mists, low cloud and darkening days. Beet was harvested there this month, for animal food during the winter. After slaughtered cattle, pigs and goats were salted down for food stocks, as happened everywhere, the Welsh gathered mussels from beaches and mud-flats, and made them into **Mussel Stew** *(see p.204 for recipe)*.

It was also the custom in Wales for neighbours to invite each other in turn to share a feast from their newly provisioned storeroom with them and their relatives, and other villagers may be taken portions.

It was a strong tradition for the family to settle down in front of the fire for weaving and knitting, harp and other instrumental music, singing and story-telling, the latter still alive and well in Brittany.

Towards the end of the month Clementing and Catterning festivities, associated with traditional holidays taken by rural craftworkers at a time when the shortening days meant a loss of good working light, were widely held, and these were scarcely over when Advent began.

Variable Dates

CORNWALL On a night in November boys in Padstow celebrated Skip-skop Night, by going from door to door asking for money to buy food for a feast. They used sling and stone to strike the door. If there was no reply and the door was open they would throw dirt, winkle shells and other rubbish in.

Fixed Dates

1st November **All Saints' Day, All Hallows' Day, Hollantide Day, All Souls' Eve, St Cadfan's Day**
CELTIC On this day people prayed for their departed relatives, leaving food and lighted candles for them in case their souls revisited the house. This custom lasted longest in Catholic areas after the Reformation. There was some transference of Hallowe'en customs, for example bonfires, mischief, guising and mumming. This was not as solemn a day as All Souls' Day tomorrow.

Souling, the visiting of each house in the village begging for soul-cakes in return for a song or blessing, was practised in Wales, probably as a result of English influence because it was such a strong tradition in the border county of Cheshire.

All Saints' Day was treated as a quarter day.

St Cadfan lived in 5th-century Rhyl, Clwyd, and a stone in the church at Towyn is said to mark his grave.

IRELAND Candles for departed relatives were put in windows before nightfall.

As the end of the farming year it was the time to start winter storage. Turf, bog-deal (partly fossilised pine trees), and wood were laid up. Winter wheat would have all been sown by now. Labourers were paid their summer wages and rents and hiring agreements honoured. There were many fairs and markets, notably Snap-apple Fair at Kilmallock.

ISLE OF MAN Mummers went round on this day used to begin their play by saying 'Tonight is New Year's Night, The Moon shines Fair and Bright.' This comes from an Old Hollantide Eve (11th November) rhyme chanted by boys as they went from house to house whacking the door with a cudgel and running off. In some areas boys carried sticks with cabbages or turnips stuck in the top and knocked with these to ask for herrings, potatoes or other gifts.

Hollantide Fair was held at St John's until the end of the 19th century and was an important hiring fair. Land and property was let or leased today, and rents fell due.

SCOTLAND Children go around as guisers, with blackened faces, from door to door, begging for food and money.

Today was the day when pranksters were tried in Kail Courts, so called from the common mischief of throwing cabbage stalks the previous evening.

WALES This day was retained by the Protestant Church in Wales after the Reformation, but the following day was not.

As it was the start of winter, today was when many farm workers ended their summer contracts, or it was on 13th November according to the old calendar.

Soul cakes were collected from house to house and offered to local priests to say a prayer giving hope for the souls of the poor to come out of purgatory.

Caernafon Hiring Fair was held today.

CORNWALL In St Cubert's parish in East Cornwall is a holy well whose virtues were discovered on this day. It is covered by high spring tides.

BRITTANY Today is a public holiday (Toussaint). To die is to be visited by Ankou (death). The souls of ancestors return today, and in some places the Feast of the Dead was held, with only family members present. At Spézet in the Ménez a meal of buckwheat crêpes, cream, smoked bacon and milk was left for returning souls. The Ménez is an Anaon, a place of waiting and penance for the souls of the dead from Purgatory. Travellers there sang to warn the souls, who tried to avoid meeting a living person. People who had left their home village returned this night to attend Black Vespers for the dead, visit their graves and the ossuary (in which was sung the Hymn of the Charnel House), then await returning souls in the family home. Long ago the whole village made the Procession of the Tombs to honour all dead, but this lapsed to a family custom for its own departed. There was fear of the vengeance and haunting by the unlamented dead. The toasts were 'Good Health to the Living' and 'God Pardon the Souls of the Dead'. The fire would be lit and stocked from the shavings from the manufacture of the coffin, and the virtues of the deceased would be recalled as cider was drunk. A bell was rung in the village by the Forerunner of the Dead warning of the approach of midnight, the Hour of the Dead. The Feast of Souls would then be laid on a clean tablecloth and all would retire to bed, for it was inviting retribution to try to eavesdrop on the feast. The Death Singers went from door to door singing the Hymn of the Souls of the Dead at midnight, then all fell quiet.

Sunday nearest All Saints' Day

CORNWALL This is St Just's Feast Day. It was a popular feast among miners of this district. On the Feasten Monday games were played, such as Kook (games of quoits in which the winner cast furthest, or cast nearest a goal), wrestling, and kailles (keels) which is a form of ninepins. A small street fair was held. Beer and moonshine (home-made spirits) were drunk.

2nd November All Souls' Day

CELTIC This was a solemn day in commemoration of, and prayer for, the faithful who remain in purgatory, in the hope that they will progress to heaven. This Feast Day was established in AD 998. In many places the customs were the same as on All Saints' Day. As then, Souling was only done in Wales.

IRELAND This night was when the souls of the dead (or faithful dead, according to the Church) returned to their old haunts. Prayers for their souls to rest in peace were said, and the living room was made ready for the visit with food, a bowl of spring water, and a candle – for each dead family member – on the table and a fire lit. The door was left unlocked. Graves were visited and cleaned.

WALES The Protestant Church in Wales did not celebrate this day after the Reformation. However, the custom of requesting soul cakes from householders did survive for a time. Originally for the departed, they were latterly collected for themselves. The giving of soul cakes to relatives is a substitute for the departed being unable to give them on their own behalf. They often contained salt, as this was a purifying agent, often put in coffins. Recipes for soul cakes varied from one district to another. Cheese and small loaves of bread (salted barley meal cakes in Clwyd) were distributed to the poor, as this was regarded as something the dead would approve of.

BRITTANY This was called The Day of the Dead, and churches were illuminated from All Saints' Day evening so that the souls of the departed could take part in a nocturnal mass with a phantom priest. People stayed in their homes for fear of meeting the deceased in their wanderings, and some stayed indoors for as long as a week.

3rd November St Winefride's Day, St Clydog's Day

CELTIC St Winefride was martyred in the 7th century, defending her virtue. St Clydog was a 6th-century king of the southern border lands between England and Wales, buried in the village of Clodock.

First Monday in November

WALES This was the date of the annual election of the Portreeve of Laugharne, Dyfed.

4th November St Cleer's Day

CELTIC St Cleer was a 6th-century Cornish hermit. The village named after him is near Liskeard, and contains a well.

CORNWALL This was Ringing Night, not only for many groups of parish bellringers, but to remind people to prepare for Gunpowder Plot celebrations next day.

5th November Guy Fawkes' Day, Bonfire Night

CELTIC This night commemorates deliverance from Guy Fawkes' unsuccessful attempt to carry out Robert Catesby's plot to blow up with gunpowder the King, House of Lords and House of Commons this day in 1605. It has inherited some features of Hallowe'en, banned during the Reformation, particularly the use of fires, torches or burning tar barrels to drive out evil and the burning of an effigy, originally a witch. The custom was taken into the Welsh marches and Cornwall by the English. See the author's 'A Chronicle of Folk Customs' for details.

8th November St Cybi's Day, St Tysilio's Day, Old St Simon and St Jude's Day

CELTIC St Cybi lived in the 6th century and St Tysilio in the 7th century, both associated with Anglesey, Wales. St Cybi lived on Holy Island, so called after his devotion to duty, and St Seiriol, his friend, lived on another island to the east. The most famous association with this saint is the village of Llanfairpwllgwyngythgogerychwyrndrobwllllantysiliogogogoch, which any villager will be pleased to pronounce and translate as 'The Church of St Mary in the hollow of the white hazel near a rapid whirlpool and the Church of St Tysilio near the red cave'.

10th November Martinmas Eve

CELTIC Although it was customary to slaughter an animal for the Martinmas feast tomorrow, this was quite usual anyway at this time of year if stored fodder was deemed to be insufficient for the number of animals on the farm, and those not eaten were salted down.

IRELAND Some of the blood from slaughtered animals was sprinkled around the house and animal quarters, and a cross made on each forehead, to keep evil spirits at bay in the year ahead. The Church created the story that in return for St Martin conferring a monk's tonsure on Patrick, the latter gave a pig, for every monk and nun, to be killed on the eve of St Martin's Day.

SCOTLAND This evening is a traditional time for unmarried people to do marriage divination.

In Huntly, Grampian, and nearby places, an old Martinmas custom called The Horseman's Word is still carried out. When a horseman reaches 18 years of age he is blindfolded and put through a number of secret rituals, after which he is given a magic word said to put a horse in his power. A similar secret society exists on Orkney.

Until 1924, at Fortingall, Tayside, a bonfire was built on a tumulus called the Mound of the Dead, and danced round until dawn. Blackthorn was never used for fear of revenge from its guardian spirits, known as Lunantishee.

11th November Martinmas, St Martin's Day, Old Hollantide Eve

CELTIC This festival is much older than the time of St Martin, who was given this saint day by the Church to try to displace the pagan rites to the ox god Hu, part of the Samhuinn celebrations, and the Roman feast of Bacchus (the wine god). A slaughtered ox was called a mart in Scotland. Another reason for the tradition of feasting was the fact that many farm labourers were paid off today after the expiry of summer and harvest hiring agreements, and they or grateful employers would buy food to celebrate. The alternative term Pack-rag Day referred to the labourers bundling up their belongings, slinging them over their shoulders, and going to seek new employment. In some areas this day was also a quarter day for rent settlements and land payments.

Among Catholics, jobs involving any vehicle or implement with a wheel were avoided.

IRELAND Wealthy farmers and landowners gave some portions of meat from the slaughtered animal to employees and poor neighbours. Blood from the beast was used to purify the house and ensure a fruitful year by sprinkling it on the step and at the four corners.

Fishing boats stayed in port, and jobs involving wheels turning were not attempted, or not done before noon, such as ploughing, pulling a cart, spinning and milling.

ISLE OF MAN Hollantide Eve today was known as Hop-tu-Naa. Mummers went from door to door, knocking on them with turnips or cabbages on sticks and singing the Hop-tu-Naa song which asked for a bonnag (oatmeal cake). Potatoes and herrings were also given. This celebration was transferred to 31st October. The traditional supper was potatoes, parsnips and fish mashed with butter. The remains, with crocks of fresh water, were left for the faeries. Marriage divination was practised by unmarried girls.

SCOTLAND This was a Scottish term day.

In the Hebrides no wheels were turned today, so activities like spinning and grinding ceased.

Many labourers were paid off today, and were treated by grateful employers to a foy or feast (usually bread, cheese and ale or whisky) before they flit (left with their belongings). Old Martinmas Eve, 21st November, was known as Flitting Day. Hiring fairs were held on both days.

BRITTANY This is Armistice Day (1918) and a public holiday.

It is also St Martin's Day, when a downpour is expected.

Saturday before the nearest Sunday to Martinmas

CORNWALL In Camborne, marrow-bones were acquired from local butchers and the jelly eaten. 'The Homage Committee' was formed for this purpose, which, after collecting the bones, toured local public houses tasting the ale.

12th November Old Hollantide Day, Old Samhain

ISLE OF MAN This was the traditional day for letting land, paying rent and hiring men-servants for the year. Hollantide customs were generally observed on this day even after the calendar change, including the bringing in of cattle for housing or slaughter for the winter.

Hop-tu-naa processions still occur, either early in the morning or on the previous evening, though some have moved to 31st October. Children with turnip lanterns go from door to door asking for contributions. This originally served as a way to bless every household and wish it free from ill luck throughout the year, this being the end of the Old Celtic Year.

Hollantide Fair was held at Douglas and as well at other places, a speciality sold was **Hollantide Fairings** *(see p.205 for recipe)*.

SCOTLAND A career divination called Stapag was done on Skye, using items placed in porridge.

WALES Templeton Fair, Dyfed, was held today. Among the speciality fairings were **Katt Pie** *(see p.205 for recipe)* and **Treacle Toffee** *(see p.205 for recipe)*.

14th November St Dyfrig's Day

CELTIC St Dyfrig lived in the 6th century, and was said to have been the Bishop that crowned King Arthur.

16th November St Margaret's Day

CELTIC St Margaret of Scotland, who died in 1093, was the wife of the 11th-century Anglo-Saxon King Malcolm III.

18th November

ISLE OF MAN This was the Winter Feast Day of Hospices (Hospitals), six months after the Summer Feast Day of Hospices on 18th May. As on that day a fair was held at St John's until 1834.

19th November

CORNWALL Truro Fair, a glove fair, was held.

21st November Old Martinmas Eve

CELTIC In some areas casual seasonal workers on farms and in fishing ports would work their last day today, and would feast to celebrate, sometimes at the expense of a satisfied employer and sometimes at their own.

SCOTLAND The end-of-season feast was called the Foy. This was Flitting Day, when employees who had been paid off left after the feast.

22nd November St Cecilia's Day, St Clement's Eve

CELTIC St Clement was the patron saint of blacksmiths, carpenters, anchormakers, lighthousemen and hatters. St Clement's Eve was a day when hatters had a holiday in honour of their patron saint St Clement. Details of trade celebrations today and tomorrow in areas of English settlement are given in the author's 'A Chronicle of Folk Customs'.

23rd November St Clement's Day

WALES Clementing was recorded from south-west Dyfed in the 18th century, where carpenters paraded an Old Clem effigy, and were given its clothes at the end before the effigy was kicked to pieces.

Owners of fishing boats in Tenby used to give their crews a feast today of roast goose and **St Clement's Day Rice Pudding** *(see p.205 for recipe)*.

BRITTANY Saint Clément governed the sea and the wind, and those dependent on them commemorated the day.

24th November St Catherine's Eve

CELTIC St Catherine is patroness of spinners, lacemakers, ropemakers, wheelwrights and spinsters.

25th November St Catherine's Day

BRITTANY Spinners maintained this trade holiday in Brittany.

26th November

ISLE OF MAN This is Maughold's Feast Day of Winter, his second feast day, the first being on 31st July. Most of Ramsey lies within the old parish of Maughold, and the second St Maughold Fair was held there.

Saturday before Advent Sunday

CORNWALL St Ives Fair-Mo (Pig Fair) was held today. 'Stannens' (stalls) were set up, and among the fairings sold were **Fairing Biscuits** *(see p.205 for recipe)*, sugared almonds, **Gingerbread** *(see p.205 for recipe)* – made into figures (possibly images of saints originally) – and pastry pigs with currant eyes. There was wrestling and an acrobats' show. The fishing season (mainly for pilchards) for St Ives' boats ended in November so people had money to spend.

Advent Sunday

IRELAND Regular prayers were said from today, marking the start of the Christmas season.

CORNWALL The Feast of St Maddern, or Madron Feast, is celebrated in Madron and Penzance, the latter formerly in the parish. On the Feasten Monday bull-baiting was held until 1813. An anchor was brought from Penzance quay, fixed in the centre of a field and the bull tied to it.

Monday after Advent Sunday

CORNWALL People used to go shooting birds today.

30th November St Andrew's Day, Andermass

CELTIC St Andrew was a fisherman and is the patron saint of Scotland. He was crucified on a cross shaped like an X at his own request, as he felt too humble to be accorded the same shape of cross as Jesus had. This gave rise to the saltire on the Scottish flag. However, the connection between St Andrew and Scotland is not one that has been historically verified. This ceased to be a religious festival after the Reformation, and became a patriotic one in Scotland instead.

SCOTLAND In the north of Scotland today was to be the end of harvesting and the beginning of preparations and slaughtering for winter. The day would end with everybody enjoying a feast. Throughout Scotland squirrel- and rabbit-hunting was traditionally done today, although nowadays haggis, singed sheep's head, sheep's head broth, **Salt Cod with Egg Sauce** *(see p.205 for recipe)* and **St Andrew's Cake** *(see p.206 for recipe)* are more commonly served at a St Andrew's Day feast, with **Oatmeal Posset** *(see p.206 for recipe)* and whisky to drink.

Piping and ceilidhs are also a feature, in what is perhaps celebrated most vigorously by ex-patriot Scots.

✸ **St Andrew's Day Commemoration, St Andrews**   Fife

Since 1980 the St Andrew's Society has organised a day of commemoration, including religious services, music and drama.

TAKE THE A91 EAST FROM CUPAR.

December
customs

The Bretons called December the Indolent Month, or the Very Black Month, but for the Manx fishermen at least it was the time to make and mend nets and other fishing gear. The year's wool crop on the island had to be carded and spun for weaving, as all the thread used in making clothes and soft furnishings was handspun at home. These tasks would have been done by the light of home-made tallow candles or of torches made from rushes.

With little productive to do in the Celtic rural heartlands there was time to enjoy the string of festivities, from Advent, through St Nicholas' Day and the election of Boy Bishops, then the preparations for Christmas Eve, or for Yule in areas of former Norse settlement such as the north of Scotland. Both have evolved into a complex mixture of pagan and religious elements, both devotional and festive. After the indoor recreation on Christmas Day came the outdoor activities, such as wrenning and sports, on St Stephen's Day, then further indulgence towards children on Holy Innocents' Day, before New Year's Eve and its fire festivals and prognostications brought the annual calendar to a close.

Fixed Dates

1st December
CELTIC St Barbara was invoked by miners and soldiers for protection against injury by explosions.
BRITTANY Today is Saint Éloi's Day. He is the patron saint of horses, but pilgrimages to chapels dedicated to him were made in the summer months.

4th December St Barbara's Day, Old St Clement's Day
BRITTANY Sainte Barbe protects people from thunder and thunderbolts. After making devotions to her a sou is given to the first poor person who passes. Sainte Barbe and Sainte Fleur both hold the thunder by a woollen thread, one white, the other blue. Sainte Barbe's Day, Christmas Day and New Year's Day all fall on the same day of the week.

5th December St Justinian's Day
CELTIC St Justinian travelled from his native Brittany to Ramsey Island off the coast of Dyfed, Wales, where he lived as a hermit. St Justinian's Spring on the island is a healing spring.

6th December St Nicholas' Day

CELTIC Cathedral towns, and some smaller towns, used to elect a boy bishop on this day, who served until Holy Innocents' Day (28th December), in commemoration of St Nicholas' compassion towards children. Records exist from Scotland and of an election by choirboys at Par, Cornwall. The boy bishop undertook all duties except taking mass. Schoolboys in many places 'barred-out' their teachers on this day, as on Shrove Tuesday, in another display of boys taking an adult role.

BRITTANY In the village of Gausson children learning to walk are dipped into St Nicholas' fountain

✠ Enthroning of Boy Bishop, Par   Cornwall

The Boy Bishop holds office until Holy Innocents' Day (28th December).
PAR IS ON THE A3082 WEST OF FOWEY, BETWEEN FOWEY AND ST AUSTELL.

ISLE OF MAN This was the old feast day of St Catherine. On the south side of the island new occupiers of land had to take possession of it on this day.

Colby Fair at Colby in the parish of Arbory was held today, starting with a procession that featured the display of a live hen, called St Catherine's Hen. The next day the hen was paraded dead and plucked, and a rhyme chanted: 'Catherine's hen is dead; The head take thou, and I the feet, And we shall put her under ground.'

There is an old custom that people settled differences on St Catherine's Day by plucking feathers and burying them, and this may relate to this. Another story says that Katherine, heiress of Colby Mooar, gave the land for the fair on St Catherine's Day as St Catherine's Church was on her estate. Moreover, she gave a hen to be killed and eaten, and ale to be drunk, at a village feast. One hen for a village feast is scarcely the height of generosity!

First Sunday in December
BRITTANY

✠ Pardon de la Sainte-Barbe, Le Faouët   Côtes d'Armor

This sometimes takes place on 3rd or 4th December.
LE FAOUËT IS ON AN UNCLASSIFIED ROAD, SOUTH OF PAIMPOL.

The Boy Bishop blessing his fellow scholars, 1937

8th December Feast of the Conception, St Budoc's Day

CELTIC St Budoc was a 6th-century saint, linked to the south-west of England, for example with Budock in Cornwall and St Budeaux in Devon, but who may have in fact been born in Waterford, Ireland.

10th December

SCOTLAND St Obert of Perth, Tayside, was the patron saint of bakers and the subject of a play performed by them before the Reformation. The bakers, in disguise, held a torchlit procession. One was dressed as St Obert, riding a decorated horse, and another wore 'The Devil's Coat'. The play was denounced as pagan by the kirk in 1588, and it ceased under pressure of participants losing the rights of their trade.

Second Thursday before Christmas

CORNWALL In East Cornwall tinners (tin miners) had a holiday in honour of one of the reputed discoverers of tin. The day was called White Thursday or Picrous Day.

11th December Old St Andrew's Day

ISLE OF MAN On the north side of the island new occupiers of land had to take possession of it today.

Andreas Fair was held today.

12th December St Finnian's Day, St Lucy's (Lucia's) Eve

CELTIC Formerly in Scandinavia St Lucy's Eve was similar to our Hallowe'en, with belief in witches and faeries strong, but although this tradition survived longest in the areas of Britain settled by Vikings, there are few remnants of it. Those that still exist seem to have found their way into stories about St Finnian, a 6th-century Welsh saint.

Second Sunday in December

BRITTANY

✠ Pardon de Notre-Dame-de-Bonne-Nouvelle, Paimpol   Côtes d'Armor

PAIMPOL IS ON THE D786 NORTH-WEST OF ST BRIEUC.

13th December St Lucy's Day

CELTIC St Lucy was a 4th-century virgin of great charity and virtue, who gave all her possessions away to the poor, preferring poverty and austerity. She was invoked by those of poor sight, because of a story that she blinded herself to make herself unattractive to men. Before the calendar change, festivities in Lucy's honour (Lucia Day) were held in Norse areas of Britain as part of the Yule celebrations around the winter solstice. The predominance of fire in these celebrations may be partly a consequence of the fact that she was burned to death. Crowns of candles were worn by girls, perhaps symbolic of the passage of the winter sun.

17th December Sow Day

CELTIC In Roman times this was the start of Saturnalia, a week-long feast and orgy, from which many of the Christmas characteristics come, such as over-indulgence, giving presents, decorating houses with greenery, and general merry-making. In the court of Mary Queen of Scots a Lord of Misrule was in charge of festivities, a custom that was borrowed from France and then copied in England.

SCOTLAND Sows were slaughtered today in readiness for preparation for Yule, a custom surviving longest in Orkney. They were never killed when the moon was waning lest the meat shrank.

Boar's head was a favourite dish at festive times among the Celts and Norsemen, who admired the strength, stamina and ferocity of the boar and hoped to acquire these characteristics themselves. In Norse mythology the sun was a golden boar called Gulliburstin. A few customs involving boar's heads remain.

18th December
IRELAND

✵ **Closing the Gates Ceremony, Derry**   Northern Ireland

This ceremony commemorates the action of 13 apprentices in preventing the army of James II from entering the city. They closed the Ferryquay Gate despite the preparations made by Governor Lundy to receive the army.

After the installation of new members at the Apprentice Boys' Hall there is a parade to the Cathedral and a symbolic burning of an effigy of the disloyal governor.

DERRY, OR LONDONDERRY, IS ON THE A6 WEST OF BELFAST.

Last clear Thursday before Christmas Day

CORNWALL This was Cherwidden Thursday, or White Thursday, a holiday for tinners. Traditionally this was the day on which 'white tin' (smelted tin) was first made or sold in Cornwall. Sadly there are no working mines left there.

20th December St Thomas' Eve, Fingan's Eve

CELTIC Traditionally, this was a holy day on which no work was done. Unmarried girls practised divination.

ISLE OF MAN Although the origin is unclear, it is said that people used to cut a great turf of peat on this evening. Perhaps this is a Manx equivalent of the Norse Yule Log.

21st December St Thomas' Day, Midwinter Day, Winter Solstice, Fingan's Day

CELTIC The Church was a force in displacing Celtic Fingan in favour of Christian St Thomas.

There are several common elements in our Christmas imagery and that in the cult of the ancient Phrygian sun god Attis, the cult of Mithras, the Persian sun god, and in Norse Yule customs. This may explain why features such as resurrection, child effigies, burning logs, fire and light can be found throughout Europe, the Middle East and East Asia. But there have been other influences too, such as from Saturnalia, the Roman celebration of the winter solstice, when the sun was welcomed back after the shortest day. When the Roman Emperor Constantine was converted to Christianity in the 4th century the Christianisation of Christmas customs began, leading to the modern Christmas on 25th December in western Europe, but which was celebrated on 6th January in eastern Europe.

The old Norse festival of Yule fell on this day, where evergreens (holly, ivy, conifers) were used to symbolise the eternity of life and fires were lit in honour of Thor and kept alight until the shortest day was passed and the new year dawn had started. The Norse sun god Frey rode across the sky on a boar (Gulliburstin) with golden bristles (the sun's rays). The Yule log was kept burning throughout, symbolising warmth, and is remembered by the chocolate Swiss roll cake. Candles were lit, Yule cakes eaten and cider drunk. A remnant of the Yule log was preserved and used to light the next one, symbolising the continuance of life. The Church replaced Thor and the rebirth of the sun with Christ and his birth. The Celts retained a few Yule customs such as cutting mistletoe, bringing in evergreens and the eating of gruel, for example, in the form of the Scottish sowans or Yule Brose for the poor and plum porridge for the better off.

The English custom of Thomassing, where poor people went from door to door asking for gifts or ingredients to make Christmas food was recorded in Cornwall only. Another English custom, Calling the Waites, was also found in some Celtic areas. Waites were groups of musicians, hired by town authorities to go round singing and playing carols. In Ireland, Cornwall and the South Wales Marches the groups were of local poor. They were not normally found in Scotland, but in the Catholic Hebrides guisers sang Gaelic carols dressed in long shirts and tall white hats, reminiscent of surplices and mitres. Babies from the households visited would be put on a white lambskin and taken thrice round the fire, as though they were being blessed as the Christ Child.

On St Thomas' Day children barred out their teachers as on Shrove Tuesday and asked for a holiday.

ISLE OF MAN St Fingan's Fair was held in Ramsey until 1834. Keeill Ingan, a church dedicated to St Fingan, was in Kirk Christ Lezayre, near Ramsey. The estate name Ballakillingan preserves the name, and was formerly the site of the fair.

SCOTLAND Yule traditions in Scotland were brought by the Norsemen in the 6th century, and Norse areas remained pagan until at least the 10th century. In the French-influenced medieval Court a character like the Lord of Misrule, called the Abbot of Unreason, was in charge of all festive occasions from Hallowmas until Candlemas, which included Yule. His assistants were dressed in various guises, including those of Robin Hood and Little John.

In the Highlands, a log was carved into human shape and burned under the name of the Old Wife (a name also used for a corn dolly).

BRITTANY On St Thomas's Day people prepared for Christmas by doing the baking and washing the linen.

Saturday before Christmas
ISLE OF MAN

🖐 **White Boys' Mumming Plays, Douglas, Peel, and Ramsey**
These were revived in the 1970s, and usually take place between 10 am and 5 pm. The general theme is that St Denis kills St George, who in turn is killed by St Patrick. The Doctor then brings them back to life, and asks the audience for his fee – which they contribute. A sword dance concludes the proceedings.
DOUGLAS IS THE PRINCIPAL TOWN OF THE ISLE OF MAN. PEEL IS ON THE A1 WEST FROM DOUGLAS. RAMSEY IS ON THE A2 NORTH FROM DOUGLAS.

23rd December
CORNWALL

⚙ **Tom Bowcock's Eve, The Ship, Mousehole**   Cornwall
According to locals, 200 years ago the villagers were near to starvation because fishing boats were coming back empty when Tom Bowcock managed to bring in a catch, containing seven different sorts of fish. This event is celebrated with **Starry Gazy Pie** *(see p.206 for recipe)*, containing seven different sorts of fish, and the singing of a folk song written about it. This pie is so called because it is served with the fish whole and their heads sticking out of the pastry. Cooking the fish whole ensures that the oil from the fish head drains into the meat.
MOUSEHOLE IS SOUTH OF PENZANCE ON AN UNCLASSIFIED ROAD.

24th December Christmas Eve
CELTIC The Yule Clog or Block had to be found, not acquired in any other way, and was doused in cider or ale and sprinkled with corn before lighting. It kept winter and the forces of darkness away, and in earlier times the lighting may have been accompanied by human sacrifice. In Cornwall a human figure came to be chalked on the log (called the Christmas Brand), and in the Scottish Highlands the figure of Cailleach Noillaich (Christmas Old Wife, Old Hag or Carline) was carved. Ireland (Christmas Block) and Wales (The Festival Block) also kept this custom. Everywhere the last bit was kept to kindle next year's block.

Yule candles were made by pouring fat and colouring into a mould, and these too were kept alight throughout the Eve and Christmas Day to protect the household and bring good fortune throughout the coming year. These were found in Ireland, north Scotland, including Orkney and Shetland, and in Cornwall.

Mistletoe was revered by the Celts, who thought it could cure all ills. Kissing under it may be a remnant of a Druidic fertility rite, though the custom was introduced into Ireland by the English and possibly also elsewhere. The use of decorations of holly, ivy and other evergreens may be through Norse influence. Like the Block they were not brought in until today. Holly has male associations in folklore and ivy female, so the entwining of them in wreaths and other decorations symbolises harmony in the home at Christmas. Churches were similarly decorated. In Wales and Ireland greenery decorations were removed on Twelfth Night or the day after. Paper decorations appeared in the late 19th century.

Events in the 12-day period of the Christmas season, which traditionally starts on Christmas Eve, were thought to reflect on the good or bad luck in the months of the year to come. For the same reason there was much weatherlore at this time. Christmas Eve became a traditional time for divination, as if it were effectively the end of the year. Most customs involved with looking into the future persisted longest among unmarried women, the unlucky and impecunious. There was also the feeling that all tasks must be completed, as at the end of the year, including house cleaning.

The Wallail Bowl was taken round in both Cornwall and Wales, and survived into the 20th century in Cornwall.

Christmas Eve was a traditional time in some Celtic areas for nativity plays and for mummers plays, the latter often including the legend of St George and the Dragon.

First-footing was done on Christmas Eve long ago, but is now generally associated with New Year's Eve.

For the other customs associated with this day, introduced from England, see the author's *A Chronicle of Folk Customs*.

IRELAND A feature of the decorations in Munster was a wooden cross with two holly sprigs attached. The animal houses were also decorated. There was a belief that today at midnight cows and donkeys kneel in adoration of the Christ child and receive the gift of speech. They were never intruded upon. Many a meal had in poor homes was the result of generosity from employers or richer neighbours, or meat won in raffles or by gambling.

This was the last day for shopkeepers to give little gifts to regular customers, and also for families to visit relatives' graves before festivities started.

Work ceased at midday and families gathered together. Meat for the Christmas Day dinner was prepared today; beef, mutton, bacon, boiled ox-head, goose and chicken were all eaten. In Co. Wexford Cutlin Pudding was a favourite, a thick wheaten porridge containing sugar, spices and dried fruits, wrapped in a greased cloth and boiled. As this was a fast day the evening meal was simple, usually potatoes with fish and white sauce. Afterwards the festivities began, and there was also divination.

Before going to bed, the family would lay places at the table for Mary, Joseph and Jesus, put a candle in the window for each member of the family, and leave the door unlocked.

In Co. Cavan Christmas was heralded from hilltops by the blowing of horns.

ISLE OF MAN Today was known as the Eve of Mary's Feast Day.

The traditional Christmas Eve service was the Oie'l Voirrey, which, with its Carval-singing, was attacked by the Methodists but never completely suppressed. The parish church was lit with candles, and each parishioner took their own candle. The church was decorated with ivy and holly ('hibbin as hollan'). After a prayer and hymn the parson would go home, leaving the parish clerk to direct the singing of the Carvals. Carvals were religious poems of parishioners' own composition. The golden age of Carval writing was the 18th century, but some are older, some newer. Themes may be on the nativity; the life of Christ; sin and repentance; death, judgement and the torments of hell; or on biblical events, especially if of a moral character.

Starting at the west end of the church, opposite the altar, the singer (or pair doing alternate verses), with Carval book and candle, would sing as he/she advanced slowly to the altar, timing the step to finish just before it. It could be that most adults would want to sing, and this made the service very long. Afterwards the mood lightened and unmarried girls would throw parched peas at bachelor friends, a custom that often became disorderly. Then, all would adjourn to a house or ale-house to drink ale spiced with pepper. Before retiring, the Arrane Oie-Vie (The Good Night Song) would be sung.

Eventually the Oie'l Voirrey was stripped of its carvals, pea-shooting and ale-drinking, and in this modified form was held in Methodist chapels. It has survived in unbroken tradition only in Kerrowkeil chapel, but has been revived elsewhere.

Visitors to the house were treated like New Year's Day first-footers. Farmers and fishermen gathered at public houses for a jough-vie (good ale). Every house lit a big Christmas candle and merry-making continued until it was burned out. The traditional drink was hot ale with spice, ginger and pepper.

SCOTLAND Incomplete activities were looked upon with foreboding.

The 12 days of Christmas (Daft Days) ran from today until Twelfth Night, or from Christmas Day to Uphalieday. Boys often did mischief during the Daft Days. Traditionally, festivities were presided over by the 'Abbott of Unreason' (like the English Lord of Misrule).

The Yule log was traditionally of oak, Thor's sacred tree, in contrast to the English preference for ash. Burning large Yule candles was a custom transferred by Protestants to New Year's Eve, which became known as Candle Night. Between sunset and sunrise Yule-bread was baked – **Selkirk Bannocks** *(see p.206 for recipe)* with a cross, one for each member of the family. In Shetland each bannock had a hole in the centre and cut edges to resemble the sun's rays.

Rowan branches were suspended over lintels, and evergreens also hung tonight, symbolising the continuance of life. Holly was lucky for men, ivy for women, and bay, box and yew were also hung. In the Highlands, holly kept faeries at bay.

Carol singers came round this evening. Caralles (carols) have been recorded in Scotland since before the Reformation. In Catholic areas carollers, called Christmas Lads, wore long white shirts and high white hats, a costume which may show Church influence.

In December 1841 Charles Drummond from Kirkgate, Leith, a publisher and bookseller, made and sold the first Yuletide greetings card. The message read: 'A Gude New Year, And mony o' them.'

Guisers may have originated as a way of linking people with gods and spirits by wearing parts of sacrificial beasts and branches or sprigs of sacred trees. The Church adopted them to enact biblical tales and perform nativity plays at Yule and Passion or Resurrection plays at Easter. A 'costume' worn by guisers in some places was a straw suit and beribboned hat. They carried a straw-stuffed effigy on a pole, possibly originally of a fertility god. A surviving secular play is the Goloshan in which the hero of that name is slain by the Champion and revived by the Doctor. Regional variations exist, but all have a presentation, then the drama, and lastly the collection. Shetland had a drama called the Seven Champions of Christendom (who were St Andrew of Scotland, St Patrick of Ireland, St David of Wales, St George of England, St Denis of France, St Anthony of Italy and St James of Spain) which was followed by a Norse sword dance.

WALES At Laugharne and Tenby, in Dyfed, people went in torchlit procession down the main street rolling a tar barrel. At Llanfyllin, Powys, the procession was candlelit, and this may have been part of the custom of taking candles to church for the plygain service.

In the Welsh borders a little of the Festival Block was burnt during each of the 12 days of Christmas. In parts of north Powys the ashes of the Festival Block were put on fields as fertilizer.

The Kissing Bush was introduced into Wales from England, and sometimes in the Marches it was lit up for a whole year as protection. It was a small decorated bush of holly or yew, hung upside down from the ceiling.

Wassailers being offered the wassail bowl by the lady of the house, 16th century

Wassailing was done by taking round the Wassail Bowl, and in South Wales gifts of money were given in return for some of the hot, spiced ale and a wassail song. The custom was essentially an exchange of good wishes for a successful growing and breeding season, and good health to all, for ale and hospitality. The wassail bowl had 12 handles. **Welsh Cakes** *(see p.206 for recipe)* and apples were arranged round it and warm ale and spices added. It was then offered round. A custom involving a wassail bowl was the carrying round of the perllan, a small rectangular board with an apple at each corner and in the centre a wren in a tree. This was carried round by young men with the wassail bowl, and appears to be a variant of the Twelfth Night wren custom.

Welsh miners carried a board from house to house on a wheelbarrow. It was covered with clay, had candles stuck in it, and was called the Star of Bethlehem. The miners knelt in front of each house, sang a carol and asked for a Christmas gift.

This was the last day on which to clean family graves and supply fresh flowers before Christmas. **CORNWALL** Poor women went 'a-gooding', asking for alms from richer neighbours. This is the same custom as Thomassing on 21st December. At Falmouth, shopkeepers were expected to give regular customers a slice of cake and a small glass of gin.

Saffron Currant Cakes or Buns *(see p.207 for recipe)* were baked today. The centre of the dough was pulled up and shaped into a smaller cake on top. This centre-piece was called 'The Christmas' and everyone in the house, including servants, had their own. It was unlucky to eat them before Christmas Day.

Christmas Eve supper for ordinary folk was pilchards and unpeeled potatoes boiled together in a crock, with egg-hot (or eggy-hot) to drink. This drink was made from eggs, hot beer, rum and sugar, poured from one jug to another until frothy.

Painted candles were placed in a box of sand and lit. Children danced around them. The Christmas Block (Mock, Stock) – a log on which a rude figure of a man was carved or chalked – was set alight with ceremony, using a piece of charred wood saved from last year's Block. This was thought to give protection against witchcraft. Children and adults alike sat up until midnight drinking to the Block and singing carols. Many Cornish towns once had their own folk carols, but sadly these have all too frequently been lost, although they survive in Padstow.

Church towers were illuminated today, for example, Zennor church. Church and chapel choirs went from door to door singing 'curls' (carols) and money or food was offered to them. At Par Chapel Well, where there is the ruined baptistry of St Levan in West Cornwall, all carol singers in the district, after going round their own villages, met for a big sing-song.

Hero-combat mumming plays starring St George were staged. These had the usual theme of principal character defeating villain, who was then revived by a comic doctor. The play at Mullion was a mime.

Wassailing was done at Warleggan today, accompanied by the firing of guns into the branches of the cider-apple trees. The custom of carrying the wassail bowl around the town is still kept up in Bodmin and Truro, after a revival in the 1970s.

Carrying the Wassail Bowl, Bodmin   Cornwall

Four men in evening dress carry the wassail bowl around the town, singing and collecting money for charity.

TAKE THE A38 WEST FROM PLYMOUTH.

Carrying the Wassail Bowl, Truro   Cornwall

Local families have maintained the custom, carrying the apple-wood bowl around and singing a wassail song which asks for a contribution, then expresses good wishes for a good apple crop for the coming year.

TAKE THE A390 SOUTH-WEST FROM ST AUSTELL.

BRITTANY Midnight mass was attended.

At Matignon and elsewhere there are records appertaining to the bringing in of the Yule log, which was sprinkled with consecrated water. It purified the chimney for the infant Jesus to come down, and a ladder was scribbled on and put up the inside. The log was sprinkled again on Christmas Day and kept burning until the evening. Yule log brands were kept as protection against lightning, and to put in wells to keep the water pure and retain the water sprites. The Christmas tree was unknown.

A custom already lapsed by the mid-19th century was done in Matignon, Ploubalay and probably also Guilaneuf today. Groups of boys carrying pointed sticks and sacks went round knocking on the doors of farmhouses. 'Who is there?', the farmer would say. 'Le hoguihanneu!', replied the boys, and they sang a traditional song for the household. The piece of bacon they were given in return was put on a pointed stick, to save for a meal called Le Bouriho. At Montauban the boys cry, 'Au guyané, au guy l'an neuf!', and receive bacon or salted beef. At Ploërmel they cry, 'Au gui gouroux!'

Yuletide Candlelighting Ceremony

Children would climb into trees or on stacks of straw to sing, and children in a neighbouring village would reply in kind. Carol singing was done, and the children of Dinan and St Malo would ask for apples, pears and cider.

In Pleudihen the story of the Three Magi was acted by children of the village. In national costume, with ribbons added, they went round and announced the venue of the midnight mass.

In the area around Ercé cod was eaten for the evening meal, and children visited their parents for it, playing truant from school.

Tonight people used to pray to St Joseph and the Virgin Mary where there were hazel trees, on behalf of the souls delivered to Purgatory today, of which there were a large number.

During the Christmas Season

IRELAND Calling the Waits happened in the days before Christmas, when bands of musicians rose early and went from door to door greeting and entertaining the household, and giving the time and state of the weather. Money or refreshments were offered in return. In Leinster and parts of west Ireland this tradition survived until recently. Carol singing was also done, surviving in Kilmore, Co. Wexford.

Traditional Carol Singing, Kilmore   Co. Wexford
A carol for every one of the 12 days of Christmas is sung, led by a member of the Devereux family.
KILMORE IS ON THE N25 SOUTH OF WEXFORD.

ISLE OF MAN At Christmas, dances in barns to a fiddler were popular, and thoughts turned to matchmaking. Christmas mummers, the White Boys, and the Mollag Band gave performances at Christmas. They were purveyors of good luck and prosperity like the feathers of the wren.
WALES Mari Lwyd was out and about.

Mari Lwyd Mummers, Pencoed   Mid Glamorgan
Traditional Welsh carol singing is still done in the Tanad Valley, Denbighshire and Montgomeryshire.
PENCOED IS ON THE A473 EAST OF BRIDGEND.

Traditional Welsh Carol Singing, Llanrhaeadr-ym-Mochnant, Tanad Valley   Clwyd
The service of carols is called a plygeiniau. Male groups go from church to church during Christmas and give unaccompanied performances.
LLANRHAEADR-YM-MOCHNANT IS ON THE B4580 WEST OF OSWESTRY.

CORNWALL Evergreens were used to decorate houses, sold in bunches called 'Penn'orths of Christmas'. A Kissing Bush was made from two hoops fixed at right angles and decorated with evergreens, apples, oranges, and other items. It was suspended from the middle of the kitchen ceiling. At night a lighted candle was put on the bottom junction of the hoops.

In East Cornwall there were wassailing customs at Christmastide. Parishioners visited each orchard, selected one tree in each, said an incantation, and sprinkled it with cider. In another variation, apple dipped in cider were hung from the branches before the sprinkling, then after the incantation everybody danced around it. The rest of the cider was drunk back at the farmhouse. In parts of East Cornwall small sugared cakes were left on the branches.

From Christmas until Twelfthtide mummers known as Goose- (or Geese-) Dancers paraded the streets masked and in disguise. If a door was found open they would go in, and fool around until given money to leave. A hobby-horse with snapping wooden jaws covered with horse-hide accompanied. Some guisers had skins of the heads of bullocks with horns on. Sometimes they acted the play 'St George and the Dragon' – or, in West Cornwall, 'Duffy and the Dragon' – a tale similar to Rumpelstiltskin. There were efforts to ban goose-dancing because it often degenerated into rowdyism, particularly in Penzance.

At Christmas Cornish miners hung a holly bush on the pit headgear.

During the 12 days of Christmas games were very popular, especially cards.

Whist with swabs *This is played like conventional whist, except that before play each player puts money in the kitty, for the player who wins the four swab cards (Ace and Deuce of trumps, Ace of Hearts and Knave of Clubs). The cards are of equal value, but if hearts are trumps the Ace counts double.*

Board 'em *This card game is a round game for 2–8 players. It is played for 'fish' – coins which are put in the pool (there must be at least six) before each trick. Each player is dealt six cards and the next card turned up for trumps. Play is like whist; you must follow suit or trump or discard. Each trick taken gets a fish. If you decline to play you lose your stake. If you play and lose you pay out to each player – you are 'boarded'.*

Ranter-go-round or Miss Joan *Any number of players can play this card game, where players match the value of the card played. Mark four divisions in chalk on a tray. The first player puts a card down:*

> *'Here's a _____ as you may see.'*
> *'Here's another as good as he.'*
> *'And here's the best of all the three.'*
> *'And here's Miss Joan, come tickle me (wee, wee).'*

The holder of the fourth card wins the trick. If you have no card of the same value as the first laid then you pay one to the pool. The player who wins the most tricks gets the pool.

Pinny-ninny *In this game a basin was turned upside-down on the table. Children dropped pins on it (the pound-pins with wire heads) and if one fell so as to form a cross on top of the heap that player took them all. The winner is the one who ends up with all the pins. Poor children often begged for pins to play the game, and were always given two.*

Pins were dropped into a wishing-well near St Austell, hence the name Pennameny Well. 'Pedna-a-mean' is Cornish for 'heads-and-tails'.

25th December **Christmas Day**

CELTIC The day started with mass in Catholic regions like most of Ireland, and then the rest of the day was given over to hunting (while the food was prepared), feasting, and sports and games, usually in that order. Hunting the wren was done, and paraded next day, or the whole custom was done tomorrow. Guisers and mummers were about. Yule fire ceremonies were found in various parts of Scotland, but today was not as festive as Hogmanay, a legacy of the successful curtailment of enjoyment by the Calvinists. The same relative lack of festivity was true of Wales, except in English south-east Dyfed, compared with New Year, but later the pattern of hunting, feasting and sports and games was followed there too. In Victorian times the community Christmas changed to the family Christmas, with its trappings of tree, cards, etc.

Christmas Day was in some places a quarter day.

IRELAND Roast Goose, **Limerick Ham** *(see p.207 for recipe)* and **Spiced Beef** *(see p.207 for recipe)* were popular for Christmas dinner, which marked the end of Advent, a fast period until 1917. The spiced beef recipe is typical of the way that salted meat was made more palatable for special occasions.

Ball games were held afterwards between parishes, on the beach in coastal areas.

ISLE OF MAN Hunting the wren involves thrashing the hedges with sticks to flush it out for capture and killing, but in living memory the bird was not killed. The last verifiable killing was in the 19th century, but the hunt was still active in the 1930s, surviving today only at Peel. No work was done between today and the 6th January (Old Christmas Day). Goose pie was a traditional dish.

The White Boys at Christmastide went round houses performing the mumming play of St George and the Dragon. This had characters like St George, Prince Valentine, King of Egypt, Sambo and the Doctor. The Doctor, with bladder-stick and collecting box, injected amusement.

Another scene to be witnessed in the past was the sight of young boys with blackened faces, dressed in women's white caps and aprons, going around dancing and singing.

SCOTLAND Yule in Scotland ran from today until 6th January. Before the Reformation the day would have started with mass, followed by feasting, music and dancing. Servants were handselled with money, which they tended to spend in ale-houses. The Calvinist Kirk in Lowland Scotland vigorously opposed the excesses of Christmas, and it was officially banned from about 1574 to 1642, but celebrated privately. Some transferred festivities to Hogmanay and Ne'er Day. When it was reinstated it was no longer such a big community event, more of a family get-together, with New Year's Day keeping its place as the biggest festivity of the winter.

Traditional Yule fire rites to encourage the return of the sun included, in various parts of Scotland, blazing tar-barrels, bonfires, burning boats, clavies, fire-balls, flambeaux and torches, some of which were later transferred to Hogmanay. Many local customs have lapsed, including Burning the Boat at Bettyhill and other towns on the Moray Firth, blazing tar-barrels in Galloway, rolling blazing tar-barrels through Campbeltown in Kintyre, the Yule Fire at Minigaff, and 'Shooting the Old Year Out' in Angus where farmers fired their guns into the air at midnight.

Yule Brose was made by making a broth overnight from bullocks' heads and knees, then adding oatmeal, keeping it simmering until ready to serve. All members of the family dipped their spoons into it at the table. Haggis was also eaten for Christmas breakfast. Other Yule foods were oat farl with Yule kebbuck (cheese); sour and sweet scones, the latter with currants and spices); sowans (oat gruel sweetened with honey or treacle, plus whisky); cloutie dumpling; Yule Mart (salted ox killed at Martinmas); and in rich homes goose and boar's head. Many Scots, however, avoided pork because the boar was sacred to Druids. Plum porridge was replaced by plum pudding, with mince pies introduced from England in the 16th century.

Something new was worn on Yule morning. First one to rise used to take a bowl of sowans to everybody still in bed. Traditional Christmas afternoon games were shinty (Highlands); football (Lowlands); bowls; foot-races; barrow races; and throwing the hammer blindfolded.

🏐 Christmas Day Ba' Games, Kirkwall, Mainland   Orkney
These are essentially warm-up games for the main events on 1st January.
KIRKWALL IS THE PRINCIPAL TOWN OF ORKNEY.

WALES As in Scotland, Christmas in Wales was formerly overshadowed by New Year celebrations, except in south-west Dyfed where there was much English influence. Christmas Day here in the

19th century was the start of a three-week holiday for farm workers. The plough was taken inside and placed under the dining table. Dinner would have included **Goose with Apple Sauce** *(see p.207 for recipe)* or stuffed with tongue, beef and Christmas pudding.

Up to Epiphany groups of men went from door to door to give greetings, and were given beer, warmed in small brass pans. Some was always saved to sprinkle on the plough.

In some parts people went to an early morning plygain service, at cock-crow, after staying up all night decorating the house with holly and mistletoe, making cyflaith (treacle toffee) and generally making merry. This service is still held in northern parts of mid-Wales. To cut down a mistletoe-bearing tree was considered very unlucky. Mistletoe tea was used to cure epilepsy, and heart and nerve complaints.

Parents told their children Christmas legends this morning, for example that singing could be heard in the air, that oxen knelt, that the hardest frost would thaw, and that the rosemary and the Glastonbury Thorn, said to have sprouted from the staff of Joseph of Arimathea, bloomed.

In the decorated, candlelit churches the plygain included the performance of solo and group carols, many written in traditional metre by local poets. This pre-Reformation tradition resembles the Oie'l Voirrey in the Isle of Man, and it survived the attentions of the non-conformists quite well, attracting many chapelgoers. However, by the end of the 19th century it had become an ordinary carol service.

After the plygain, which usually finished around 9 am, the rest of the day was festive in mood. A typical breakfast would have been toasted bread and cheese with hot ale, or perhaps also brwes (oatcake steeped in broth, hot milk or water), swig, cakes and cold meats. A Yule log was burnt. Dinner would often be goose. A Christmas Pie was made for visitors, from boned roast goose stuffed with boiled tongue, encased in pastry lined with mincemeat, and eaten cold.

Games were popular, including mass football, which was especially popular in central Dyfed. A match was played each year at Maentwrog. In the match between Cellan and Pencarreg both men and women participated on each side, and the same was true of the match at Llanwenog, near Lampeter, between the Bros and Blaenaus. Traditionally the Bros were immigrants to the town, living in the hills and said to be from Ireland, while the Blaenaus in the old town were the indigenous inhabitants. The match began at midday, after the service. The Bros' goal was the hamlet of Rhyddlan and the Blaenaus' goal was New Court. Injuries were frequent.

Decorations were left up until Candlemas and then used to kindle fires to cook pancakes on Shrove Tuesday.

✦ Plygain Service, Llanfihangel-yng-Ngwnfa, near Llanfyllin   Powys
LLANFIHANGEL-YNG-NGWNFA IS ON THE B4382, NORTH-WEST OF WELSHPOOL.

CORNWALL In Scilly it was customary for girls to go to church dressed in white.

At Pendeen Cove, north of St Just, there is a Christmas spirit in the form of a beautiful lady dressed in white with a red rose in her mouth. It is disaster for anyone to intrude upon her while she takes her morning walk at dawn.

On Porthminster Beach, St Ives, at 9 am, boys played Cornish Rounders and Catchers.

Cornish Rounders *From those available the two captains chose their teams of six alternately. They tossed for first innings. Four bickens (piles of sand) were made 10 yards apart in a square. In the centre of the square is the bowler, and behind the batsman is the tip. The other four are fielders. The object is to hit the ball and run through all four bickens. If the tip or fielders threw the ball and hit the batsman between bickens he was out. If the ball was caught the whole team was out.*

Catchers *Only one bicken is required. If picked up by a fielder he asked the batsman to say how near he thinks he will throw it to the bicken. A reply might be 'Two a good scat, Try for the bat.' This means within two bat lengths of the bicken. 'Scat' means blow or slap. If the fielder does it the batsman is out.*

Christmas Day dinner was often giblet pie, containing the giblets of a goose, boiled and finely chopped, with sugar, raisins and apple added.

BRITTANY Today is a public holiday (Noël). Children believed that the infant Jesus in a white gown and bare feet came down the chimney to deliver presents as a reward for good behaviour. Father Christmas was unknown.

Wren Boys, Brosna, Co.Kerry

From today until New Year's day was called the Old Week, and originally the first Monday was St Étienne's Day, the Saturday St Sylvester's Day, regardless of the date. Farmhands and servants had a holiday all Old Week, and some got married then. Others broke their contracts and went to look for a better job.

Week after Christmas Day

CORNWALL Giglet Fair was held in Launceston (giglet, giglot means giddy young woman). There was also one in Okehampton, Devon. Part of it was a wife-market for young bachelors.

26th December Boxing Day, St Stephen's Day

CELTIC Hunting foxes and squirrels was traditional on this day, as was shooting birds – particularly the wren. Wrens like to nest in dark places including tombs and caves, and so acquired the reputation of being go-betweens with the underworld and the forces of darkness. Killing it was a way of ensuring that the sun's light would win through and return. The bird was also the Druids' messenger.

Wren Boys, having caught a wren on Christmas Day, paraded it, singing a wrenning carol. The bird's carcass was hung on a pole, or carried in a garland of holly or gorse, and paraded around the town. Donations were given in exchange for a wren's feather, which was considered lucky. The latter custom was prevalent in Cornwall. Another explanation for this custom is that it represents a seasonal role reversal, when servants and masters changed places, and the smallest bird became king of the birds. If the wren could be killed then perhaps the temporary role reversal would become permanent. Among sailors a wren killed on St Stephen's Day was thought to protect the killer from shipwreck or other disaster. A justification for the wrens' persecution is the claim that one's song alerted the Roman guards to the appearance of Jesus in the Garden of Gethsemane, and that another woke St Stephen's jailer by landing on his face, thus preventing St Stephen's escape.

Two other common activities today were mumming and sports, the latter still widespread.

IRELAND This was a fast day in many places.

The wren was attached to a beribboned holly bush on top of a pole, and taken round the village for collection of money and food for the Wren Party in the evening. In earlier times paraders dressed as for combat, and the Wren Boys would even be accompanied by mummers and a hobby-horse. Sometimes Wren Boys wore straw masks and animal skins or horns, or they dressed as women, symbolic of fertility. If anyone failed to contribute to their feast they were liable to have

184 December customs

the wren's burial place outside their house. Today, wrenning is still done in parts of rural Ireland but the bird is not killed. The Irish justified killing the wren by claiming that on two occasions one alerted invaders to the presence of Irish soldiers stealing up to attack – Vikings and Cromwell's army respectively.

In south-west Ireland the robin was hunted and its tail pulled out, but the bird was not killed.

From today in West Meath mummers used to travel round and perform, collecting money for Christmas boxes. Sometimes their strange appearance, including men in women's clothes, and old weapons caused alarm, hostility and even police action. Mumming in Ireland may be an English import. The plays were in verse, of the type where two protagonists engage in combat, the loser being revived by a comic Doctor. They were also called Hogmanay Men or Christmas Rhymers, and played throughout the 12 days of Christmas. In Co. Wexford there has been a recent revival of this tradition.

Horse-racing, hunting, cock-fighting and bull-baiting were all activities pursued this day in the past, the latter until the 1830s.

ISLE OF MAN The Wren Boy who killed the wren was praised, made King for the day, and assured of good luck in the coming year. In early times, the wren was plucked, laid on a bier with great solemnity, taken to the parish church, and buried. Dirges were sung over the grave in Manx. Later, another way of parading the dead bird was adopted, to suspend it from two wooden hoops, crossed at right angles, fixed on the end of a pole decorated with evergreens and coloured streamers. This was paraded with drums beating and flags flying in a triumphal procession. The feathers were distributed as charms against evil influences and hazards in the new year. These were much sought after by herring fishermen. A wren-song, 'The Hunting of the Wren' was sung when the pole was set up outside a house on the processional route. Still more recently the ceremonial was held, in Peel, but the wren was not actually killed. Nowadays a live bird is not used and the garlanded wren-pole has a model bird.

Hunting the Wren
Douglas

At 10 am the Wren Boys go round the town, perform the 'Hunt the Wren' dance and sing the 'Hunting of the Wren' song.

DOUGLAS IS THE PRINCIPAL TOWN OF THE ISLE OF MAN.

SCOTLAND In Kirkmaiden, Dumfries and Galloway, the captured wren was adorned with ribbons and released. Scots gave the wren the title Lady of Heaven's Hen.

The Masons' Walk, Melrose
Border

Masonic Lodges in Scotland traditionally celebrated on St John's Eve, when their officials were elected for the year and a parade held in honour of St John the Apostle. This walk was moved to 27th December and then a day earlier.

TAKE THE A609 SOUTH-EAST FROM GALASHIELS TO MELROSE.

The Masons' Walk, Melrose

WALES There was a custom called holly-beating, or holming, in which men and boys thrashed the naked arms of female domestics with holly branches. This was last recorded in 1879. A similar custom is the holly-beating of the last one in the house to get up this morning, who is called a tapster. These may have an association with the martyrdom of St Stephen, or there may be a connection with the ancient practice of holming (bleeding animals) on this day. It was done in the belief that the animals' health and stamina would be improved, especially if done under the rejuvenated sun following the winter solstice. People also holmed themselves.

BRITTANY This is St Étienne's Day, and if it rains then next year's cherry harvest will be spoiled. From today until 31st January, and sometimes longer but never beyond the Sunday before Shrove Tuesday, friends and family arranged a once a year get-together, each taking a turn, called New Year's Coffee. It started about 4 pm with women and children, and the men joined them when they returned from work. A typical meal was cold pork and wine (white for women and red for men), roast meat with bread and butter, coffee, crêpes and rice pudding. Fruit was never put on the table.

28th December Holy Innocents' Day, Childermas

CELTIC Boy Bishops, elected on St Nicholas' Day, gave their sermons today, with good records from Scotland.

As it was regarded as an unlucky day, no new task or journey was started, nor marriage contracted.

IRELAND The day of the week on which this festival fell was regarded as an unlucky day for the whole year.

Last Monday in December

CELTIC This is traditionally Judas' birthday, and was considered an unlucky day.

31st December New Year's Eve, St Sylvester's Day

CELTIC The ancient custom of burning the old year out has its origins in the midwinter fires lit to encourage the sun to return, a custom which survives still in Scotland. Saining as at Beltane and Hallowe'en was done in rural areas.

Dressing up as animals, for example bulls, goats and deer, on this day was a custom descended from pagan animal-god worship, one fiercely attacked by the church.

Divination games and fortune-telling are traditional on this day, some resembling those done on Hallowe'en. New Year's Resolutions were often made on this day, and still are, though perhaps not so resolutely kept! In similar vein the weatherlore was taken for signs of conditions in the coming year. Another ritual was the placing of a silver coin outside the house. If it was still there next morning it would be brought in with joy as the year would be prosperous. An extension of this custom was to put out a piece of coal, a piece of bread and a silver sixpence, and bring them in on New Year's morning to ensure the family has warmth, food and prosperity during the year. As a preparation for next year, to set the right tone, all tasks were finished, the house and contents cleaned, debts paid and borrowed items returned. The old year was let out through the back door, then the new year admitted through the front as the chimes of midnight sound. It was a time for giving gifts, and first-footers prepared for their rounds. The singing of the Scottish song 'Auld Lang Syne' has become common everywhere, as the church bells sound and toasts and well-wishing are done.

In Wales and Cornwall the wassail bowl was taken round.

Watchnight services at midnight were started by the Methodist Church in the 18th century, and similar are held in many churches and cathedrals today. It was also a favourite time for bell-ringing.

IRELAND This and the following day were not significant festivals in Ireland, although the new year was welcomed with bonfires, fireworks, church bells ringing and well-wishing.

Everyone had a large supper to ensure plenty to eat in the year ahead. Another custom done in the west of Ireland to keep hunger at bay was for the man of the house to throw a bairín breac at the doors of the house and byre, imploring hunger to stay away. This custom has been transferred from Hallowe'en. No food was allowed out of the house.

First-footing was done. This custom may have been brought from Scotland. In the north of Ireland children visited local houses to hand wisps of straw as New Year tokens to the occupants, and were given small gifts in return.

ISLE OF MAN This day was also called Little Christmas Eve.

SCOTLAND In the days when horned gods were worshipped people dressed up today as horned animals, particularly as bulls, deer and goats. Dressing in bull's hide survived the longest, the 'bull' being beaten in front of villager's doors to bring luck. The 'bull' gave out sticks whose end was wrapped in bull-hide, to be passed between the family members before being carried three times sunwise round the house. Whisky, cakes and cheese were eaten, the latter alleged to bring luck in the New Year. Looking through holes in cheese was thought to give you the ability to see through darkness or mist.

In the Hebrides, the Hogmanay Lads performed the Procession of the Bull. A complete bull-hide was kept in the rafters all year and taken down today for one of the guisers to put on. The others had a stick, often a shinty stick, to which a sheepskin bag was attached (traditionally from a sheep slaughtered for a sacred festival) to collect alms from householders after going sunwise round their house and singing at their door until admitted. The bull's tail was singed in the fire and everyone sniffed it for protection and fertility. After refreshments they left, and went sunwise three times round welcoming houses and the other way if not, cursing loudly.

Today, in Scotland, it is mainly children who go guising, sometimes wearing white sheets and carrying a bag for gifts of food, hence the name Cake Day. In eastern Scotland a traditional gift was a red herring.

In Fife, the tradition of finishing all tasks before midnight was taken very seriously, particularly with respect to spinning and weaving, lest the Gyre-carlin take the flax left.

There are big gatherings in places like Tron Kirk, Edinburgh, and George Square, Glasgow. At midnight arms are linked, 'Auld Lang Syne' is sung, strangers are kissed and bells peal. Traditionally the old year is rung out with muffled bells and the new year rung in with unmuffled bells. Then, the main door was opened to let the New Year in, and everyone beat on metal objects to make a noise sufficient to drive out malevolent spirits. Many traditional foods are eaten, including stovies and **Potted Hough** *(see p.207 for recipe)*.

Stovies are layers of sliced potatoes and sliced onions, browned in bacon fat or beef dripping and layered with seasoning and a little stock, and sometimes added cooked chopped meat.

In Shetland this was called Tulya's E'en, seven days before Yule Day on 6th January. The Yules started today and ended on Twenty-Fourth Night (24 days after Yule Day) or Up-Helly-Aa. When toasting this evening the sign of Thor's hammer was traditionally made, later becoming a cross.

A Yule stack of peat was made by householders to keep fires stocked during this time. As trolls were abroad saining was done. Blazing peat was carried round for this purpose. A cross made from two straws was placed on stiles next to cornfields, and a cross of plaited animal hair on the door of the animal house.

In Newburgh, Fife, there used to be a procession today combining that of the Merry Freemasons and the Oddfellows. The former ceased to attend, and the latter continued until 1965. This inebriated, fancy-dress parade was a remarkable sight, walking from the Town Hall, round the town, and back for a pie supper.

The Hogmanay Revels at Newton-Stewart in Galloway no longer take place. It was the custom for youngsters to raid premises for barrels to fill with combustibles and tar, and these were carried at midnight in a torchlit fancy-dress procession from Market Field through Minigaff and back. The villages of Minigaff and Blackcraig were involved in the event. Afterwards bonfires were lit in Newton-Stewart and Minigaff.

A lapsed Hogmanay (Old Calendar) festival which started this evening was the Burning of the Crate at Dingwall. A crate filled with combustible materials was set alight and dragged through the town by a horse ridden by a villager dressed as a Red Indian. It was preceded by a 'band' playing home-made instruments, and was timed to reach the Mercat Cross as the first stroke of midnight sounded, at which signal the contents of the crate were scattered. Not surprisingly, this highly dangerous custom was banned in the 1860s.

New Year's Eve Fireballs, Stonehaven

Grampian

Fireballs on wire strings are made by packing paraffin-soaked combustible material into a ball enclosed by wire mesh. These are whirled round the paraders' heads. The procession starts at 11.30 pm from the Mercat Cross, and when it reaches the beach the fireballs are flung into the sea, as befits its origin as a fishermen's festival before the middle of the 19th century. It was then a purification ritual, but the decline of the fishing fleet led to the custom becoming a community affair in the hope that it would restore prosperity.

TAKE THE A90 SOUTH FROM ABERDEEN.

The Flambeaux Procession, Comrie

Tayside

Originally, smoke from burning material on poles was used to purify a farmer's animals. When this custom ceased it became a procession with locals dressed in horned headdresses as animals. Starting at the last stroke of midnight in the village square, three birch poles, 10 feet high, each with a bundle of burning sacking on top, are paraded by guisers, with a piper in the lead. More bundles are lit on the way, and, on returning to the square, they are all thrown together in a heap at the end of the march (formerly into the River Earn). Everyone dances round the pile until it is burned out. General festivities follow round the bonfire, with some revellers in fancy dress. Then first-footing begins. This ceremony has survived through strong local interest and participation.

TAKE THE A85 WEST FROM CRIEFF.

Burning the Old Year Out and Mischief Night, Biggar

Strathclyde

Bonfire-building starts after the November fair, on Tinto, the Druidic Hill of Fire, a traditional site of Beltane and Samhuin fires. Seguisers go round the town performing Goloshan to collect money for combustibles and fireworks. Across the Biggar Burn from the town lies Westrow, and these rival villages would try to steal fuel from each other's bonfires. The bonfire is lit in the town square in the evening, followed by fireworks, dancing and other festivities. Traditionally red herrings are cooked in the fire - symbols of plenty in the New Year. After the last chime of midnight 'Auld Lang Syne' is sung, then it is Mischief Night in the town for children and first-footing for adults.

BIGGAR IS ON THE A702 SOUTH OF EDINBURGH.

New Year's Eve Bonfire, Wick

Highland

This is built in Bignold Park, formerly on Shilling Hill. Combustible material may be pilfered so locals guard their property. The bonfire is lit at midnight and afterwards first-footing begins.

WICK IS AT THE NORTHERN END OF THE A9.

Other Scottish towns used to burn out the Old Year, either as at Wick with a bonfire or by sounding volleys of gunfire. This purified the air for the coming year, witches and evil driven out, and the power of the feeble winter sun augmented. Domestic fires would be kept burning past midnight and were not re-lit until noon on New Year's Day if they went out. No-one would risk giving away or lending a burning brand, or allow candles to be lit from the fire by anyone outside the family, lest their luck and warmth for the New Year be taken with the departing flame.

A vestige of the once-common custom of dressing up as bulls, goats or deer as part of the worship of horned gods was the leading of a many in bull's hide from door to door to be beaten symbolically for luck. The bull-man handed out sticks wrapped in bull hide, and these were singed in the fire and passed round the family, then taken three times sunwise round the house, as another cleansing ritual. The evening concluded with refreshments including cheese, which brought good luck in the New Year if eaten today.

WALES Children went round collecting gifts or money. The Wassail Bowl, with its hot spiced ale, was taken round and wassail songs sung.

On the first stroke of midnight the back door was opened to release the old year, then locked, and the front door opened on the last stroke of midnight.

CORNWALL In East Cornwall parties of men (Warsail Boys) went round with a small begging bowl for money to buy food for a feast in exchange for the hot spiced ale in the bowl, a custom recently revived.

St Tibbs is a saint of unknown sex. A false promise made is said to be fulfiled next St Tibbs' Eve – a day that falls 'between the old and new year', or that comes 'neither before nor after Christmas' – a day that never comes.

Seeing in the New Year was common, with parties and wishes for health and happiness to all. Before retiring tonight elderly women opened a bible at random to see what luck was indicated for the New Year, by where the forefinger fell on the page.

BRITTANY Today was not a religious feast day.

Pardon de Notre-Dame-de-Callot, Carantec

Finistère

CARANTEC IS ON AN UNCLASSIFIED ROAD NORTH OF THE D58, NORTH-WEST OF MORLAIX.

Additional customs

Annual Customs of Variable Date

CORNWALL

⚙ Summercourt Fair, Summercourt   Cornwall
TAKE THE A3058 SOUTH-EAST FROM NEWQUAY.

BRITTANY

✋ International Celtic Harp Festival, Dinan   Côtes d'Armor
DINAN IS ON THE N176, SOUTH OF ST MALO.

✴ Theatre production of life in the Château in the Middle Ages
and the Wars of Breton Succession, Château de la Hunaudaye   Côtes-d'Armor
This takes place every summer.
CHÂTEAU DE LA HUNAUDAYE IS ON AN UNCLASSIFIED ROAD, SOUTH-WEST OF PLANCOËT.

⚙ Foire Teillouse (Chestnut Fair), Redon   Ille-et-Vilaine
At the fair, which takes place in Autumn, you will find stalls, street peddlers, story-tellers, music,
and roasted chestnuts to buy.
REDON IS ON THE D177 SOUTH–WEST OF RENNES.

Customs Held Regularly at Intervals

SCOTLAND

♕ Key Ceremony   Edinburgh Castle
This 800-year-old ceremony lapsed in the mid-19th century but was revved in 1936. On the
appointment of a new General Officer Commanding Scotland the holder is also made Governor

of the Castle. Accompanied by the Lord Lyon King of Arms (the chief herald of Scotland and authority on all such matters), other Scots Heralds and the Scottish State Trumpeters, the Governor-elect walks to the gates. After a fanfare the alarm is raised inside, the garrison commander, with sword drawn, challenges the Lord Lyon from the battlements. The Lord Lyon commands that the gates be opened, whereupon the garrison commander requests a true copy ('just double') of the warrant to be passed through a small door in the gate. After the warrant has been inspected the key is handed over.

EDINBURGH IS THE PRINCIPAL CITY OF SCOTLAND.

Occasional Customs

SCOTLAND

Riding of the Marches, Forfar   Tayside

Now an irregular event, it was held triennially until World War I, and then replaced by a Town Council inspection of its farms, properties and water courses. The last time the Riding took place, largely by car and on foot, was in 1965, to mark the 300th anniversary of the granting of the town charter.

TAKE THE A90 NORTH FROM DUNDEE, THEN RIGHT ON THE A929.

Walking of the Marches, Newburgh   Fife

The marchers, led by the Provost, start at the East Port at 1 pm. The Town Officer puts a paint mark on each march stone.

TAKE THE A913 NORTH-WEST FROM CUPAR.

The Riding of the Marches in Crieff, Tayside, has now ceased. Another lapsed festival is St Serf's Festival at Culross, for which he is the patron saint. There was a parade in which branches and greenery featured, the Cross and Tron being decorated with flowers. This parade of the burgesses of the town is known to have happened on a 1st July, but ceased in the mid-19th century. Culross, Fife, is said to be the birthplace of St Kentigern. The three-day Riding of the Marches of Inverness's extensive town lands, in Highland, was last done in 1768.

WALES

Courts Leet of the Barony of Cemaes and the Manor of Mynachlogddu   Dyfed

These combined proceedings convenes to manage the Common Lands of the Preseli Hills in Dyfed.

MYNACHLOGDDU IS ON AN UNCLASSIFIED ROAD WEST OF THE A478.

🤼 Cornish Wrestling at St Columbs, St Wenn (where the championships are held), St Kew, St Merryn and Perranporth

TAKE THE A3059 EAST FROM NEWQUAY. ST COLUMB MINOR IS REACHED FIRST THEN ST COLUMB MAJOR. TAKE THE A39 NORTH FROM ST COLUMB MAJOR, RIGHT ON THE B3274, THEN LEFT ON AN UNCLASSIFIED ROAD TO ST WENN. FOR ST KEW TAKE THE A39 NORTH-EAST FROM WADEBRIDGE, THEN LEFT ON AN UNCLASSIFIED ROAD. FOR ST MERRYN TAKE THE B3276 NORTH FROM NEWQUAY. FOR PERRANPORTH TAKE THE A3075 SOUTH FROM NEWQUAY, THEN RIGHT ON THE B3285.

Dates for Movable Feasts

	1999	2000	2001	2002
Shrove Tuesday	16th Feb	7th Mar	27th Feb	12th Feb
Ash Wednesday	17th Feb	8th Mar	28th Feb	13th Feb
Mothering Sunday	14th Mar	2nd Apr	25th Mar	10th Mar
Easter Sunday	4th Apr	23rd Apr	15th Apr	31st Mar
Hock Sunday	11th Apr	30th Apr	22nd Apr	7th Apr
Rogation Sunday	9th May	28th May	20th May	5th May
Ascension Day	13th May	1st June	24th May	9th May
Whit Sunday	23rd May	11th June	3rd June	19th May
Trinity Sunday	30th May	18th June	10th June	26th May
Corpus Christi	3rd June	22nd June	14th June	30th May
Advent Sunday	28th Nov	3rd Dec	2nd Dec	1st Dec

	2003	2004	2005	2006
Shrove Tuesday	4th Mar	24th Feb	8th Feb	28th Feb
Ash Wednesday	5th Mar	25th Feb	9th Feb	1st Mar
Mothering Sunday	30th Mar	21st Mar	6th Mar	26th Mar
Easter Sunday	20th Apr	11th Apr	27th Mar	16th Apr
Hock Sunday	27th Apr	18th Apr	3rd Apr	23rd Apr
Rogation Sunday	25th May	16th May	1st May	21st May
Ascension Day	29th May	20th May	5th May	25th May
Whit Sunday	8th June	30th May	15th May	4th June
Trinity Sunday	15th June	6th June	22nd May	11th June
Corpus Christi	19th June	10th June	26th May	15th June
Advent Sunday	30th Nov	28th Nov	27th Nov	3rd Dec

	2007	2008	2009	2010
Shrove Tuesday	20th Feb	5th Feb	24th Feb	16th Feb
Ash Wednesday	21st Feb	6th Feb	25th Feb	17th Feb
Mothering Sunday	18th Mar	2nd Mar	22nd Mar	14th Mar
Easter Sunday	8th Apr	23rd Mar	12th Apr	4th Apr
Hock Sunday	15th Apr	30th Mar	19th Apr	11th Apr
Rogation Sunday	13th May	27th Apr	17th May	9th May
Ascension Day	17th May	1st May	21st May	13th May
Whit Sunday	27th May	11th May	31st May	23rd May
Trinity Sunday	3rd June	18th May	7th June	30th May
Corpus Christi	7th June	22nd May	11th June	3rd June
Advent Sunday	2nd Dec	30th Nov	29th Nov	28th Nov

Recipes appendix

January

Potted Stilton
8 oz (225 g) Stilton cheese crumbs
2 oz (50 g) softened butter
Pinch of mace
Milk
Clarified butter

Mix together the cheese, butter and mace, adding just enough milk to make a creamy paste. Put into small dishes and cover each with a little clarified butter. Put into the refrigerator to cool before serving.

Het Pint
4 cups (32 fl oz/1 litre) ale
½ cup (4 fl oz/120 ml) Scotch whisky
4 tablespoons sugar
1 egg

Heat the ale until it just boils. Beat the egg, and add the sugar and whisky, mixing well. Add this mixture to the gently boiling ale, stirring constantly to prevent any curdling. Pour from a height into mugs so that a froth is created, put in a spoon and drink while the froth remains.

Athol Brose
3 heaped tablespoons oatmeal
2 tablespoons honey
1 fl oz (30 ml) whisky

Add cold water to the oatmeal in a jug, and mix to a thin paste. Allow to settle and strain the liquid off. Heat the liquid gently in a saucepan, take off the heat and stir in the honey and whisky. Serve in a glass when cool enough. This drink is said to have been a favourite of, and named after, the 15th-century Earl of Athol. It is traditionally stirred with a silver spoon.

Black Bun
For the pastry
12 oz (350 g) plain flour
6 oz (175 g) butter
For the filling
8 oz (225 g) plain flour
2 oz (50 g) brown sugar
1 lb (450 g) currants
1 lb (450 g) raisins
3 oz (75 g) blanched, chopped almonds
4 oz (100 g) crystallised peel
1 teaspoon ground cinnamon
1 teaspoon ground ginger
1 teaspoon grated nutmeg
Pinch of ground cloves
½ teaspoon baking soda
3 eggs
1 tablespoon whisky

To make the pastry, rub together the flour and butter and add water to produce a stiff-textured dough. Roll out thinly and line a greased 8 in (20 cm) cake tin with it. Keep the rest for the lid.

To make the filling, mix all the dry ingredients together. Beat the whisky and eggs together and add to the dry mixture, stirring in thoroughly. Add milk if it is too dry. Put into the pastry-lined tin, smooth over and put on the pastry lid. Pierce the cake in several places and brush the top with beaten egg. Bake for about three hours in a moderate oven at 350°F/180°C.

Petticoat Tails
1 lb (450 g) plain flour
4 oz (100 g) caster sugar
8 oz (225 g) butter
1 egg
Almond essence

Cream the flour, sugar, butter and egg together with a few drops of almond essence. Roll out on a floured board until thin and cut four circles of 7 in (18 cm) diameter. Score radially, prick over with a fork, and remove a small circle from the centre. Place on a greased baking sheet and bake in the centre of a cool oven at 225°F/110°C for about 1½ hours until firm and pale gold in colour. Allow to cool on a rack, and serve warm with a little caster sugar sprinkled over.

Kelso Gingerbread
¼ lb (100 g) oatmeal
½ lb (225 g) butter
¼ lb (100 g) minced peel
2 fl oz (60 ml) cream
¾ lb (330 g) flour
¾ lb (330 g) treacle
1 oz (25 g) preserved ginger
Pinch of salt

Beat the butter to a cream, and stir in sifted flour, oatmeal and cream. Mix the treacle, ginger and peel together and add this to the other mixture. Mix thoroughly and put into a buttered loaf tin. Bake in a moderate oven at 325°F/160°C for ¾ hour.

Brunies
6 oz (150 g) flour
6 oz (150 g) medium oatmeal
1 oz (25 g) butter
4 oz (100 g) sugar
Pinch of salt
2 teaspoons ground ginger
½ teaspoon baking powder
2 tablespoons black treacle
1 egg
½ pint (300 ml) buttermilk

This recipe for brunies comes from Orkney, but is very close to what was used to make Yule brunies. Sift the flour into a large bowl and add the oatmeal. Mix, then rub in the butter. Add the sugar, a pinch of salt, the ginger and baking powder. Mix thoroughly. Beat the egg and melt the treacle. Stir the egg into the treacle with half the buttermilk, then add this to the large bowl. Stir as the rest of the buttermilk is gradually added until the mixture can be dropped from a spoon. Pour into greased, shaped moulds, or grease a rectangular tin and pour in the mixture, baking in a moderate oven at 350°F/180°C for about 1¼ hours, until an inserted skewer comes out clean. Let the brunie cool overnight before cutting.

Bara Brith

3 oz (75 g) currants
3 oz (75 g) sultanas
3 oz (75 g) butter
1 oz (25 g) crystallised peel
2 eggs
¼ teaspoon mixed spice, ground
3 oz (75 g) brown sugar
12 oz (350 g) self-raising flour
Honey

Put the dried fruit in a saucepan, add water and simmer for 15 minutes. Strain the fruit and put in a bowl, to which is added the butter (softened if necessary) and peel. Beat in the eggs, and stir the mixed spice, sugar and flour in thoroughly. Tip the mixture into a greased 2 lb (1 kg) loaf tin and bake in a slow oven at 300°F/150°C for 1 hour. Allow to cool for 15 minutes and turn out on to a wire rack. Warm a little honey and use to glaze the loaf.

Teisen Lap ('Moist Cake')

8 oz (225 g) plain flour
1 teaspoon baking powder
½ teaspoon ground nutmeg
4 oz (100 g) butter
1 oz (25 g) lard
4 oz (100 g) currants
4 oz (100 g) caster sugar
2 eggs
2 tablespoons milk

Sift the flour into a bowl and add the baking powder and nutmeg. Mix, then rub in the butter and lard. Add the currants and sugar and stir thoroughly. Beat the two eggs together and mix into the dry mixture, adding sufficient milk to give a soft texture. Grease and flour an 8 in (20 cm) sandwich tin and pour the mixture in. Spread evenly and bake in a moderate oven at 350°F/180°C for 20 minutes, and at 325°F/160°C for a further 30 minutes.

Twelfth Night Cake (Teisen Galan Ystwyll)

1 lb (450 g) sugar
1 lb (450 g) butter
½ teaspoon cinnamon
½ teaspoon coriander
½ teaspoon ginger
2 teaspoons allspice
9 eggs
1 lb (450 g) self-raising flour
1 cup brandy
4 oz (100 g) candied peel
4 oz (100 g) ground almonds
1 lb (450 g) sultanas
1 lb (450 g) currants
Pinch of salt

Line a 9 in (22.5 cm) cake tin with greaseproof paper and butter it lightly. Cream the butter and sugar, then mix in the spices. Separate the egg yolks, beat, and mix in alternately with portions of the brandy and flour. Add the nuts and dried fruit. Whip the egg whites and fold in, then add a pinch of salt and mix thoroughly. Tip into the cake tin, cover, and bake in a moderate oven at 325°F/160°C for 3–4 hours, removing the cover halfway through. Decorate with marzipan and icing if required.

Haggis

1 sheep's stomach
Sheep's pluck (heart, lungs and liver)
1 large onion
4 oz (100 g) grated suet
1 lb (450 g) oatmeal
8 oz (225 g) blanched, chopped almonds
1 oz (25 g) salt
Black pepper
Cayenne pepper
½ teaspoon mixed herbs
1 lemon

Prepare the ingredients first. The stomach must be washed and scraped thoroughly and soaked overnight in water. The sheep's pluck is also prepared the night before, by boiling for 2 hours in water, with the wind pipe hanging over the edge of the pan and a bowl underneath to catch the drips. Leave in the liquor overnight.

On the day, grate the rind of the lemon and extract the juice. Toast the oatmeal and chop the onion. Cut off the windpipe and mince the pluck. Keep the liquor. Add the suet, onion, oatmeal and almonds, and mix well. Then add the salt, two types of pepper, herbs, lemon juice and rind, followed by the pluck liquor. Mix thoroughly again and put into the sheep's stomach until it is half full. Sew up and prick with a fork. Put into boiling water and simmer for 3 hours, pricking again from time to time to prevent the stomach bursting. Make a saltire cross (the symbol of St Andrew) cut in the top and fold back the flaps before serving.

Scotch Broth

1 lb (450 g) mutton (use neck with fat trimmed off)
4 pints (2.5 litres) stock
3 teaspoons salt
Mixed herbs
1 oz (25 g) pearl barley
1 leek
1 onion
2 carrots
2 oz (50 g) peas
2 oz (50 g) white cabbage

Prepare the ingredients:. Rinse the barley thoroughly, shred the cabbage, peel and dice the carrots, trim and slice the leeks and peel and chop the onion.

Add the stock, salt, herbs and barley to the mutton in a saucepan and bring to the boil. Skim, cover and simmer gently for one hour. Then add the onion, carrot and leek and continue simmering for 25 minutes, and for a further 10 minutes after adding the peas and cabbage. Remove the mutton and cut off the lean meat, discarding the remainder of the neck. Chop up the meat and return it to the pan. Reheat and serve.

Colcannon

Take 1 lb (450 g) kale or green leaf cabbage
1 lb (450 g) potatoes (unpeeled)
6 spring onions or chives
¼ pint (150 ml) milk or cream
2 oz (50 g) butter
Salt and pepper

Remove stalks from the kale and shred. Chop the onions finely and simmer in the milk or cream for about 5 minutes. Boil the potatoes and kale in salty water until tender, drain and peel the potatoes. Mash the potatoes and mix with the hot milk and onions. Mash the kale and add to the potato mixture, then add half the butter and season with salt and pepper. Heat through and serve each portion with a knob of butter. Buttermilk is a traditional accompanying drink.

Champ

1 lb (450 g) potatoes
4 onions
1 cup (8 fl oz/240 ml) milk
Salt and pepper
2 oz (50 g) unsalted butter

For this type of colcannon, peel and slice the potatoes and slice the onions. Boil the potatoes until tender and mash. Put the onions and milk into a saucepan and bring to the boil. Simmer for a few minutes until the onions are tender. Stir the whole mixture into the mashed potato and season. Mix in the butter and serve hot.

Dumplings

4 oz (100 g) self-raising flour
2 oz (50 g) shredded suet
2 tablespoons chopped parsley
1 egg
Salt and pepper

Beat the egg with 4 tablespoons cold water. Sift the flour into a bowl and add the suet, parsley, pepper and salt. Mix thoroughly, then add the egg and water. Mix again to make a dough, roll into balls and cook in hot water for about 15 minutes, or in a simmering stew 15 minutes before serving.

Boxty Bread and Pancakes

2 oz (50 g) dripping
8 oz (225 g) plain flour
½ teaspoon bicarbonate of soda
8 oz (225 g) potatoes
2 oz (50 g) cheese
2 fluid oz (50 ml) buttermilk
1 tablespoon chopped parsley
Salt and black pepper

To make the bread, boil and mash the potatoes, and grate the cheese. Melt the dripping in a saucepan and stir in the flour and bicarbonate of soda. Add the mashed potatoes and cheese and mix thoroughly. Sprinkle on the buttermilk, mixing in well, and then add the parsley, salt and pepper. Stir until the mixture is soft like dough. Roll it out on a floured board, not too thinly (about ½ in (1.25 cm) thick), and cut into 3 in (7.5 cm) rounds. Make a cross on each so that when cooked they will divide into farls. Transfer to a greased baking sheet and cook in a fairly hot oven at 400°F/200°C for 15 minutes or until golden-brown and well risen. Split and serve with butter.

To make the pancakes, use the same ingredients as for the bread but add enough milk to make a batter of dropping consistency. Drop on to a hot greased pan or griddle, cook both sides and serve with butter.

February

Feasten Cakes

1 lb (450 g) plain flour
½ teaspoon cinnamon
4 oz (100 g) unsalted butter
2 teaspoons dried yeast
2 oz (50 g) sugar
¼ teaspoon of saffron
¼ pint (150 ml) milk
6 fl oz (175 ml) clotted cream
2 eggs
4 oz (100 g) currants

Warm the milk and make an infusion of the saffron. Cream the yeast with a little sugar. Sieve the flour and cinnamon into a bowl and mix. Rub in the butter. Strain the saffron milk and beat in the cream. Add the yeast to this mixture and leave for the yeast to activate. Beat the eggs.

Pour the frothy yeast mixture into the flour and cinnamon and add the eggs, currants and remaining sugar. Knead well, cover and leave for dough to rise. Later, shape dough into small, flat cakes and leave again until dough is springy to the touch.

Put on to a lightly greased baking sheet, brush milk and sprinkle sugar on each, then bake in a fairly hot oven at 375°F/190°C for about 25 minutes. Serve cold with whipped or clotted cream.

Shrovetide

Scotch Collops (recipe 1)

8 slices (¼ in (5 mm) thick) beef steak
4 onions
Salt and pepper
1 tablespoon walnut, mushroom or oyster ketchup

Melt butter in a pan and add the meat slices, searing on both sides. Slice the onions and add them, seasoning to taste. Cover and cook gently for 10 minutes. Remove collops and keep warm. Add the ketchup to the pan juices and bring to the boil. Pour over the collops and serve hot.

Scotch Collops (recipe 2)

1½ pounds (675 g) minced meat
1 cup stock (8 fl oz/240 ml)
1 teaspoon salt (for fresh meat)
1½ tablespoons dripping
2 small onions
1 dessertspoon oatmeal

Fry the onion in the dripping for a few seconds then add the mince. Brown carefully while stirring to prevent lumping. Add the stock, and the salt if needed. Cover and simmer gently for ¾ hour. Finally, add the oatmeal and continue cooking until the oatmeal is ready. Serve hot with toast or mashed potatoes.

Pea Soup

1 pint (600 ml) dried split peas
Selection of root vegetables, peeled and chopped
(for example, 2 each of carrots, onions, turnips,
celery sticks)
3 pints (1.8 litres) stock
½ pint (300 ml) milk
1 teaspoon chopped mint (optional)
Pinch of mustard powder (optional)
Black pepper
1 teaspoon sugar
Chopped ham
2 oz (50 g) butter

Soak the peas overnight, and then bring to the boil with
the root vegetables and stock. Simmer for 2½–3 hours.
Blend in a food processor, or through a sieve, return to
the pan and add the milk and extra ingredients. Season
with pepper and simmer for 15 minutes, stirring in the
butter during the last minute.

Irish Pancakes

2 cups (16 fl oz/500 ml) flour
½ teaspoon salt
2½ cups (20 fl oz/750 ml) milk
2 eggs
1 oz (25 g) unsalted butter
Caster sugar
Lemon juice

Beat the milk and eggs together in a bowl. Sift the flour
and salt into another bowl and add half the mixture to
them, stirring constantly. Melt the butter and whisk it in,
doing the same as the rest of the egg and milk mixture
is added. Allow the batter to stand for at least two hours.

  Melt 1 tablespoon butter in a frying pan, add ¼ cup
batter and tip until the pan is evenly coated. Keep the
pan moving as you cook to prevent sticking. When the
underside is golden-brown flip the pancake and cook
the other side. Sprinkle with sugar and lemon juice and
serve rolled up.

Boxty Pancakes or Stamp

1 lb (450 g) potatoes
2 tablespoons plain flour
1 teaspoon baking powder
Salt and pepper
¼ pint (150 ml) milk

Peel the potatoes and grate coarsely into a bowl. Add
sifted flour and baking powder. Mix thoroughly, then
add salt and pepper and mix in the milk. Stir and drop
tablespoons of the mixture on to a hot, oiled frying pan
or griddle. Cook for about 5 minutes each side until
golden-brown. Serve hot with butter and sugar.

Crowdy (Sollaghyn)

Brown porridge oatmeal in a pan and stir in a knob of
butter. Skim the Cowree pot (see May) and stir in the
liquid until a homogenous consistency is obtained.

Fastyn Cock

8 oz (225 g) oatmeal
4 oz (100 g) shredded beef suet
1 onion
1 egg
Salt and pepper

Beat the egg and finely chop the onion. Mix all the
ingredients together and mould into a chicken shape.
Scald a pudding cloth, sprinkle flour over it and put the
mixture in the centre. Tie up securely, allowing room for
the mixture to swell, and cook in boiling water (or
steam) for 2 hours.

Sauty Bannocks

2 tablespoons syrup
1 pint (600 ml) milk
8 oz (225 g) oatmeal
Bicarbonate of soda
Pinch of salt
2 eggs

Beat the eggs. Warm the syrup and stir in the cold
milk. Add the oatmeal, a pinch of bicarbonate of soda,
a little salt and the beaten eggs. Stir and allow to stand
for 20 minutes. Grease and heat a griddle, and drop
table-spoons of the mixture on to it. Cook on both sides
until brown.

Cock-a-leekie Soup

5 lb (2.25 kg) stewing chicken, with bones
removed
5 pints (3 litres) water
2 teaspoons salt
½ teaspoon pepper
12 leeks
1½ cups rice

Partially cook the rice in boiling water. Cook the chicken
in the measured water until tender, adding the salt and
pepper after an hour. Remove the chicken and keep
warm. Slice the leeks, and add with the rice to the soup,
cooking for 25 minutes. Add the chicken meat to the
soup, and cook for another 5 minutes. Serve hot.

Pancakes with Beef

4 oz (100 g) plain flour
½ teaspoon salt
1 egg
½ pint (250ml) milk
Lard or fat for frying
Thin slices of beef

Sieve flour and salt, make a well in the centre and
add the egg, working the flour in from the sides. Add
the milk gradually, beating to make a smooth batter.
Melt just enough lard to coat the bottom and sides of
a pan; when hot and just beginning to smoke pour in
a little pancake batter. Spread evenly and cook until
set and browned underneath, toss or turn and cook
the second side. Spread the slices of beef on and roll
up. Place in an oven dish, cover with foil and reheat
in a moderate oven.

Welsh Pancakes

4 oz (100 g) self-raising flour
Pinch of salt
1 oz (25 g) caster sugar
2 eggs
¼ pint (150 ml) milk
2 oz (50 g) butter
1 oz (25 g) currants (optional)

Crack one egg into a bowl and add the milk and the
yolk of the other egg. Melt the butter and add this to
the bowl, stirring until the mixture is smooth. Sift the
flour into a large bowl and add a pinch of salt and the
sugar. Pour in the mixture and beat to a smooth batter.
At this point add the currants and fold in.

  Heat a greased or oiled frying pan, or griddle, and
add sufficient batter to cover. Cook both sides. Serve
warm.

Welsh Oatmeal Pancakes (Crempog Geirch)

4 oz (100 g) flour
1½ oz (40 g) fine oatmeal
¼ oz (6 g) yeast
Sugar
Milk
1 egg
Pinch of salt
Lard

Beat the egg. Sift the flour into a bowl and add the oatmeal, a pinch of salt and the yeast creamed with sugar and milk. Mix and stir in the beaten egg. Cover and leave in a warm place for 1 hour. If the mixture thickens add a little warm milk. Melt the lard in a frying pan, drop a tablespoonful of mixture in and cook both sides until golden-brown. Serve hot with butter, honey or jam.

Periwinkle or Limpet Soup

periwinkles or limpets
Beef stock
1 onion
Peppercorns
Allspice
Flour

About half a bucketful of periwinkles or limpets are needed, which should be thoroughly washed in cold tap water and the shells cleaned. Using a large pestle and mortar grind them up, transfer to a large saucepan, cover with water and boil for a few minutes. Take about a quarter of this volume of beef stock, add the sliced onion, and boil it until the onion is soft. Strain the periwinkle or limpet broth through muslin and add the stock to it, together with the other ingredients, using flour to thicken. Boil for a few minutes while stirring and serve hot.

Lenten

Lenten Kail

1 lb (450 g) spring greens or mixture of available green vegetables
2 tablespoons oatmeal
5 fl oz (150 ml) single cream
Salt and black pepper

Cover greens with water in a saucepan and bring to the boil. Simmer until tender. Strain and keep only half the liquid. Blend in a food processor, or through a sieve, and return to the saucepan. Mix the oatmeal to a smooth paste with a little of the soup and add to the saucepan. Stir it in, and season. Bring to the boil and simmer for 15 minutes, adding the cream during the last minute.

March

Laverbread with Oatmeal and Bacon

8 oz (225 g) laverbread
4 slices smoked bacon
Oatmeal
Salt and black pepper

Dice and fry the bacon, and stir in the laverbread. Add oatmeal to the frying pan, with black pepper and a little salt to season, and stir together while continuing to fry gently. When crisp and brown on both sides serve hot.

Leek and Ham Soup

1 onion
1 oz (25 g) butter
1 oz (25 g) flour
1 pint (600 ml) water or white stock
6 leeks
Ham, 5 thin slices or cuts off the bone
¼ pint (150 ml)
Salt and black pepper
Single cream

Slice the leeks and chop the ham. Chop the onion and fry in the butter until soft. Add the flour and cook for another minute while stirring. Continue stirring while the stock or water is added and boil gently until the soup thickens. Put in the leeks and ham and simmer for 30 minutes, stirring occasionally. Pour into a blender and blend for a few seconds. Add the milk and stir in, then season with salt and pepper to taste. Before serving, remove from heat and stir in a little cream.

Leek and Potato Soup

1 lb (450 g) potatoes
2 carrots
1 lb (450 g) leeks
½ pint (300 ml) chicken stock
½ pint (300 ml) milk
Salt and black pepper
1 teaspoon mace

Peel and slice the potatoes and peel and chop the carrots. Add to the chicken stock in a saucepan and boil for 15 minutes. Cut the leeks into rings and add, continuing to boil until all the vegetables are soft. Pour into a blender and blend for a few seconds. Put back in the saucepan, season to taste and add the milk. Reheat and serve.

Cawl

For the stock
Diced, lean Welsh lamb and the bones with fat removed
1 tablespoon barley
1 onion with skin on
1 leek
1 large carrot
For the soup
Diced vegetables as available, such as onions, carrots, turnips, celery, leeks and parsnips
Salt and pepper
Chopped parsley

To make the stock, first chop the vegetables. Then, brown the bones and trimmings in a roasting tin in the oven, for about 30 minutes, and transfer the bones to a large saucepan. Pour off the juices and use the roasting tin to sauté the stock vegetables for about 10 minutes. Add them to the bones, cover with water and simmer gently for about 3 hours. Strain, cool and skim. Reboil if necessary down to 4 pints (2.25 l).

To make the soup, sauté the diced lamb and add with the barley to the stock. Add a bayleaf if desired, and simmer for 45 minutes. Sauté the remaining chopped vegetables, except the leeks, in some of the lamb fat, drain off the fat and add the vegetables to the lamb and stock. After simmering for 30 minutes add the leeks and continue for a further 10 minutes. It is traditionally served decorated with marigold petals. Years ago it was served as two courses, the liquid soup first with the meat and vegetables to follow.

Easter

Anglesey Eggs (Wyau sir fôn)
6 leeks
1 oz (25 g) butter
2 oz (50 g) grated cheese
8 eggs
1 lb (450 g) mashed potato
Salt and pepper
½ oz (25 g) flour
½ pint (300 ml) milk

Slice the leeks and boil in salty water for 10 minutes. Strain and mix with the mashed potato. Season, add half the butter and beat. Pack around the edge of an ovenproof dish. Melt the rest of the butter and stir in the flour and milk, keeping warm and stirred whilst the cheese is added. Slice or cut the eggs and put into the ovenproof dish, covering with the cheese sauce. Sprinkle more grated cheese on top and cook in a fairly hot oven at 400°F/200°C until golden-brown on top.

Salt Beef and Cabbage
1 lb (450 g) salt beef
¾ lb (330 g) cabbage
2½ oz (62.5 g) butter
4 or 5 juniper berries
Black pepper

Soak the beef overnight to leach out most of the salt, then boil it until tender (about 40 minutes). Leave to cool, remove from water and slice. Boil the cabbage in salty water until tender and chop. Melt the butter in a deep frying pan and add the juniper berries, beef slices and pepper to season. Fry gently until the meat is just brown. Remove the beef and keep warm. Add the cabbage to the frying pan and fry for 3–4 minutes. Serve together, hot.

Welsh Toasted Cheese (Welsh Rarebit or Tost Caws)
Thickly sliced bread
Welsh Caerphilly cheese
Butter
Slices of raw onion
Green salad
Ale

Cut ¼ in (6 mm) slices of cheese and toast on both sides. Do not melt completely. Toast the bread on both sides, spread thinly with butter and place slices of onion on. Put the toasted cheese on top and serve warm with green salad and ale.

Saffron Cake
¼ teaspoon saffron
Pinch of salt
5 tablespoons water
1 lb (450 g) plain flour
¼ teaspoon bicarbonate of soda
8 oz (225 g) butter
2 oz (50 g) candied peel
8 oz (225 g) currants
6 oz (175 g) sultanas
6 oz (175 g) sugar
2 eggs
Milk

Put the water in a basin and add a pinch of salt and the saffron. Stir and leave overnight. Sift the flour and bicarbonate of soda into a bowl and rub in the butter. Add the dried fruit, peel and sugar, and mix. Beat the eggs and stir in. Strain the saffron off and add the saffron water to the bowl and sufficient milk to get a pouring consistency. Beat well and pour into a 9 in (23 cm) round baking tin lined with greaseproof paper. Bake for 1½–2 hours in a moderate oven at 350°F/180°C until the centre is cooked. A skewer should come out clean. Leave to cool before serving.

Dulse (Dillisk, Dillesk)
Dulse can be eaten raw, but to cook it, soak it first for 3 hours in cold water, then put in a saucepan with milk, a knob of butter and black pepper. Simmer for a further 3 hours. Add it to mashed potato to make Dulse Champ, or to soups. It can also be served with meat or fish.

Sloke
Sloke is like the Welsh laver. Wash it, then simmer in water for 4–5 hours. Drain and shake with butter, cream, and lemon juice. Serve as a vegetable with roast lamb, ham or fish.

Willicks (Willocks)
These periwinkles are boiled in their shells for 10 minutes in sea water. Remove the bodies with a pin and roll in fine oatmeal.

Jugged Hare
1 hare, jointed and boned
2 pints (1.2 l) stock
2 oz (50 g) streaky bacon
2 oz (50 g) butter
2 onion
3 carrots
2 sticks of celery
Salt and black pepper
1 oz (25 g) flour
4 tablespoons port
1 tablespoon redcurrant jelly

Put the bones into a saucepan. Peel and chop one onion, peel and slice one carrot, and chop one stick of celery. Put in the saucepan and cover with water. Bring to the boil and simmer gently for 30 minutes. Strain and keep the stock. Prepare the remainder of the vegetables similarly.

Partially fry the bacon in a deep casserole dish (which has a close-fitting lid), add the butter and hare joints and continue frying until the hare is browned. Put in the remainder of the vegetables, pepper and salt. Cover with the stock and bring to the boil. Put the lid on and cook in a slow oven at 300°F/150°C until the meat is tender. This should take from 2½ to 3 hours. Make a paste from the flour by mixing it with water and stir the paste in. Cook for a few minutes longer, then add the port and redcurrant jelly. Stir in and serve immediately.

April

Manx Dressed Crab
Remove the white flesh from the shell and claws and mix with mayonnaise and bread crumbs. Add salt, pepper and a spot of mustard to taste. Serve in fresh bread rolls.

Elderflower Wine
6 elder flowers
2 tablespoons (25 g) white wine vinegar
Juice of 1 lemon
1½ lb (675 g) caster sugar
1 gallon (4.5 litres) cold water

Put all the ingredients into a large bowl, stir, cover and leave for a day. Strain through muslin and pour into sterilised bottles. Leave for 2–3 weeks before drinking.

Beltane Bannocks and Beltane Caudle
For the bannocks
4 oz (100 g) medium oatmeal
Pinch of salt
Baking powder
1 teaspoon lard
For the caudle
1 egg
1 tablespoon oatmeal
1 tablespoon milk
1 tablespoon cream

To make the bannocks, put the oatmeal, a pinch of salt and a pinch of baking powder in a bowl, mix and create a well in the centre. Melt the fat and pour in. Mix to a dough and add hot water if necessary to make the dough pliable. Rub oatmeal over the surface and roll out to ⅛ in (0.25 cm) thickness. Cut into 2½ in (6 cm) rounds and cook lightly on a griddle or frying pan, turning once.

To make the caudle, beat the egg and mix a little with the other ingredients for the caudle. Brush on to the top of the bannocks, turn them over and cook. Brush on the other side (now on top), turn and cook this side. Repeat twice more. Cool before serving.

Welsh Oatcakes (Bara Ceirch)
Take 6 oz (175 g) medium oatmeal
6 oz (175 g) whole-wheat flour
1 teaspoon salt
¼ teaspoon bicarbonate of soda
3 oz (75 g) butter
2 tablespoons water

Mix the oatmeal, flour, salt and bicarbonate of soda in a large bowl and rub in the butter. Add sufficient water to create a soft, smooth dough. Sprinkle flour on a board and roll out half the dough to a large circle, say 10 in (25 cm) diameter. Cut into circles or leave whole and score radially into portions. Bake in a moderate oven at 325°F/160°C for about 20 minutes until just golden-brown, or cook both sides on a griddle.

May

Grilled Manx Kippers
Dot the kipper with butter and grill for about five minutes. Serve with bread and butter.

Hasty Pudding
1 pint (600 ml) milk
1 tablespoon plain flour
1 tablespoon fine or medium oatmeal
Pinch of salt

Mix the dry ingredients with a quarter of the milk to make a sloppy paste. Bring the remainder of the milk to the boil and stir in the paste. Keep stirring as you cook until the mixture thickens.

Cowree
Steep oat husks in water, with a little fine oatmeal added, for 9 days. Strain the now bitter, fermented liquid into a large pot and heat, with stirring, until thick. Cool and boil portions with milk to serve. The liquid, called Sooslagh, was sometimes drunk on its own.

May Junket
Milk
Rennet
Cream
Sugar
Cinnamon

Warm the milk and put in a bowl. Turn it with rennet, then put scalded cream, sugar and cinnamon on top, but do not break the curd.

Irish Whiskey Syllabub
1 lemon
6 tablespoons clear honey
8 tablespoons whiskey
½ pint (300 ml) double cream
Grated nutmeg

Chill the cream. Grate the lemon rind and put this in a bowl with the lemon juice. Add the honey and whiskey and leave to stand for 1 hour. Whisk in the cream until the mixture thickens, then spoon into glasses or dishes. Serve chilled with grated nutmeg sprinkled on top. Syllabub separates into two layers on standing.

Fuggan ('Heavy Cake')
2 cups flour
2 oz (50 g) fat
Currants
Pinch of salt
Sour milk or clotted cream

Mix all the ingredients together and roll out until 1 in (2.5 cm) thick, in an oval shape. Make criss-cross scores with a knife and bake for about half an hour. It is traditionally accompanied by parsnip wine or sloe gin.

Helston Pudding
4 fl oz (100 ml) milk
½ teaspoon bicarbonate of soda
2 oz (50 g) plain flour
2 oz (50 g) currants
2 oz (50 g) raisins
2 oz (50 g) sugar
2 oz (50 g) breadcrumbs
Pinch of salt
1 tablespoon candied peel
2 oz (50 g) ground rice
2 oz (50 g) shredded suet
½ teaspoon mixed spice

Add the bicarbonate of soda to the milk and stir until dissolved. Mix together the dry ingredients and add the milk. Stir well and put into a greased 2 pint (1.2 litre) pudding bowl. Cover with greaseproof paper and tie a linen cloth or foil over the top. Steam for 2 hours. Serve with custard.

Whitsuntide

Squab Pie
For the pastry
12 oz (350 g) plain flour
½ teaspoon baking powder
6 oz (175 g) butter
1 egg
Salt and pepper
For the filling
2 lb (900 g) lean pork pieces
1 lb (450 g) onions
1 lb (450 g) apples
1 teaspoon dried sage
Salt and black pepper
1 pint (600 ml) stock

To make the pastry, sift the flour into a bowl and stir in the baking powder. Rub in the butter. Beat the egg and add, with salt and pepper, mixing to produce a stiff dough. Knead and leave in the refrigerator for 15 minutes.

To make the pie, grease a large pie dish. Peel and slice the onions, and core, peel and slice the apples. Add these, with the pork, to the dish so as to make layers, sprinkling sage, salt and black pepper on each layer. Pour on the stock. Roll out the pastry on a floured board and cover the dish. Pierce the top and cook for 10 minutes in a hot oven at 425°F/220°C. Reduce the temperature to moderate at 325°F/160°C and cook for 2 hours. Serve hot, but it can be eaten cold.

Junket
1 pint (600 ml) fresh milk
1 tablespoon caster sugar
1 teaspoon rennet essence
Grated nutmeg
Clotted cream

Warm the milk and sugar to blood heat, take off the heat then add the rennet essence. Stir for 10 seconds before pouring into warm dishes. Keep warm for 20 minutes to allow for setting. Sprinkle each with nutmeg and serve with clotted cream and available fresh fruits.

June

Shearing Cake
1 lb (450 g) plain flour
1 heaped teaspoon baking powder
8 oz (225 g) butter
Pinch of salt
12 oz (675 g) soft brown sugar
1 tablespoon caraway seeds
1 lemon
1 teaspoon grated nutmeg
½ pint (300 ml) milk
2 eggs

Sift the flour and baking powder and rub in the butter. Grate the lemon rind and extract the juice. Put both in the flour, with the sugar, caraway seeds, nutmeg and a pinch of salt. Mix, and continue to stir as you pour in the milk. Beat the eggs and add these, mixing again. Fold into a 9 in (22.5 cm) cake tin lined with greaseproof paper and bake in a moderate oven at 350°F/180°C for half an hour and at 300°F/150°C for about 1½ hours.

Cockles, Laverbread and Bacon
4 oz (100 g) laverbread
1 oz (25 g) fine or medium oatmeal
2 rashers bacon
2 eggs
Cockles

Mix the laverbread and oatmeal together and form into rissoles. Remove cockles from shells and wash them thoroughly. Fry the bacon dry so that the fat runs out. Remove bacon and keep warm. Now fry the rissole-shaped lavercakes on both sides and keep with the bacon. Beat the eggs and add the cockles, then pour the mixture into the frying pan and cook. Serve hot.

July

Galettes
2 oz (50 g) buckwheat flour
2 oz (50 g) plain flour
Pinch of salt
1 egg
¼ pint (150 ml) milk
¼ pint (150 ml) water
2 oz (50 g) butter
Groundnut oil

Sift the plain flour into a bowl and add the buckwheat flour and a pinch of salt. Break an egg into a well in the centre and mix, gradually adding the milk and water as you do so. Beat well and add the butter. Beat again until the mixture is like thick cream. Leave the batter to stand for 2 hours.

Get the griddle or frying pan really hot then lightly grease. Pour in 2–3 tablespoons of batter and spread thinly with a wooden spatula. Cook until the underside is just crisp, then flip over and cook the other side. Serve on a warm plate, folded in half.

Crêpes

Follow the recipe for galettes but use 4 oz (100 g) plain flour only. To make sweet crêpes, add 1–2 tablespoons caster or vanilla sugar and a tablespoon of calvados or brandy. They can also be flavoured with cinnamon or aniseed. Crêpes can be spread with butter, cream, jam, honey or chestnut purée, then folded into four. To make filled pancakes, use fillings of cooked apple or pear, or of thin strawberry slices cooked in a little butter and sugar. Vanilla sugar can be made by storing some caster sugar in a jar with a couple of vanilla pods added.

The speciality from Quimper called Crêpe-dentelle is made using equal amounts of flour and sugar, flavoured with vanilla. The sugary mixture is harder to handle and cook, but, if successful, cut the pancake into strips and roll into flat cylinders around the blade of a knife. Eat with a sweet wine.

Tynwald Fudge

2 cups caster sugar
2 oz (50 g) plain chocolate
¼ teaspoon salt
1 cup evaporated milk
¼ cup honey
2 tablespoons butter

Put the sugar, chocolate, salt and milk into a saucepan and bring to the boil. Heat for 5 minutes then add the honey. Heat at 240°F/115°C until soft. Remove from the heat and add the butter. Stir and allow to cool a little naturally. Pour on to a buttered baking tray and cut when cold.

Teisen 'Berffro

8 oz (225 g) butter
8 oz (225 g) sugar
8 oz (225 g) self-raising flour

Cream the butter and sugar together, and add the flour gradually, working the mixture with the hands. Roll out then press pieces in the scallop shells. Bake in a moderate oven at 325°F/160°C for about 20 minutes. Remove from the shell and serve curved side up, sprinkled with sugar.

August

Mutton Pie

3 lb (1.4 kg) lean mutton
2 large onions
2 leeks
2 oz (50 g) unsalted butter
1 oz (25 g) flour
Shortcrust pastry (using 1 lb/450 g flour)

Slice the onions and leeks. Put them into a saucepan with the mutton, boil and simmer for about an hour until the mutton is tender. Strain and keep the liquor. Cut the meat into bite-sized pieces and put with the vegetables into an 8 in deep pie pan. Melt the butter in a frying pan and stir in the flour. Gradually add 2 cups of the liquor, stirring constantly. Bring to the boil then cool slightly before adding to the pie pan. Allow to cool. Now cover with the shortcrust pastry, trim and make vents for the steam to escape. Brush with milk and bake in a fairly hot oven at 400°F for 15 minutes. Turn the heat down to moderate at 350°F/180°C and bake for another 10–15 minutes until the crust is golden-brown.

Barm Brack or Bairín Breac

¾ oz (18 g) fresh yeast
¾ cup caster sugar
1 cup milk
4 cups unbleached white flour
1 teaspoon salt
1 teaspoon grated nutmeg
1 teaspoon cinnamon
1 teaspoon grated allspice
½ cup unsalted butter
2 eggs
1½ cups sultanas
¾ cup currants
½ cup chopped candied peel
1 lemon

Cream the yeast with a teaspoon of sugar and the same amount of milk. To a large bowl add the sifted flour, salt and spices, and mix together. Rub in the butter and blend in the sugar. Beat the eggs and warm the milk, then add both to the yeast mixture, stirring well. Now add to the flour mixture and mix to form a dough. Knead until it is fairly firm but pliable. Add the dried fruit, peel and grated lemon rind, mixing with the hands. Cover and allow to stand in a warm place until the dough has risen to twice its size. Transfer into a round 10 in baking tin lined with greaseproof paper and allow to stand for a further 30 minutes. Bake in a fairly hot oven at 400°F for about 1 hour, until golden-brown.

Orkney Bride Cakes

5 oz (150 g) self-raising flour
2 oz (50 g) butter
1 oz (25 g) caster sugar
1 oz (25 g) caraway seeds
3–4 tablespoons milk

Sift the flour, soften the butter and rub together. Add the sugar and caraway seeds and mix, adding sufficient milk to make a firm dough. Roll out on a floured board until ½ in (1.25 cm) thick and cut out a circle 7 in (18 cm) diameter. Score radially to make eight segments. Cook on a griddle, with medium heat, for about 10 minutes, or until golden-brown on each side. Turn only once to avoid crumbling. Cool before serving.

Trout with Bacon (Brithyll â Chig Moch)

Trout, cleaned and de-boned
Bacon rashers
Salt and pepper
Parsley

Line an oven-proof dish with bacon rashers, lay the trout on top and cover with more rashers. Season with salt and pepper and sprinkle the parsley over. Bake in a fairly hot oven at 400°F/200°C for 15–20 minutes.

Salmon (Eog) with Lemon Butter

Rub the whole fish with lemon and butter, double-wrap in foil and bake in a moderate oven at 350°F/180°C according to the weight, say about 15 minutes to the pound (per 450 g).

Yellowman

1 lb (450 g) golden syrup
½ lb (225 g) brown sugar
1 teaspoon baking soda
½ oz (12.5 g) butter
2 tablespoons vinegar

Melt the butter in a pan, covering the bottom, then add the sugar, syrup and vinegar. Stir until a homogeneous liquid is obtained. Boil without stirring until drops put in cold water become brittle. Add the baking soda, stir and pour into a greased dish. When cool enough pull the toffee until yellow. Cut up as desired.

Harvest

Manx Herring Pie
Shortcrust pastry(using 1 lb/450 g flour)
6 fresh herrings
Butter
½ teaspoon mace
Salt and black pepper
3 large cooking apples
2 onions

Grease a large pie dish and line with the pastry (a half to two-thirds should be needed, rolled out). Prepare the herrings by removing the heads, tails, fins, scales and guts. Butter the pastry at the bottom of the dish and lay the herrings on. Season with the mace, salt and pepper. Core, peel and slice the apples thinly. Put the slices in the dish on top of the fish. Peel and slice the onions and make a layer on top of the apple. Dot with butter and add a cupful of water. Roll the remaining pastry and use to cover the pie. Pierce and cook in a moderate oven at 350°F/180°C for about 35 minutes.

Cranachan or Cream Crowdie
¼ pint (150 ml) whipping cream
½ pint (300 ml) cream cheese
2 oz (50 g) medium oatmeal
1 small glass malt whisky
1 tablespoon honey

Soak the oatmeal in whisky and honey for at least 3 hours. Whip the cream and fold it into the cream cheese. Then add the oatmeal mixture and blend. Serve with fresh soft fruit.

Flummery (Llymru)
4 oz (100 g) medium oatmeal
2 tablespoons clear honey
1 tablespoon lemon juice
2 tablespoons brandy (optional)
8 oz (225 g) fresh chopped fruit in season (optional)
¼ pint (150 ml) buttermilk, double cream or fromage frais

Soak the oatmeal in water overnight. Strain off excess water and stir the honey, lemon juice, brandy and fruit into the oatmeal. Whisk the cream and fold into the mixture.

Teisen Blat (Harvest Cake)
For the tart
1 lb (450 g) self-raising flour
8 oz (225 g) butter
¼ pint (125 ml) cold water
2 teaspoons sugar
½ teaspoon cinnamon
Mixed spice
Milk
For the filling
Purée made from 1½ lb (675 g) cooked fruit, sweetened to taste and stones removed

Sift the flour into a bowl, and add the sugar, cinnamon and a pinch of mixed spice. Mix, then rub in the butter. Add the water and work the mixture into a pliable dough. Roll thinly on a floured board and cut into four rounds. Put two rounds on to a greased baking tray and cook in a fairly hot oven at 400°F/200°C for 10 minutes. Remove and add filling, cover with the other rounds and seal. Prick the tops, brush with milk and bake in a moderate oven at 350°F/180°C until golden-brown. Serve warm or cold, with buttermilk to drink.

Llandysul Harvest Pie (Poten Ben Fedi)
Boil potatoes and mash with a handful of wheaten flour. Boil together minced pieces of bacon and beef and chopped onion. Add to the mashed potato, mix and warm through.

September

Roast Goose
1 goose
3 cooking apples
Salt and pepper

Prepare the goose. Cut the apples in half and remove the cores, but not the peel. Place them inside the goose. Season with salt and pepper and place in the centre of the oven, with a drip pan on the lower rack. Cook according to weight, and baste and pierce the skin every 30 minutes so that the fat runs out freely.

Potatoes were also used to stuff the goose, as they absorb both the fat and the flavour.

Gooseberry and Fennel Sauce
1 cup gooseberries
1 oz (25 g) sugar
½ oz (12.5 g) unsalted butter
1 oz (25 g) chopped fennel

To make the sauce, top and tail the gooseberries and boil gently with ½ cup of water until soft. Add the sugar, turn the heat down and simmer for 10 minutes. Remove from heat and stir in the butter and fennel.

Onion Sauce
Boil chopped onions and mash. Mix with a knob of butter, pepper, salt, a pinch of nutmeg and a little cream. Beat until smooth.

Apple Sauce
Cook peeled and cored apples in a minimum of water until soft. Mash and mix with butter, sugar, a pinch of nutmeg and salt.

Manx Michaelmas Goose with Apple Sauce
1 goose
Sage and onion stuffing
2 lb (450 g) cooking apples
1 oz (25 g) butter
Sugar

Prepare the goose and remove some fat from the inside. Stuff it with sage and onion stuffing and spread the fat over the breast. Roast in a moderate oven at 325°F/160°C for 30 minutes. Add a cupful of hot water to the fat and continue cooking, basting regularly. Allow about 20 minutes per pound (225 g).

To make the sauce, peel, core and slice the apples and stew very slowly in a pan with the lid on. Stir and add the butter, beating until smooth. Add sugar to taste if desired.

October

Blackberry Wine
3 lb (1.4 kg) blackberries
Sugar
Brandy

Put the blackberries into a stone jar and add 3 dessertspoonsful (6 g) of sugar. Cover and stir every day for three weeks, then strain through muslin. For every pint (600 ml) of juice add 1 lb (450 g) of sugar. Stir well and pour into sterilised bottles. Add to each a dessertspoonful (2 g) of brandy. Cork and leave for a few weeks before drinking.

Potato Apple Cake
8 oz (225 g) mashed potato
½ teaspoon salt
1 oz (25 g) butter
2 oz (50 g) plain flour
Caster sugar
Butter
10 oz (300 g) sliced Bramley apples

Mix the mashed potato, salt and butter together in a large bowl, and stir in the flour until the dough is pliable. Cut into two pieces and roll each out into an 8 in (20 cm) circle. Put half the apple slices on to each circle, covering only one half of it. Moisten the edges and fold the uncovered halves over, pressing the edges together. Bake the cakes on a griddle for 15–20 minutes each side. Take off the griddle and cut the curved edges to open the cakes. Sprinkle the apples with sugar and add small knobs of butter. Press the edges together again and cook for a further 5–10 minutes.

Champ
Boil and mash potatoes. Chop spring onions (one for each potato) and boil in milk for 5 minutes. Add to the mashed potato and stir thoroughly. Season with salt and black pepper, make a hollow in the top and add a knob of butter. Serve immediately. Champ can also be made with chopped parsley, chives, nettle tops or peas.

Tea Brack
9 oz (250 g) sultanas
9 oz (250 g) raisins
8 oz (225 g) soft brown sugar
16 fluid oz (500 ml) hot, strong tea (without milk!)
12 oz (330 g) plain flour
2 teaspoons baking powder
2 teaspoons mixed spice
2 eggs

Put the dried fruit and sugar into a bowl and pour in the tea. Add the sugar immediately and stir to dissolve. Cover and leave overnight.

Line an 8 in by 3 in (20 cm by 7 cm) cake tin all over with greaseproof paper and grease with melted butter. Sift the flour and mix in the baking powder and mixed spice. Beat the eggs. Add in portions to the fruit mixture alternately with portions of the flour mixture. Beat well before adding the next portion. Pour into the cake tin and bake in a moderate oven at 325°F/160°C for about 1½ hours. Serve when cool.

Currant Soda
1 lb (450 g) soda bread flour
1 teaspoon bicarbonate of soda
Pinch of salt
2 oz (50 g) caster sugar
4 oz (100 g) dried fruit
15 fl oz (450 g) buttermilk

Sift the flour into a large bowl and add the bicarbonate of soda, a pinch of salt, the sugar and fruit. Stir well and make a well in the centre to pour in half the buttermilk. Stir to make a loose dough, adding as much of the rest of the buttermilk as necessary. Grease an 8 in (20 cm) round cake tin with melted butter and turn in the dough. Sprinkle with a little flour and bake in a fairly hot oven at 400°F/200°C for 30 minutes, then for a further 30 minutes in a slow oven at 300°F/150°C until crisp on top and golden-brown in colour. Check that the centre is cooked by inserting a skewer, which should come out clean. Cool wrapped in cloth, and serve as buttered slices.

Nut Biscuits
3 oz (75 g) whole hazelnuts
5 oz (150 g) plain flour
Pinch of salt
4 oz (100 g) butter
2 oz (50 g) caster sugar
Honey

Toast the hazelnuts first, then remove their skins and crush into small pieces. Mix the flour and salt in a bowl, blend in the butter (softened if necessary) and sugar, and finally add the nuts and flour. Mix thoroughly and knead the dough until smooth. Put into the refrigerator for 30 minutes. Roll out the dough on a floured board and cut into 2 in (5 cm) rounds. Grease a baking tray and spread rice-paper over it before placing the rounds on. Bake in a fairly hot oven at 375°F/190°C for about 8 minutes. Cool on a wire rack, slice in half and make a sandwich of each with honey.

Irish Oatcakes
8 oz (225 g) fine or medium oatmeal
2 oz (50 g) plain flour
½ teaspoon bicarbonate of soda
¼ teaspoon cream of tartar
½ teaspoon salt
2 oz (50 g) butter

Sift the flour, add to the oatmeal in a bowl, and mix together with the bicarbonate of soda, cream of tartar and salt. Put the butter in a saucepan and add 2 fl oz (50 ml) of hot water. Bring just to the boil. Make a well in the centre of the mixture in the bowl and pour the boiling liquid into it. Stir until a uniform texture is obtained then roll into a round cake on a board dusted with oatmeal. The cake should be ⅛ in (3 mm) and about 9 in (23 cm) in diameter. Sprinkle oatmeal on to the surface and press in. Cut radially into eight portions, put on a floured baking sheet and bake in a moderate oven at 350°F/180°C for about 40 minutes. Serve with butter, cheese, and buttermilk to drink.

Apple Dumplings
Shortcrust pastry (using 1 lb/450 g flour)
6 apples
2 oz (50 g) sugar
2 oz (50 g) butter
6 cloves
Milk

Chill the pastry for 15 minutes, then roll out thinly and cut into 6 rounds. Cream the sugar and butter together. Core and peel the apples and fill with the sugar and butter mixture. Put a clove in each apple and place one on each pastry round. Brush milk on the edges of the rounds and mould around the apple, pressing the edges together. Put upside down on to a greased baking tray, brush with more milk and bake in a fairly hot oven at 400°F/200°C for about 30 minutes, longer for large, unripe apples.

Brown Cake (Soda Bread)
1½ lb (675 g) plain flour
2 teaspoons baking powder
1 teaspoon salt
½ pint (300 ml) natural yoghurt
¼ pint (150 ml) water
1 egg

Mix the flour, baking powder and salt together in a bowl. In another bowl put the yoghurt, egg and water and beat. Add the flour and mix until a stiff dough is formed. Knead well and mould into a round loaf shape, scoring a cross into the top. Place on a greased baking tray and bake in a fairly hot oven for 40 minutes at 375°F/190°C. Wrap it in a cloth and allow to cool.

Fortune-telling Crowdie
2 heaped tablespoons oatmeal
½ pint (300 ml) double cream
1 oz (25 g) caster sugar
2 teaspoons whisky

Toast the oatmeal and whip the cream, both lightly. Put both in a bowl and stir in the sugar a little at a time to taste. Pour in the whisky, mix and chill for a few minutes. Add the charms, stir and take to the table. Allow to cool before serving.

Cloutie Dumpling
6 oz (175 g) self-raising flour
2 oz (50 g) butter
6 oz (175 g) caster sugar
4 oz (100 g) raisins
4 oz (100 g) currants
1 oz (25 g) candied peel
½ teaspoon mixed spice
1 teaspoon cinnamon
Pinch of salt
1 egg
Milk

Measure and mix all the dry ingredients. Beat the egg and add with a little milk. Stir until homogeneous, then put into a greased pudding bowl. Cover with greaseproof paper and tie a cloth over the top. Steam or boil for at least 3 hours. Serve with custard. Traditionally the dumpling was left in front of the fire to dry and brown before serving.

Ginger Biscuits
2 oz (50 g) lard
2 oz (50 g) margarine
2 teaspoons golden syrup
6 oz (175 g) self-raising flour
3 oz (75 g) caster sugar
½ teaspoon bicarbonate of soda
1 teaspoon ground ginger

Melt the lard, margarine and syrup together in a pan but do not boil. Sift the other ingredients together and add to the pan. Stir thoroughly and remove pan from heat. Make portions of the mixture into balls and put on to a baking tray. Flatten slightly before baking in a fairly hot oven at 375°F/190°C for 10–15 minutes.

Mash o' Nine Sorts (Stwmp naw Rhyw)
4 small to medium potatoes
2 carrots
2 parsnips
2 turnips
½ lb (225 g) peas
Butter
1 large leek
Salt and pepper
Milk

Peel and dice the potatoes, and peel and slice the other root vegetables. Boil them until just soft, drain and mash. Boil the peas, drain and add to the mash. Fry the leeks in butter until soft and also add to the mash. Mix and season with salt and pepper, adding a little milk to blend the mixture. Serve immediately.

November

Mussel Stew
2 cups mussels
½ cup water
1 tablespoon oil
1 small clove garlic
3 mushrooms
1 small onion
2 oz (50 g) white breadcrumbs
1 teaspoon lemon juice
1 tablespoon chopped parsley
Salt and pepper
1 egg yolk
2 tablespoons cream

Wash the mussels thoroughly, cover with water in a saucepan and heat gently until all the shells have opened. Remove the mussels and keep the liquid for later. Add to it any juices from the shells. Break the mussels apart and remove the beards. Crush the garlic and chop the onion and mushrooms. Fry lightly in the oil, and remove the latter. Add to the mussel juice in a saucepan, and put in the breadcrumbs, lemon juice, parsley and seasoning. Bring to the boil and simmer gently for 5 minutes. Beat the egg yolk and cream together and add to the saucepan. Reheat, but do not boil. Serve hot.

Hollantide Fairings

3 oz (75 g) butter
2 tablespoons golden syrup
2 oz (50 g) caster sugar
2 oz (50 g) plain flour
½ teaspoon bicarbonate of soda
½ teaspoon mixed spice
1 teaspoon ground ginger

Put the butter, syrup and sugar into a saucepan and melt and stir over a low heat. Remove from heat. Sieve the flour and spices into a mixing bowl and add to the saucepan. Dissolve the bicarbonate of soda in sufficient water and stir into the mixture in the saucepan. When a dough consistency has formed transfer to the bowl and cover for an hour or so. Roll thinly and cut out shapes, traditionally men on horseback. Bake in a moderate oven at 325°F/160°C for 15 minutes. When cold decorate with icing, lemon peel and currants.

Katt Pie

For the pastry
1 lb (450 g) flour
8 oz (225 g) grated suet
½ teaspoon salt
For the filling
1 lb (450 g) minced lamb or mutton
8 oz (225 g) currants
6 oz (150 g) brown sugar
Salt and pepper

To make the pastry, boil the suet in ½ pint (300 ml) water for 5 minutes, then add the flour and salt. Mix thoroughly and roll out on a floured board to a thickness of about ⅜ in (1 cm). Cut into circles and put half on a greased baking tray.

Build up layers of the filling on the pastry circles, first the currants, then sugar, mutton and seasoning. Moisten round the edges with water and press the lids on. Make sure the filling cannot fall out, pierce the tops and brush with milk. Bake in a moderate oven at 325°F/160°C for about 35 minutes. Serve warm.

Treacle Toffee (Cyflaith)

1 lb (450 g) demerara sugar
12 oz (675 g) butter
12 oz (675 g) golden syrup

Put the ingredients in a saucepan, bring to the boil and stir gently for 10 minutes, or until drops poured into cold water harden at once. Pour into an oiled flat tin and score surface into squares. Loosen before it sets too hard, and when cold cut into pieces. While still liquid dried fruit or chopped nuts could be added.

St Clement's Day Rice Pudding

3 oz (75 g) pudding rice
½ pint (300 ml) milk
½ pint (300 ml) cream
3 oz (75 g) demerara sugar
1 oz (25 g) butter
4 eggs
Pinch of salt
½ teaspoon grated nutmeg
4 tablespoons caster sugar

Put the rice in a greased pie dish and add the milk, cream, demerara sugar, butter, nutmeg and salt. Mix together. Separate two egg yolks (keep the whites), beat them and add to the mixture. Stir again and bake in a moderate oven at 325°F/170°C for 2 hours. Separate the yolks from the other eggs and whisk the whites from all four eggs. Fold in the caster sugar, put turn on to the top of the rice and bake at 350°F/180°C for another 30 minutes or until the meringue is golden on the top.

Fairing Biscuits

4 oz (100 g) flour
1 teaspoon baking powder
1 teaspoon bicarbonate of soda
1 teaspoon ground ginger
½ teaspoon mixed spice
Pinch of salt
2 oz (50 g) butter
2 oz (50 g) caster sugar
3 tablespoons golden syrup

Sift together the flour, baking powder, bicarbonate of soda, ground ginger, mixed spice and a pinch of salt. Rub in the butter until the mixture is crumbly, then mix in the sugar. Stir the warmed golden syrup into the mixture, making a firm, smooth paste. Roll into a long sausage and cut off slices 1/4 in (0.6 cm) thick, putting these on to a greased baking tray. Cook in a hot oven at 400°F/200°C for about 10 minutes.

Gingerbread

1 lb (450 g) honey
6 oz (150 g) sugar
1 oz (25 g) ground cinnamon
2 oz (50 g) sliced candied lemon
4 oz (100 g) sliced, blanched almonds
4 oz (100 g) flour

Melt the honey in a saucepan, and when hot and fluid stir in the other ingredients, with sufficient flour to make a stiff paste. Roll out three times so that it has a smooth, uniform texture and put into buttered tins of the desired shape, about ¼ in (0.6 cm) deep. Cook in a moderate oven at 350°F/180°C for about half an hour.

Salt Cod with Egg Sauce

1 lb (450 g) salt cod
Fresh parsley
Vinegar
4 eggs
2 oz (50 g) unsalted butter
Black pepper
Mace

Soak the cod overnight in water with a cupful of vinegar added. Change the water several times, to remove salt that has leached out. Boil the fish in a little water (just sufficient to cover) until tender. Hard boil the eggs. Drain the fish and remove the flesh in flakes. Place on a warm dish and sprinkle parsley over it. Keep warm.

For the sauce, chop the hard-boiled eggs into smallish pieces and heat in a pan with the butter. When just on the boil add a pinch of mace and season with black pepper. Stir and pour over the fish. Serve at once.

St Andrew's Cake

1 lb (450 g) plain flour
1 teaspoon salt
½ oz (12.5 g) fresh yeast or ½ tablespoon dried yeast
1 teaspoon caster sugar
½ pint (300 ml) water
1 egg
4 oz (100 g) lard
4 oz (100 g) currants
4 oz (100 g) sugar
1 oz chopped, crystallised lemon peel

Mix flour and salt and sift into a mixing bowl. Warm the water in another bowl and to it add a mixture of the yeast and caster sugar. Blend and leave until the frothing stops. Then mix in a beaten egg, and add the mixture to the flour and salt. Melt the lard slowly and, when cooled, add it to the mixture and stir until smooth. Knead, cover and leave to rise.

Knead in the currants, sugar and peel and transfer to a 2 lb (1 kg) loaf tin. Leave until the dough has risen to the top, then bake in a moderate oven at 350°F/180°C for about 1 hour or until golden-brown. Cool, and serve sliced with butter.

Oatmeal Posset

1 pint (600 ml) milk
½ teaspoon cinnamon
½ teaspoon grated nutmeg
2 tablespoons fine oatmeal
3 tablespoons ale
3 tablespoons sweet white wine
2 tablespoons sugar

Put the milk, spices and oatmeal in a saucepan and bring to the boil. Continue until the oatmeal is soft. In another saucepan put in the ale, wine and sugar and heat gently to dissolve the sugar. Do not boil. Add this to the other saucepan, stir and simmer gently for two minutes. Serve hot.

December

Starry Gazy Pie

6–8 whole pilchards
2 eggs
Pie pastry
Breadcrumbs
Parsley
Salt and pepper

Hard boil the eggs and slice. Grease a pie dish and sprinkle with breadcrumbs. Line it with the pastry, put in the pilchards with heads up, add the sliced eggs and season with parsley, salt and pepper. Put the pastry top on so that the pilchard heads poke through. Cook in a moderately hot oven at 375°F/190°F for 10 minutes, then reduce to a moderate oven (325°F/160°C for about 50 minutes, until the pastry is golden-brown.

This recipe can be used with herrings, and the tails and bones (except the heads) can be removed if desired.

Selkirk Bannocks

2 lb (900 g) flour
2 packets instant yeast
Pinch of salt
4 oz (100 g) lard
4 oz (100 g) butter
8 oz (225 g) granulated sugar
¾ pint (450 ml) milk
1 lb (450 g) mixed sultanas and seedless raisins
2 oz (50 g) chopped candied orange peel
1 egg

Sift the flour into a bowl and add a pinch of salt and the yeast. Make a well in the centre. Warm the milk in a pan and add the lard and butter. When the fats have melted allow to cool to blood heat 99°F/37°C. Pour this mixture into the well in the flour and mix to a dough. Knead on a floured board for five minutes and return to the bowl. Cover and allow to rise in a warm place until its volume has doubled. Knead again while working in the dried fruit, peel and sugar. Shape in to rounds, flatten slightly, put on a buttered baking tray and allow to rise for 30 minutes. Bake in hot oven at 425°F/220°C for 15 minutes and then continue in a fairly hot oven at 375°F/190°C until golden-brown. When they start to brown, beat the egg and use for glazing. Test that a skewer inserted comes out dry.

Welsh Cakes

8 oz (225 g) self-raising flour
1 teaspoon mixed spice
Pinch of salt
2 oz (50 g) butter
2 oz (50 g) lard
3 oz (75 g) caster sugar
3 oz (75 g) currants
1 egg
1 teaspoon golden syrup

Sift the flour into a bowl and mix with the spice and a pinch of salt. Rub in the butter and lard until the mixture is crumbly, then add the sugar and currants. Mix together. Beat the egg and add this and the syrup to the mixture, stirring constantly until a firm dough is obtained. Roll out the dough on a floured board until ¼ in (5 mm) thick and cut into 2 in (5 cm) rounds. Bake on a medium-hot griddle until golden-brown on each side. The middles should be slightly soft.

Saffron Currant Cake or Buns

1 small packet of saffron
2 oz (50 g) lard
1 oz (25 g) fresh yeast
2 oz (50 g) margarine
1 lb (450 g) flour
½ teaspoon salt
3 oz (75 g) sugar
2 oz (50 g) currants
2 oz (50 g) sultanas
Milk

In a low oven, crisp the saffron for a few minutes, but do not allow to turn brown. Powder, and cover with hot water. Leave for 2 days.

Sift the flour with the salt and rub in the fats and yeast until a crumbly texture is achieved. Add the sugar, fruit and saffron water. If the dough is not pliable add water and milk as required. Knead until smooth, place in a plastic bag and keep it in a warm place until it has doubled in size. Put into a greased, lined 2 lb (900 g) loaf tin. Allow to rise again and bake in a moderate oven at 350°F/180°C for about an hour.

For a shaped cake mould as required, place on a greased baking tray, and allow to rise. Brush top surfaces with milk and bake as above.

For buns, cut up the dough into the size pieces desired and knead again. Shape and allow to rise, then put on a greased baking tray. Brush with milk and bake at 375°F/180°C for 15 to 18 minutes, until they sound hollow when tapped.

Limerick Ham

1 smoked ham
10 cups water
2 tablespoons brown sugar
1 teaspoon mace
1 tablespoon ground black pepper
Whole cloves

Soak the ham overnight by covering with water to dissolve all the salt. Next day, put the ham into a roasting pan and add the water, sugar, mace and pepper. Cover with foil and cook for 20–25 minutes per pound at 300°F/150°C until tender. Remove any skin, but not fat, from the ham and score to make a diamond pattern. Stud the intersections with cloves and sprinkle on some brown sugar. Bake for 15 minutes in a hot oven at 425°F/220°C until glazed.

Spiced Beef

1½ lb (675 g) topside or silverside beef
For the marinade
2 cups of ale
1 bay leaf
1 teaspoon each of black pepper, ground cloves, allspice, cinnamon and salt
1 tablespoon black treacle
½ tablespoon brown sugar
For the sauce
2 onions
2 carrots
2 sticks of celery
1 turnip
Butter

To make the marinade, mix all of the ingredients together and marinade the beef in it for up to 12 hours. Put the beef and marinade in a saucepan, add enough water to cover the meat, and simmer for 3 hours. Allow to cool.

To make the sauce, prepare and chop the vegetables and sauté in butter in a frying pan for 5–10 minutes. Add the beef stock and simmer until the vegetables are tender. Serve the meat cold and the sauce hot.

Goose with Apple Sauce

1 goose
Lard for roasting
For the stuffing
4 oz (100 g) breadcrumbs
1 apple
1 onion
½ oz (12.5 g) chopped sage
1 egg
Salt and pepper
For the sauce
½ lb cooking apples
1 small onion
1 oz (25 g) sugar
1 teaspoon vinegar
1 oz (25 g) breadcrumbs
Mustard
Cinnamon

To make the stuffing, separate the egg white and beat. Mix the stuffing adding the egg white last. Stuff the goose and roast according to weight, basting regularly. Pour off surplus fat at the end. While the goose is in the oven prepare the apple sauce.

To make the sauce, peel and core the apples, peel and chop the onions, and cook together with the sugar. When soft add the remaining ingredients, with stock to make up any liquid loss. Simmer for 10 minutes.

Potted Hough

1½ lb (675 g) hough or shin of beef
1 jointed oxtail
1 nap or shin bone
Salt and pepper

Put the hough, oxtail, nap bone and salt to taste in a large saucepan, cover with water and bring slowly to the boil. Simmer gently for at least 4 hours. Remove the bones from the pan and take off all the meat. Shred or mince the meat and return it to the pan, seasoning with salt and pepper. Boil rapidly for 10 minutes then leave to cool. Skim off any fat and pour the liquid into moulds. Chill thoroughly. Serve with boiled potatoes, cooked or pickled beetroot, and redcurrant jelly.

Acknowledgements

in Source Order

AKG, London Front Cover top. **Barnabys Picture Library**/David Simson 82, /David Alexander Smith 40. **Collections**/Brian Shuel 12, 53, 57, 85, 129, 136, 141, 188. **Cornwall County Library**/Cornish Studies LIbrary 51, 69, 84, 91 left, 91 right, 151, /George Ellis 145. **Association Le Doare-Archives** Front Cover left, Frontflap, Backflap, 9 Bottom, 88, 96, 120, 138. **Courtesy of the Carluke and Lanark Gazette** 187. **Doc Rowe Collection** 18, 27, 29, 34, 77, 79, 103, 113 left, 113 right, 121, 124, 134, 161 right, 173 left, 182 /Manners and Customs of Mankind 125, /Topical Press 161 left. **Celtic Designs and Motifs by Courtney Davis/Dover Publication** 1, 8, 28, 42, 46, 52, 58, 62, 68, 70, 78, 80, 92, 95, 97, 98, 112, 128, 146, 150, 158, 164, 170, 190. **Mary Evans Picture Library** 15, 23, 71, 87, 106, /F.W. Buss 178, /Illustrated London News 54. **Fortean Picture Library** 32 left, 174, /Paul Broadhusrt 179. **Historic Scotland**/Crown Copyright: Reproduced by Permission of Historic Scotland 191. **Hulton Getty Picture Collection** 38, /Fox Photos 45 left, 45 right, 100, /Picture Post 90, 118, /Radio Times 153, /The Observer 108, /Topical Press 60. **The Illustrated London News Picture Library** 166, 171. **Bord Failte - Irish Tourist Board** 48, 105, 184. **Billie Love Historical Collection** 72 left, 72 right, /Billie Love 149. **Courtesy of the Manx National Heritage** 177, /G.B. Cowen 59. **Morrab Library, Penzance** 39. **National Museums of Scotland** /Courtesy of the Trustees of the National Museums of Scotland 111 left, 111 right, 159, 173 right. **The National Museum of Wales** 32 right, 33. **National Library of Ireland - Photographic Archives** 67, 137. **The National Library of Wales** 114 left, 114 right. **Pat Hodgson Library** 30. **Royal Institution of Cornwall, Truro**/A.W.Jordan 155. **Ron Davies©**/Courtesy of The National Library of Wales 142 right. **Scotland in Focus**/© Clapperton 185, /J. MacPherson Front Cover bottom, Back Cover. **The School of Scottish Studies, University of Edinburgh**/ Ian MacKenzie © 37. **Wales Tourist Board Photo Library** 142 left